Online Counseling

P 35
391

Online Counseling

A Handbook for Mental Health Professionals

Second Edition

Ron Kraus

George Stricker

Cedric Speyer

ELSEVIER

Amsterdam • Boston • Heidelberg • London • New York • Oxford
Paris • San Diego • San Francisco • Singapore • Sydney • Tokyo
Academic Press is an imprint of Elsevier

Academic Press is an imprint of Elsevier
32 Jamestown Road, London NW1 7BY, UK
30 Corporate Drive, Suite 400, Burlington, MA 01803, USA
525 B Street, Suite 1800, San Diego, CA 92101-4495, USA

First Edition 2003
Second Edition 2010

Notice
No responsibility is assumed by the publisher for any injury and/or damage to persons or
property as a matter of products liability, negligence or otherwise, or from any use or
operation of any methods, products, instructions or ideas contained in the material herein.
Because of rapid advances in the medical sciences, in particular, independent verification
of diagnoses and drug dosages should be made

British Library Cataloguing-in-Publication Data
A catalogue record for this book is available from the British Library

Library of Congress Cataloging-in-Publication Data
A catalog record for this book is available from the Library of Congress

ISBN: 978-0-12-378596-1

For information on all Academic Press publications
visit our website at www.elsevierdirect.com

Typeset by MPS Limited, a Macmillan Company, Chennai, India
www.macmillansolutions.com

Transferred to Digital Printing in 2011

Working together to grow
libraries in developing countries

www.elsevier.com | www.bookaid.org | www.sabre.org

ELSEVIER   BOOK AID International   Sabre Foundation

Contents

Foreword

Unprecedented Change is Upon Us

The twenty-first century is rapidly becoming an era of educated consumers utilizing the most up-to-date technology to assume control over their own health care. This evolutional journey from passive compliance to active participation by psychology's clients/patients will require a significant shift in perspective for most practitioners. Inherent in this new orientation is the underlying notion that clients/patients will increasingly become equal partners in all health care decisions affecting them. This will clearly take time as, for example, the Institute of Medicine (IOM) of the National Academy of Sciences estimates that nearly half of the US population today has difficulty in understanding and using health information, especially our nation's elderly and low-income populations (IOM, 2004). Yet, change is definitely upon us.

Equally important for our practitioners to appreciate will be the steady realization that the unprecedented advances occurring within the communications and technology fields will have an increasingly direct impact upon the daily delivery of health care and, ultimately, upon society's definition of "quality care." Data-based gold standards of care will soon be the norm for all of health care. Across-provider and diagnostic comparisons will become commonplace. No longer will geographical location and restrictive state licensure requirements determine who can provide care. We must expect the establishment of around-the-clock virtual consultation systems, with the most up-to-date scientific and clinical research becoming readily available to both providers and their clients/patients.

In this light, it is important to expressly emphasize that psychology (and many of the other traditional mental health disciplines) is steadily maturing into becoming one of the nation's bona fide *health care* professions (Kenkel et al., 2005). For most training programs and many senior colleagues, this is an entirely new orientation. Very few psychology programs possess clinical training "homes of their own" (Rodgers, 1980). Few of our colleagues have been trained in providing collaborative, interdisciplinary care. Nevertheless, at the 2010 annual State Leadership Conference, anticipating the enactment of President Obama's health care reform vision, Katherine Nordal, Executive Director of the American Psychological Association (APA) Practice Directorate, accurately highlighted several underlying and related themes: "We need an integrated health care delivery system, and psychologists must be part of the health care teams in that system [...] We also need to help more of our members become comfortable with and accustomed to using the electronic media that increasingly shape our interactions with others" (Nordal, 2010). As we go forward as a nation, it is critical that our practitioners come to appreciate, in a timely fashion, that, as health care providers, our expertise is considerably broader in clinical scope than solely being one of the mental health care specialties. Collectively, we must not be satisfied with the status quo. The magnitude of change occurring within the nation's health care arena simply will not allow that to occur. Those professions without proactive vision will slowly disappear and the clinical services that they might have potentially provided will eventually come within the jurisdiction of other maturing professions (e.g., clinical pharmacy, advanced practice nurses, and mental health counselors). To passively stand still is simply not a viable option.

THE PAST IS PROLOGUE

Although largely absent within the psychological literature, the potential impact of technology upon the delivery of health care has been a topic of serious discussion among many health care policy experts for a significant period of time. Over a decade ago, the Pew Health Foundations Commission suggested that

> The successful practitioner of the next century will need to master information technologies in order to effectively manage the care of their patients. As the microscope allowed practitioners in an earlier era to see the microbial agents of infection, the computer allows today's generation to aggregate data about populations and understand broader patterns of health and illness. But the computer will also change the patient. As patients arrive with better and more information, health care professionals may find themselves increasingly in the role of counselor and consultant.
> **O'Neill and Pew Health Professional Commission, 1998, p. 18**

A similar perspective has been proffered by the IOM:

> Health care delivery has been relatively untouched by the revolution in information technology that has been transforming nearly every other aspect of society. The majority of patient and clinician encounters take place for purposes of exchanging clinical information [. . .] Although growth in clinical knowledge and technology has been profound, many health care settings lack basic computer systems to provide clinical information or support clinical decision making. The development and application of more sophisticated information systems is essential to enhance quality and improve efficiency.
> **IOM, 2001, pp. 15—16**

We would further suggest that the advances occurring within the field of online counseling as described in this text are exactly what the Pew Foundation and the IOM were contemplating.

LANDMARK HEALTH CARE REFORM LEGISLATION

With the election of President Obama in 2008, landmark health care reform legislation assumed central stage in the nation's public policy arena. Further, within a remarkably short period of time, the president was able to sign into law three extremely significant bills, which together will have major long-term implications for the delivery of health care, including behavioral and mental health care. The American Recovery and Reinvestment Act (ARRA) of 2009 (PL 111-5), the Patient Protection and Affordable Care Act (PPACA) (PL 111-148), and the subsequently enacted budget reconciliation legislation, the Health Care and Education Reconciliation Act of 2010 (PL 111-152), established the vision, infrastructure, and economic resources for successfully embracing the potential inherent within the ever-advancing world of technology. To provide perspective on the magnitude of change being contemplated, this was at a time when the Administration estimated that approximately only five percent of physicians had fully functional electronic health records. The Administration's stated goal is to bring utilization up to 70 percent for hospitals and 90 percent for physicians by 2019. Change is definitely coming.

THE ADVENT OF TELEHEALTH CARE

With this evolving landscape in mind, it behooves behavioral health professionals of all disciplines to make better-informed and more-appropriate use of emerging communication technologies and to no longer continue the health care community's traditional tendency to ignore the tremendous potential these new mediums of communication possess. One of the most obvious benefits is the increased access to care that online counseling offers those who live in rural or underserved areas, where behavioral health care may be extremely limited or entirely absent. This is also the case for those who live in populated areas where services are readily available and where the convenience of online counseling — which can be as accessible as one's laptop computer, hand-held data device, or cellular phone — offers distinct advantages over the standard 50-minute, face-to-face (f2f) model of therapy established a century ago.

We can appreciate that there is the perception among many behavioral health care providers, and especially among our senior colleagues, that these new means of providing therapeutic services — online counseling, webcam, etc. — are, at best, a "second tier" approach to care. This fundamental assumption, however, is increasingly being questioned and most of the emerging evidence strongly suggests that these new and highly innovative approaches provide equivalent care quality with distinct advantages. For example, active-duty members of the armed forces returning from a war zone have reported being more comfortable in disclosing very personal information via webcam or videoconference than in an f2f encounter. Among all groups, satisfaction rates with these and other long-distance or telehealth behavioral interventions appear to be equivalent to f2f intervention.

INCREASING RECOGNITION WITHIN THE FEDERAL SYSTEM

During the Summer of 2010, the Vice Chief of Staff of the US Army (Department of Defense (DoD)) testified before the Senate Armed Services Committee on the importance of providing timely behavioral health care for the invisible wounds of war:

> Web-based Behavioral Health Care Services. Today, Soldiers and Family Members can access behavioral health care services on-line through the TRICARE Assistance Program (TRIAP). The program is open to: Active duty service members; Members eligible for the Transition Assistance Management Program (TAMP) for 6 months after demobilization; [and] Members enrolled in TRICARE Reserve Select, as well as spouses and family members 18+ years. Soldiers and Family Members can access unlimited short-term, problem-solving counseling 24/7 with a licensed counselor from home or any location with a computer, Internet, required software download, and webcam. If more specialized medical care is deemed necessary, an immediate warm handoff can/will be made to a medical provider. In conjunction with TRIAP, the Army is working to build a network of locations and on-line providers for telemental health services, using medically-supervised, secure audio-visual conferencing to link beneficiaries with offsite providers. Once in place, this Network will be able to provide the full-range of behavioral health care services, including psychotherapy and medication management. Our long-term goal is to create a network of counselors and certified mental health care providers that encompasses the entire US. Then when a Brigade redeploys, for example, a gymnasium full of stations/computers could be put in place allowing every Leader and Soldier to participate in a behavioral health evaluation on-line upon redeploying [...] In my 38-year career in the Army, I have never dealt with a more difficult or critical mission than the current charge to reduce the number of Soldier suicides and properly diagnose and treat individuals suffering from TBI, PTS and other behavioral health issues. Over the past year, our commitment to health promotion, risk reduction and suicide prevention has changed Army policy, structure and processes [...] Our success notwithstanding, we still have much more to do [...] This is a

holistic problem with holistic solutions, and that's how we are going to continue to approach it with this campaign.

Chiarelli, 2010

At the same US Senate hearing, the Acting Principal Deputy Under Secretary for Health of the Veterans Health Administration (VA) also testified:

'Polytrauma' is a new word in the medical lexicon that was termed by VA to describe the complex, multiple injuries to multiple body parts and organs occurring as a result of blast-related injuries seen from Operation Enduring Freedom (OEF) or Operation Iraqi Freedom (IOF) [...] VA has developed and implemented numerous programs to ensure it provides world-class rehabilitation services for Veterans and active duty Servicemembers with TBI. VA has enhanced its integrated nation-wide Polytrauma/TBI System of Care [...] The system offers comprehensive clinical rehabilitative services including: treatment by interdisciplinary teams of rehabilitation specialists; specialty care management; patient and family education and training; psychosocial support; and advanced rehabilitation and prosthetic technologies [...] In April 2009, VA began an advanced technology initiative to establish assistive technology laboratories at the four PRCs. These facilities will serve as a resource for VA health care, and provide the most advanced technologies to Veterans and Servicemembers with ongoing needs related to cognitive impairment, sensory impairment, computer access, communication deficits, wheeled mobility, self-care, and home telehealth [...] [R]esearch has shown the value of having co-located, collaborative mental health staff that can complement the medication-focused care management programs with psychosocial interventions to address depression and other mental health problems. The mental health providers co-located in primary care also can engage with family members when appropriate to listen to their concerns, ensure they understand the care the Veteran is receiving, and describe how they can contribute to ongoing treatment for the Veteran.

One important set of requirements in the Handbook was to ensure that evidence-based psychotherapies are available for Veterans who could benefit from them and that meaningful choices between effective alternative treatments are available. VA implemented the broad use of evidence-based psychotherapies in response to evidence that for many patients, specific forms of psychotherapies are the most effective and evidence-based of all treatments. Specifically, the IOM report on treatment for PTSD emphasized findings that exposure-based psychotherapies, including Prolonged Exposure Therapy and Cognitive Processing Therapy, were the best-established of all treatments for PTSD [...] For several years, VA has provided training to clinical mental health staff to ensure that there are therapists in each facility able to provide evidence-based psychotherapies for the treatment of depression and PTSD as alternatives to pharmacological treatment or as a course of combined treatment. . ... The online version of the Hotline, Veterans Chat, enables Veterans, family members and friends to chat anonymously with a trained VA counselor. If the counselor determines there is an emergent need, the counselor can take immediate steps to transfer the visitor to the Hotline, where further counseling and referral services can be provided and crisis intervention steps can be taken. Since July 2009, when Veterans Chat was established, VA has learned many valuable lessons. First it is clear that conversations are powerful and capable of saving lives. As a result, opening more avenues for communications by offering both an online and phone service is essential to further success. Second, training and constant monitoring is very important, and VA will continue pursuing both of these efforts aggressively [. . .] Data also support the conclusion that high quality mental health care can prevent suicide.

The health policy implications of the testimony proffered by these two high-level Administration officials should be clearly evident. The twenty-first century will be an era in which the unprecedented advances occurring within the communications and technology fields will ensure provider accountability to objective standards and open the door to entirely new definitions of "quality therapeutic relationships" (Jesse, 2010). Online counseling is unquestionably one of the new visions for the future.

ONGOING PROFESSIONAL CHALLENGES

While patient satisfaction and comfort with these new forms of treatment is high, provider satisfaction appears to be less so. Training in the new modes of therapeutic service delivery is still lacking. Therapists also continue to have many unanswered questions about liability, safety, and insurance reimbursement. From our perspective, all of these complex issues will eventually be satisfactorily addressed as the entire health care delivery system becomes increasingly engaged in embracing technological advances and focusing specifically upon what is best for the patient (i.e., providing gold-standard care in a timely fashion). Change is always unsettling. Nevertheless, we would suggest that those behavioral health practitioners interested in using this technology in their practice will likely need to take an advocacy role in promoting legislative and regulatory changes such as licensure mobility in order to ensure that their unique needs are ultimately satisfactorily addressed, a process that many are unfortunately unfamiliar with. Former APA Congressional Science Fellow Neil Kirschner (2003) reflects: "If I've learned anything on the Hill, it is the importance of political advocacy if you desire a change in public policy."

We earlier noted that there is also the belief among many providers that a strong interpersonal relationship cannot be established in other than an f2f environment. The popularity of online communities and the intense emotional investment of many thousands of individuals who use them certainly call for further examination of that assumption. Online interventions are often more frequent, shorter, and timelier, and may at some point prove to result in better treatment outcomes compared to care via the now-standard 50-minute visit. Either as a stand-alone intervention or as part of a combined f2f and online treatment program, the potential applications of online technology are fascinating, as the federal government is actively demonstrating. Further research needs to be conducted in order to firmly establish the effectiveness of these interventions. Not surprisingly, integral to President Obama's vision was $1.1 billion targeted for comparative clinical effectiveness research, in order to scientifically evaluate the relative effectiveness of various health care services and treatment options. These results, combined with the "hands on" experiences of our colleagues within the DoD and the VA, will undoubtedly unalterably shape the provision of behavioral health care during the coming decade.

Reflecting upon a personal observation, the junior author recently witnessed firsthand the impact of an "online intervention" when an agoraphobic patient made her first visit in 10 years to a crowded shopping mall. She reported that the online support she received from hundreds of friends and similarly affected patients – both before the event and via Twitter during her mall walk – was the key that allowed her to engage in what she would otherwise have perceived as an impossible task. Transformative therapeutic events can occur as a result of words read on a computer or personal data device. From a behavioral health/mental health policy perspective, the recent testimony before the US Senate by the high-level DoD and VA Administration officials should underscore the magnitude of change that is definitely coming. Our maturing profession must, and we are confident ultimately shall, embrace the reality of our ever-changing health care environment.

Patrick H DeLeon
former American Psychological Association President

Raymond A Folen
Tripler Army Medical Center
(the views expressed are those of the author and not necessarily those of the Department of Defense or the US Army)

REFERENCES

Chiarelli, P. W. (2010, June 22). Testimony before the U.S. Senate Armed Services Committee.

Institute of Medicine (IOM). (2001). *Crossing the quality chasm: A new health system for the 21st century.* Washington, DC: National Academy Press.

Institute of Medicine (IOM). (2004). *Health literacy: A prescription to end confusion* Washington, DC: National Academy Press.

Jesse, R. (2010, June 22). Testimony before the U.S. Senate Armed Services Committee.

Kenkel, M. B., DeLeon, P. H., Mantell, E. O., & Steep, A. (2005). Divided no more: Psychology's role in integrated healthcare. *Canadian Psychology/Psychologie Canadienne, 46*(4), 189–202.

Kirschner, N. M. (2003, August). *QMBs, SNFs and notch babies: A hippie banker tour.* Presentation at the 111th APA Annual Convention, Toronto, Canada.

Nordal, K. C. (2010, March). Keynote address at the 2010 APA State Leadership Conference, Washington, DC.

O'Neil, E. H., & the Pew Health Professions Commission. (1998). *Recreating health professional practice for a new century: The fourth report of the pew health professions commission.* San Francisco, CA: Pew Health Professions Commission.

Rodgers, D. A. (1980). The status of psychologists in hospitals: Technicians or professionals. *The Clinical Psychologist, 33*(4), 5–7.

Introduction

Ron Kraus and George Stricker

ABOUT THE HANDBOOK

The second edition of *Online Counseling — A Handbook for Mental Health Professionals* has been written in order to update the original, groundbreaking guidebook. About 10 years have passed since work on the first edition started and much has been added to our understanding of the new modality since then. The second edition became necessary as interest in online health care grew, research accumulated, and online health-care-related interactions were formally accepted. As in the first edition, leading experts in the field have been asked to contribute their time and wisdom so that the accumulated knowledge could be shared.

Online counseling is a relatively new modality. Experience shows that it usually takes some time before new modalities are established and then integrated. Years ago, some mental health professionals considered the idea of placing a telephone in their office. Today, most practitioners are available on the phone, and telephone hotline operations continue to save people's lives. In the same way, the penetration of the Internet into our homes, workplaces, and practices is already a reality, not a question to consider. Millions of clients are looking for service online, and an overwhelming majority of clinicians use the Internet for some form of professional activity and email. With the 2010 health care reform in the US, it is expected that medical records, patient education, clinical consults, referrals, and billing will all move online. As the health care industry is positioned to move online, preparing clinicians for online practice becomes a must.

Often, the introduction of a general textbook marks the birth of a new field, much as the field of psychology is associated with the publication of William James' 1890 book, *The Principles of Psychology*. Although we did not quite reinvent the field of psychology with this handbook, we do hope that it will lay the foundations for professional online counseling. This book was made specifically to guide and educate practitioners about use of the online medium and to make recommendations for effective, professional practice strategies.

Note: The term "online counseling" is used in this handbook to refer to all clinical consultations and services that are done via various Internet-assisted modalities (text, email, chat, and videoconferencing), although some studies refer to the modality as "e-therapy," "telepsychiatry," "telemental health," and the like.

WHAT IS IN THIS HANDBOOK?

The handbook is divided into four parts. Part I, "Psychology and Counseling Online," discusses use, potential, and online counseling research findings to date. Chapter 1, "Online Behavior, Communication, and Experience," lays the foundation to the exploration of online counseling with a general presentation of the Internet and its uses for both consumers and health care professionals. The potential of online health care delivery in the twenty-first century is discussed.

Chapter 2, "The Psychology of Text Relationships," analyses and explains the nature of text-based relationships, which are either synchronous, as with text messages and chat in real time, or asynchronous, as with email exchanges, message boards, and blogs. The importance of understanding the relationship between what is said and how it is said is discussed. In Chapter 3, "Online Counseling: Does it Work? Research Findings to Date," empirical evidence, research findings, and future trends related to mental health services online are presented.

Part II presents the practical aspects of online counseling. In Chapter 4, "The Technology of Online Counseling," the author discusses the technological aspects of online counseling, explaining in detail the hardware, software, and networking infrastructure that allow mental health professionals and clients to communicate via the Internet.

Chapter 5 explains ethical issues in online counseling. The ethical framework for professional online counseling is examined. Understanding the ethical requirements related to online practice is made easy with the 10 simple principles of EthicsCode.com.

In Chapter 6, "Legal Issues for Online Counselors," the laws and regulations related to online counseling are presented. Legal issues and risks for professionals who work online are discussed, and ways in which to avoid such problems are suggested. Chapter 7, "The Business of Online Counseling," discusses the practical, financial, and business aspects of online counseling. Strategies and steps that mental health professionals need to take in order to operate a successful online practice are explained.

Part III of the handbook discusses specific clinical skills for online counseling. Online counseling via email and chat, as well as various types of group work and theory, are presented in this section. In Chapter 8, titled "Text-based Online Counseling: Email," the authors present asynchronous online counseling and discuss email counseling. Clinical approaches to e-counseling are presented, case management challenges are discussed, and an annotated case study is provided.

In Chapter 9, "Text-based Online Counseling: Chat," modalities in counseling and psychotherapy are presented. Clinical approaches to therapeutic chat are explored, phases of online chat therapy are discussed, and a case study excerpt is provided.

Chapter 10, "Counseling Groups Online: Theory and Framework," discusses the historical development and current uses of group counseling online. The various sub-modalities of online group communications are presented and analyzed, and guidelines and suggestions for successful group work online are provided.

In Chapter 11, "Clinical Work with Support Groups Online: Practical Aspects," the authors discuss the empirical, practical, and clinical aspects of group counseling online. Specific recommendations for planning, starting, and managing a group online are presented. Risks, potential benefits, and conflict resolution strategies are explained, and clinical examples are provided.

Chapter 12, "Internet-based Psychological Testing and Assessment," presents the various ways in which online assessment tools are revolutionizing the field. Uses of online assessment tools for psychological testing, clinical diagnosis, self-assessment, and research collection are discussed. Advantages and disadvantages, as well as ethical and legal issues related to assessment online, are discussed.

In Chapter 13, "International and Multicultural Issues" the authors explain multicultural issues as they relate to online counseling. Principles for clinical work in a multicultural online environment are discussed, with a review of suggested guidelines.

Part IV of the handbook, consisting of Chapter 14, explores tomorrow's health care environment. In this section the author looks into the future of health care in the US with a focus on online counseling, taking into consideration technological advancements as well as predictable patterns in tomorrow's health care field.

ONLINE COUNSELING: A NEW MODALITY IS HERE TO STAY

When pioneers started thinking about the concept of online counseling over a decade ago, many basic issues required careful consideration. At the time not much was known about the subject. As the millennium turned, regulations by state boards or professional associations were mostly nonexistent, or they expressed cautionary remarks about the risks of the yet-to-be explored field. The skeptics raised justified questions about the efficacy of text relations, and concerns were voiced about the absence of body language, facial gestures, and voice intonation. As a result, most clinicians did not rush to provide services online. After all, online counseling was a new field, research findings were scarce, regulations recommended caution, and, yes, even educated mental health professionals sometimes fear the unknown.

Today, sufficient research exists to confirm the efficacy of online counseling, regulations are in place for the practice, and current procedural terminology (CPT) codes for billing online counseling sessions exist. Most active clinicians have an email address and many are registered in various online directories, whether via the insurance company they are affiliated with or through their own website online. It is quite likely that in the future many more clinicians will be listed and available to patients online. Before long, training clinicians for online counseling is likely to become part of the way professionals are prepared for tomorrow's health care work environment.

ONLINE COUNSELING: THE HEALTH CARE ENVIRONMENT OF TOMORROW

It may be safe to assume that in the future some clients will still come to the office for f2f therapy sessions, while others will prefer to locate, schedule, consult, and settle their bills online. The same will probably be true for the clinical community. Some practitioners will be comfortable working online while others may prefer the traditional in-office sessions. Regardless, the need to educate the clinical community about the new modality already exists. Guidebooks such as this one will be useful in professional and academic settings to prepare clinicians for the online health care work environment.

ACKNOWLEDGMENTS

The editors would like to express their appreciation and gratitude to all the people who contributed and helped to create the second edition.

Ron Kraus dedicates this book to the memory of his father Otto (Ota) B. Kraus. Ron wishes to thank Edith (Dita) Kraus for her kindness, wisdom and devotion, Orna Kraus for her patience and support, and the professional team at OnlineClinics.com.

George Stricker is grateful, as always, for the support of Joan, and for the presence of his children and grandchildren.

Cedric Speyer gives thanks to Maurice and Elizabeth Speyer for their love of letters and each other; Eusebia da Silva, conscious companion on the InnerView path; Paul Wittes, E-Counseling manager and Michele Mani, E-Counseling co-supervisor, for their support and clinical wisdom; Scott Christie, for his administrative dedication; Susan Valentine, script doctor for composite cases; and to all the members of the 'E-team' who bring gifts of text-based bonding and non-local presence to countless clients in need of their guidance every day.

PSYCHOLOGY AND COUNSELING ONLINE

Chapter one

Online Behavior, Communication, and Experience

Michael Fenichel, PhD
Private practice

CHAPTER OUTLINE

To say that much has changed in the last 10 years, the first decade of a new millennium, is perhaps a vast understatement. Our society has become immersed in a lifestyle often described as the "digital decade," with an application for every whim, a communication tool for every purpose, and a vast choice of platforms and technology.

In the 1990s it was quite exciting to imagine the dawning of a new era of open world travel, via the "information highway." Now the highway leads to people's homes and inboxes and both personal and professional relationships have been revolutionized as a result. Grandmothers

3

Online Counseling. DOI: 10.1016/B978-0-12-378596-1.00001-0

watch grandchildren via Skype as the grandchildren turn from the piano to iPhone to Leapster to homework, with Facebook somewhere in between. At the same time, opportunities have opened up for new avenues of employment for entrepreneurs, researchers, students, and educators, and for computer applications involving virtual reality.[1]

Context matters. It matters in social situations, work environments, intimate relationships, and public forums. It is the context of this digital age, when an entire generation simply do not know anything else and parents and practitioners alike swear by the power of multi-tasking. This is in spite of the mounting body of applied research suggesting that the brain has not caught up with the applications through a natural process of neurological evolution. This is the prevailing *zeitgeist* for both potential clients and counselors/therapists/consultants. While some debate can be heard above the din of ringtones, instant messages (IMs), and beeps about the relative value versus the dangers of multi-tasking, of "addiction," and of human attention morphing into a state of fragmented cognition measured by the onslaught of 140-character tweets and SMS, the fact remains that this is the world in which we live. It is a candy store for some, a menu of limitless tools for others, and simply taken for granted by the generation that evolved from NeoPets and *The Sims*, to MySpace, Facebook, and various music- and art-focused sites. A new high tech enthusiasm is now trickling up from the younger generations, which were born into an era where they are surrounded by devices, networks, and myriad media options, to adults, who vary in their excitement about and adaptation to the various technologies and social activities online.

CONTEXT IS EVERYTHING

Context is key to understanding human experience and the myriad components of communication, along with the elements of interpersonal relationships. Our unique and shared experiences form the foundation for all meaningful collaborative relationships, including the therapeutic one. Thus, it is essential, in facilitating a professional therapeutic relationship, to fully understand and appreciate context and perspective. Without this there is no possibility of genuine empathy or trust. A decade ago some of the earliest efforts of online researchers and practitioners focused on understanding how online counselors might effectively determine a good "fit" in terms of therapeutic venue and modality. Long before the advent of the Internet, such variables as the matching of goals and expectations between psychotherapist and patient had been shown to constitute a powerful determinant for positive outcomes, whether these were achieved by goal-directed dialogue,

---

[1] See, for example, http://www.fenichel.com/virtual.shtml for a description of clinical and military application demonstrated to be effective in the treatment of trauma.

behavioral coaching, insight, narrative analysis, or supportive, empathic counseling. Practicing online clinicians have been adapting and adopting new procedures to ensure accurate communication and allow for expression of feeling and mood to be accurately and mutually understood; in short, to promote *online empathy*.

The multitude of options has long ago moved beyond the choice between "on-the-couch" and "face-to-face" (f2f) therapy paradigms or even the efficacy of one school versus another. People's needs vary, and yet, as H. S. Sullivan (father of interpersonal psychiatry) pointed out, people also are more alike than otherwise. Now there are many viable choices of method and venue to provide specialized treatments, with an entire continuum of communication tools, from traditional f2f office-based practice to text or video chat, support groups (with and without professional moderation), and self-help resources and communities — along with the burgeoning availability of individual online counseling services.

In the first edition of this book, long before a multitude of training manuals, institutes, and courses began to appear and offer standardized training materials, I sought to underscore how, no matter what the communication tool, it is effective communication that is vital.

In graduate school and beyond, therapists learn that the single most important factor in effective counseling and psychotherapy is the quality of the therapeutic relationship. Having the ability to understand human nature, analyze the dynamics of relationships, and probe the depths of the psyche is an essential contributor to the positive therapeutic relationship, along with the "nonspecific factors" experienced by clients, such as warmth, empathy, and genuineness. Add to the therapeutic relationship the goals and expectations of both client and counselor, along with the processes and tools that facilitate treatment that is experienced as helpful, and this fortuitous combination of an effective working relationship and appropriate clinical interventions is thought to be the key to success.[2]

With the advent of the Internet, communication has been revolutionized and basic tenets of human relationships have been intensified, broadened, and challenged.[3] Opportunities now exist for socially

---

[2] Notwithstanding the interest and novelty attached to such classic software programs as ELIZA, where in effect the "therapist" (or "fortune teller") is the computer itself, without human intervention or intelligence.

[3] For example, according to a Harris Poll, by the year 2000 57 percent of all US adults were online, at home or at work, and of this group 86 percent had sought information on health care via the Internet, up from 71 percent of users in 1998. By November 2007, a new Harris Poll found nearly 80 percent of all US adults spend time online, on average 11 hours per week. Source: Reuter News, (2007, November 5). Do you find yourself going online more and more? You're not alone. Retrieved 16 September 2010 from http://www.reuters.com/article/idUSN0559828420071106.

shy, isolated, or physically challenged individuals to reach out for connectedness or support, utilizing the web to seek information, companionship, self-validation, and, increasingly, advice or professional mental health services, such as counseling and psychotherapy.[4] Today's products and services are being driven by the generation that has been born to multi-task and who take digital options for granted, as prior generations went from wanderlust to familiarity with movies, television, video games, portable music, CDs and DVDs. Trends continue to change within and across generations. Recently, for example, the Pew Research Center (Pew Internet and American Life Project, 2010) has identified a declining interest in blogging in favor of more instant and personally interactive social media such as Facebook. Children and teens are not as interested in tweeting out bird-sized texts as in sending free-form messages and using more creative and diverse media, often simultaneously, usually favoring wireless platforms. Adults, on the other hand, are becoming more engaged by social networks designed for teens and college students, and increasingly populate professional networks and interest groups. When considering where the average person with a computer or smart phone may look for mental health support, the public landscape for seeking such help has clearly changed.

COUNSELING OR THERAPY ONLINE?

While there can be great debates around the perennial question, "what is therapy?," there is little doubt that many online clinicians, support communities, and self-help websites are offering "therapeutic" services and experiences. Counseling is available online both as an open-ended process and for a wide range of goal-directed ends, ranging from vocational decision-making to bolstering social confidence, building self-help skills and self-esteem, and fostering a more cohesive sense of self or interpersonal competency. Online mental health practitioners also serve as a bridge to referrals in the f2f community, or to online specialists with expertise in particular presenting issues.

The vast majority of American lives are now touched, if not transformed, by each of us having potential access to everybody else on earth with a computer (or smart phone) and an Internet connection. A society built on mobility via cars and highways has now completely embraced the new technology. The most promising means of getting where and what one wants is now, in many minds, readily accessible on the "information highway" or within one's social/professional networks.

---

[4] *The Wall Street Journal* (June 4, 2002, p. D6) went so far as to announce, "Online Therapy Goes Mainstream." Written by Robert J. Davis.

The potential for interactive communication and for broadening our understanding of human behavior across contexts and cultures is profound. An entire generation in the US has integrated the computer and the Internet into their lives as easily as their parents were able to embrace the telephone and television. Often, the first solution in seeking help, support, or information today is to "go online." Certainly, teens in particular are now equally at ease with IMs as with emailing, using a cell phone, or meeting a group of friends in a chat environment to swap pictures, video, or music.

It is the very *ease* and naturalness of using the Internet and the computer in daily life now, unencumbered by worries about wires, routers, and so forth, that makes turning to the Internet more commonplace than using a telephone directory or other offline sources of information and support. Add to this the populations already benefiting from telehealth services, such as the geographically isolated, physically challenged, vocationally mobile, and socially inhibited, and there is clearly a huge need that can be filled by online practitioners. The "presenting problems," can entail interpersonal relationships, addictions, work-related stress, or anxiety, to name but a few areas that mental health practitioners commonly address in all mediums. Working online, however, carries unique challenges and opportunities, which in turn demand additional skills (Fenichel, 2000; Fenichel et al., 2002). It is also incumbent upon the Internet-based mental health professional to understand and accept that not every situation or potential client is appropriate for online treatment (Suler et al., 2001).

Returning to the generally accepted model, which assumes a counseling or therapy relationship to be the sum of its parts — the client, counselor, presenting situation, treatment goal, intervention, and several nonspecific factors — it becomes quite clear that the clinician who works entirely online needs a new skill-set that includes privacy safeguards for the client, methods of clear communication (compensating for absent verbal and visual cues), a framework that is structured yet flexible, and processes that allow for a means of validating the results.

While this is still a new frontier, online mental health services and information are already being embraced internationally in a variety of ways — from Japanese support for short-message, text-based counseling provided through Employee Assistance Programs (EAPs), to American telehealth provisions for unserved and underserved populations, to an innovative Internet-based suicide-prevention hotline utilized with great success in Israel (Barak, 2001), to a growing number of referral, training, consultation, and educational offerings worldwide. Both individuals and the health care industry may be looking at online services as being the latest and most efficient means of delivering short-term services, with respect to both prevention and intervention for a variety of presenting problems.

LIFE IN CYBERSPACE *Re - read*

Much has been written about the phenomenology of life in cyberspace (Baker, 2008; Barak & Suler, 2008; Fenichel, 2002). Sometimes this involves people taking on new personas consistent with a virtual world, where one can feel anonymous while at the same time instantly disinhibited when opening up to total strangers (Suler, 2002). Similarly, relationships online may be infused with fantasy or may reflect a well-established pattern of realistic and rich communication between individuals or within groups. It is easy to reach out and become cyber-buddies through shared-interest communities such as forums, social networks, and list-servs. It is easy to walk away, too. It is easy to deceive and easy to be brutally truthful. Those who are comfortable with interpersonal relationships both online and off are often able to seamlessly integrate both aspects of experience into an over-all web of social connectedness. Many individuals, it is important to note, develop preferences for one modality over another. While not everyone loves computers or can use them without frustration, for many people the Internet spells liberation and a world of opportunity. Some fundamental aspects of traditional relationship-based therapies can change as well. For example, as widely discussed, the nature of text-based relationships lends itself not only to rapid disinhibition but also to distortions, potential miscommunication, and the development of strong (positive and negative) transference/countertransference dynamics. Each offers challenges and opportunities.

Freud *might* well have said, were he here to comment, that it is very easy to find websites, groups, and online objects inviting cathexis (and through which libido can be sublimated), and, moreover, that the Internet fosters free-association, transference, and projection. There are also opportunities to address the symbolism involved in online pursuits such as virtual farming, self-focused quizzes, and profile photos. Freud might well have wondered more generally about the "psychopathology of everyday *online* life." Similarly, object relations theorists might have good cause to wonder whether multi-tasking and message boards invite "splitting" or how social networks might evolve into a somewhat richer but more fragmented inner world of part-objects, with both toxic and non-toxic object internalization generated by the mix of "real" experi-ence and fantasy. Is it like dreaming? Just try, in between tweets, texts, and incoming chat screens, to think for a moment about "the interpreta-tion of web experience"! For some, it may in fact be dream-like. For some it can also be highly addictive (Fenichel, 1997, 2009; Morrison & Gore, 2010).

No doubt many dreams these days include web-based content and day residue from online interpersonal relationships as well as the indelibly etched repetition of online applications, from Facebook to Flickr and Google to YouTube. Many now live substantial portions of their waking lives focused upon their master social control panel, otherwise known as Facebook. Still others have severely diminished attention spans corresponding with tweet-sized cognitive processing, something increasingly being shown to have a negative impact on neurological executive functioning. Some people disappear online into alternate realities, while others manage to integrate all the activities and distractions into daily life. It is this broad range of individual experience that is highly relevant in formulating a treatment plan, and not least of the considerations must in turn be the comfort levels experienced by both client and practitioner. On a cognitive level we might speak to the "automaticity" of using the technology. On a holistic, phenomenological level, the key is individual experience. Context is crucial.

Meanwhile, back in the material world, it is a given that a myriad of counselors, therapists, consultants, coaches, and advisors are poised and ready to respond to the groundswell of requests for online help, referral, advice, and counseling or psychotherapy. Many critical questions arise in the process, and these are being addressed through hands-on experience, research, and professional dialogue. Where does one go to for the best possible treatment or counseling/advice? Where are the best-trained online counselors found? What are the elements of ethical practice? How are "best practice" skills being developed and taught? What traits are called for in the therapist or counselor when one cannot see the diplomas on the wall, the warm smile, or the books on the shelf that reveal his or her therapeutic orientation? From the would-be provider's point of view, which strategies have shown the greatest potential? Does a combination of online interaction and f2f consultation work best? Can one work with couples? Children? What works best for whom, with whom, and for what purpose? Studies to further our clinical understanding of online relationships are clearly warranted, along with a clarion call for further research by social scientists in response to these variables. Great opportunities exist for groundbreaking empirical studies in terms of how people are utilizing Internet technologies to facilitate both insight and behavioral/goal-directed pursuits as well as social/communicative endeavors.

COMMUNICATING ACCURATELY AND EFFECTIVELY

One of the great challenges confronting online mental health professionals is the accurate perception of "meaning," nuance, and tone within the context of text-based communication. Correspondingly, the client is likely to benefit most when consistently feeling understood and believing the counselor or therapist to be concerned, empathic, and expert in helping with their particular problem.

There is a substantial body of information describing the various technical and practical challenges in effective online communication (e.g., Fenichel, 2000, 2002) as well as detailed analyses of the ways in which nuance, pacing, emphasis, and meaning, can be finessed through text-based communication, either through email or during the course of chat-based communication (Suler, 2000).

John Suler and the members of the ISMHO Clinical Case Study Group observed and described some of the many ways in which clients and counselors evolve natural communication styles that facilitate transparent, meaningful dialogue. For example:

> Experienced e-mail users have developed a variety of keyboard techniques to overcome some of the limitations of typed text — techniques that almost lend a vocal and kinesthetic quality to the message. They attempt to make e-mail conversations less like postal letters and more like a face-to-face encounter. Some of these strategies include the use of emoticons, parenthetical expressions that convey body language or 'sub vocal' thoughts and feelings (sigh), voice accentuation via the use of CAPS and *asterisks*, and trailers... to indicate a transition in thought or speech. Use of 'smileys' and other commonly used symbols can convey not only facial expression but also a variety of emotional nuances.
>
> **Fenichel et al., 2002**

PHENOMENOLOGY OF TWENTY-FIRST-CENTURY DAILY LIFE

Despite the assertion that it is possible to integrate online experience into one's daily life in a positive and effortless manner (e.g., Fenichel, 2002), it is apparent that for many people cyberspace offers an alternative, or virtual, reality that can be dissociated from other aspects of daily life. Some relish the opportunities for anonymity, to be creative, to try on new personas and new behaviors, or to find supportive environments as an alternative to real-life situations, which may be dysfunctional, stressful, or simply tedious. Others see the Internet and computers merely as tools, to find information, send announcements, or make travel reservations. Still others are able to utilize the Internet in the same way that they use a telephone, television, or automobile. With the majority of American households having the means for both instrumental and social uses of technology through "going online," society is poised for blurring boundaries and distinctions between the means of accessing each other and the things we need. Already, many among us — particularly the younger and more pragmatic — do not think twice about turning to the net to contact a friend, shop for a car, find medical information, or seek help in one way or another for psychological distress. Increasingly, the mental health expert is not only easy to find online but willing to respond to requests for help.

Much has already been written about the psychological dynamics of online life for the denizens of the Internet (netizens) who spend time conversing through email, list-servs, virtual communities, and message boards. Aside from the well-known "disinhibition effect," which derives from the empowerment that anonymity and lack of visual cues provide, there are opportunities to benefit from social support as well as much leeway for acting-out online. Until we know more about which are the most salient therapeutic factors, it is possible to speculate that a combination of nonspecifics (such as warmth, empathy, and genuineness) can be powerful, and often *new*, experiences for those who discover the relative ease of sharing personal experience with others over the Internet. Add to this a mental health professional's skill and experience (online as well as off), and it is easy to see why forming an initial therapeutic alliance seems inherently easy, certainly for the purposes of developing a treatment plan or well-circumscribed goals such as are the hallmark of short-term, goal-oriented psychotherapies (e.g., Bellak & Small, 1978; Malan, 1976). Yet, despite the potential for forming a therapeutic relationship and the growing number of online clinicians who are competent, professional, and ethical, not *every* presenting problem is ideally suited for this modality (see, e.g., Suler et al., 2001). There are also challenges and risks of exacerbating a situation by providing opportunities for dissociative experience online. This underscores the need for online counselors to be sensitized to the way in which both guided and unguided dissociation can occur online. Positive examples of this are found in activities such as healthy role-playing and encouraging use of a web page for creative and self-expressive pursuits. Negative examples can be seen in the phenomena of flaming, trolling, and stalking. Counselors need to know about these aspects of online behavior and relationships as they can be very real and powerful, even if "only online." Not only can there clearly be depth and poignancy in the relationships between people online, but, as Suler, King, and others have noted, there is tremendous potential for transference to quickly develop and deepen, as well as potential for the surfacing and working through of cognitive and emotional distortions, which for some is a key ingredient of psychotherapy.

One can truly wonder at the phenomenological aspects of online communication and web-based interpersonal relationships. Basic questions arise, such as, "Where and when is the 'here and now' of Cyberspace?" (Fenichel, 2002); How does an email correspondence provide an appropriate therapeutic frame? What modality provides the right amount of structure or the optimal therapeutic holding environment? When is a message board an appropriate supplement for f2f counseling, psychotherapy, or experiential classroom learning activities? When is an online community or message board effectively a self-contained therapeutic milieu? When might real-time chat be a powerful supplement to asynchronous email exchanges or a treatment of choice in response to a given client's need for immediacy? When would mixed media provide the best of all worlds, with f2f components and/or email journals, homework, and creative expression contributing to a longitudinal and multi-dimensional portrait of the client's full range of daily functioning?

Experience demonstrates that, for the net-savvy and skillful therapist or counselor, there are amazing new opportunities for effective yet unconventional types of treatment using various modalities, separately or in combination. A number of situations have been identified for which Internet-facilitated mental health services have been clearly invaluable, often providing much-needed support (and sometimes "treatment" or referral) for a wide variety of people who have reached out for assistance but who might not have done otherwise.

ONLINE BEHAVIOR IN CLINICAL PRACTICE

In 1999, the fledgling ISMHO established the Online Clinical Case Study Group (CSG), comprised of mental health professionals from the fields of psychology, psychiatry, social work, nursing, family therapy, and community counseling. For over a half decade, on a continuous basis, this multi-national, cross-discipline group of mental health professionals provided ongoing peer supervision while working toward formulating basic principles and strategies across a wide range of online clinical practice.

While initially focusing on ethical and practical considerations, the CSG quickly learned firsthand the power of peer support, shared resources (including web pages), case presentations, and case management skill-building. One profound benefit was the ability to seek collegial input in the event of a crisis or when unsure how to respond to an initial request for help or information. Having colleagues across the globe, in different time zones, engaged in numerous specialty areas, and with knowledge of local health care systems, provided a *human* web of online resources to draw upon, at any hour of the day or night, 365 days a year. Each and every member felt this kind of synergy to be an empowering experience.

The ISMHO CSG confronted a number of situations that were thought to be impossible to address or manage online, given how difficult such clients and presenting problems can be in an f2f situation. In fact, it was discovered that the online treatment frame can be a significant advantage in containing the emotional chaos involved.

As a result of intensive ongoing work and study, the ISMHO's CSG was able to highlight and clarify many of the challenges as well as the enormous potential of online clinical work. Along the way it was recognized that there exists an obvious need for online practitioners to have access to training and supervision that combines experiential and theoretical approaches and that employs a means of studying outcome as well as process. After three years, a number of "myths and realities" about online clinical work had emerged rather clearly, and were described in a third-year report (Fenichel et al., 2002). Among the more profound of the revelations was that some online endeavors that were widely thought to be impossible were clearly successful (e.g., crisis intervention and online interventions with some types of serious psychopathology). For example,

> An advantage of online work with severely disturbed clients is that clients can choose to use emails, chat scripts, and other online exchanges (that can be saved) to rehearse, review, and reinforce therapeutic messages in a way that can be grounding, affirming, and increase reality testing. Also, the therapist's empathic words can function as a transitional object that can be internalized over time at the client's pace. Additionally, having access to an International group of online colleagues has proven very useful in making rapid, appropriate referrals, sometimes in single-session correspondence or very short-term consultation.
>
> **Fenichel et al., 2002**

After an unprecedented half decade of continuous collaboration on this project, utilizing a case study, scientist-practitioner, peer supervision model – which took advantage of this amazing new technology and allowed for instant and diverse communication tools – the CSG issued its half-decade report (Fenichel et al., 2005). Even to this day, over a decade since its inception, members still turn to one another for peer consultation in which there is deep trust and ability to communicate as if by second nature, despite the lack of f2f presence. This is a legacy of evolving online communication skills, a phenomenon inherited and embraced by the children and teens who comprise the digital generation.

For some it may be surprising to learn that, unlike using the telephone, "going online" is subjectively a very different social experience; one has the ability to employ a vast array of hardware and software to interact with others through a variety of channels/communities utilizing chat, email, video/photo/music sharing, support/self-help, message boards, list-servs, and SMS/texting, to name some of the most popular activities. One can insert or post photographs, poems, cartoons, journal articles, or brochures, as well as creatively and expressively use color, emoticons, and "text talk" (Suler, 1997) for emphasis or to help convey nuance and emotional tone. The combined use of the Internet and the personal computer is far more multi-dimensional than simply picking up or flipping open one's telephone and talking. The way in which people are using the Internet – particularly younger people, who know no world without it – covers the spectrum from instant casual communication to information-seeking and sharing to profoundly creative activities and deeply meaningful personal dialogue fueled by collaborative interaction.

A Pew Internet and American Life Project report (2002) outlined the findings of a longitudinal study whereby it was found that there is a slight drop-off in time spent online simply surfing the net as users become more efficient in seeking what they really need. At the same time, evidence suggests that the Internet is increasingly being used to seek advice on matters of major importance.

SOCIAL CONNECTEDNESS: LIFE IN THE TWENTY-FIRST CENTURY

Imagine a world in which the norm is to choose from a menu of activities in daily life that combines the methods of technology-facilitating communication − telephone, radio, television, and the Internet. All of these venues can be utilized − some passively, some interactively − in order to reach out to friends and family, pursue hobbies, shop, and find information of importance. In such a world, in a century where f2f contacts compete with fax machines, corporate and school-based email, camera phones, Blackberries, iPhones, and instant messaging/SMS, life is rife with options, obligations, and possibilities, all within a culture where multi-tasking rules. That time is now.

Research and debate continue regarding the benefits and risks of allocating interpersonal time to a computer screen rather than using the telephone or interacting f2f with friends and family, and the consequences of spending excessive time online rather than with a family-in-waiting. Yet, any teenager will likely tell you that the time spent online, in chat and casual IM, is simply *additive* to time spent on the phone or playing video games, watching television, engaging in physical activities, or conversing with family members. In a widely reported study (LaRose et al., 2001) it was suggested that, despite initial theories about why online time "paradoxically" led college students to feelings of social isolation and depression, these early studies may have reflected feelings of poor self-efficacy among people with little computer or Internet experience. It thus follows, particularly in light of the very large-scale, longitudinal studies of the Pew project, that, with increased proficiency in using the Internet and feelings of self-confidence in response to positive reinforcement from finding help and information more readily, a shift in our relationships with (and on) the worldwide web is becoming widespread. The times, to paraphrase Bob Dylan, have been a-changin'. Now an entire generation, as one teen recently stated, "doesn't know anything else." It is a new era. Online is not a place; it is a means to connect and communicate, to learn and share, to seek and provide.

We are increasingly living in a world that is interconnected, which brings both immense opportunities as well as new and unique challenges. One may well argue that much of the debate over the Internet reflects individuals' comfort levels with the medium and ability to integrate Internet-facilitated communication tools into their lives in a congruent way. In this light, the computer is in fact only a tool that allows access to diverse mediums, in addition to near-universal access to every-body on earth who has access to a computer and an Internet connection.

If we accept that for many people daily life involves Internet-facilitated communication — which it increasingly does, at least for the majority of Americans and a growing number of people around the planet — it seems reasonable to assume that the type of experience that one shares in counseling or therapy sessions is likely going to reflect relationships that exist at least in part in the "here and now" of cyber-space (Fenichel, 2002). This notion of the here and now has been central to many concepts of psychotherapy ranging from Freud's transference–countertransference model to the Gestalt Therapy process and the use of the here and now in group therapy. Why? One common thread appears to be that the here and now reflects a grounded reference point for a person's reality and the basis on which a group or therapist can reflect distortions, transference processes, interpersonal dynamics, and underlying beliefs that manifest in real-time behavior and experience.

Another aspect of traditional therapies is that they may be "state-dependent" in that the analytical session may entail the couch and a style of minimally directive therapy; the psychiatric session may involve a prescription pad; the short-term behavior therapy environment may be a setting where notes are taken on homework assignments and diaries or logs; rational emotive behavior therapy may challenge self-defeating beliefs; and dialectical behavior treatments now extend far into belief systems that underlie cognition and behavior.

The online counselor is in the unique position of being both present in and removed from the psychological space where the dramas take place. At the same time, he or she can read the words of others in a pri-vate and self-selected holding environment. Guided by a treatment plan that recognizes realistic goals and expectations combined with the ability of the clinician to *truly* be empathic from the other side of the computer screen, the *new* nonspecifics of effective online counseling might well be in evidence through client reports of online warmth, online genuine-ness, and *online empathy*. Clinicians are now at a historical juncture where such online skills are ripe for an environment in which whole new perspectives and the development of new skills and theoretical frameworks are emerging.

The online practitioner needs to be knowledgeable about the larger field of mental health theory and practice, and to be trained and super-vised in keeping with the requirements of the helping professions at large. Yet, one needs also to know about the features of twenty-first-century interpersonal relationships that have not been covered in psychology textbooks (until now). Only if one can understand how a client may feel after being "flamed" in a chat room, how easy it is to miscommunicate online, or what is meant by various emoticons and short-hand means of texting thoughts, can one truly understand and empathize with an online client. Beyond such minimal understanding of online interpersonal life, the online therapist has the ability not only to address important events in a client's life as they occur both online and off, but also to mirror a client's words (in writing), encourage use of creative expression (e.g., using font color and graphics), combine modalities during a course of treatment (e.g., email and chat or phone, f2f and message board, journal assignments, or even virtual reality exercises), and provide self-help, support, and informational resources, which are abundantly available online. For the clinician to have so many tools available to assist in the client's self-discovery, self-healing, and goal attainment is quite exciting and clearly has the potential to revolutionize the mental health care delivery systems already in place.

CONCLUSION

There are myriad ways in which counseling and psychotherapy are traditionally offered, in a multiplicity of contexts. Such endeavors have increasingly been under the scrutiny of scientific study with regards to their efficacy and professional ethics. In this new dawn in which communication is possible between anyone on earth with the resources, skills, desire, and technology to reach across previous barriers, there are tremendous challenges and opportunities at hand. As practitioners and mental health professionals, whose primary "tools of the trade" are our own good judgment and application of best practices, we rely on professional training, experience, adaptive skills, and a new technological toolset to realize the potential now on the horizon, with access to mental health care resources such as could not have been envisioned in the primordial days of the twentieth century.

You, the reader of this book, are part of a new generation of clinicians, educators, and students who will extend the limits of what we know and can do with Internet-facilitated counseling, peer consultation, online supervision, training, education, and research. This updated compendium of contributions from many of the leaders within the field of online mental health represents a diverse sampling of perspectives. Key concepts are illuminated by pioneers in the field of online mental health, with elements of both theory and practice included in this comprehensive handbook for today's twenty-first-century mental health professionals. I hope you enjoy and appreciate the collective wisdom and practice-based discussions contained herein.

DISCUSSION QUESTIONS

1. How do we reframe the perpetual question of "What is therapy?" given the new age of online interpersonal communication? How can counseling and other goal-oriented mental health services best be conceptualized in light of their online versions?

2. In Japan, counseling occurs via texting, and office workers text the person next to them rather than establish eye contact. While cultural factors may not be as obvious to Americans surfing the net, what does the American online therapist or counselor need to know about lifestyle in *this* country, among children, teens, and young adults who were raised on the Internet? What do established offline clinicians need to know about online behavior? How does research inform practice regarding the efficacy or lack thereof of multi-tasking or tweeting as a means of social discourse?

3. While several excellent conceptual models and how-to guides are presented in the following pages, what are some ideas you have about the goals and outcomes of online work as well as the risks and benefits of text-based communication? How would you evaluate the adaptability of traditional sources of training (graduate schools, continuing education, specialized training) for online practice? Now that several training programs have been flourishing for a few years (largely outside of the US), what do we know about their successes and challenges? What do we know about cultural preferences online and what must we know about legal as well as technical and professional issues?

4. How would *you* train somebody in the basics of effective online communication? Could an experienced therapist who is limited in online skills be an effective online counselor? Can the offline therapist benefit from being more familiar with the culturally prevalent online life that so many have adopted? Conversely, do online therapists need less training in traditional f2f psychotherapy approaches?

5. What legal or professional mandate should govern licensed mental health professionals providing consultation, treatment, counseling, or psychotherapy using the Internet as a basis to establish or supplement their professional practices? What if the client is distant from the provider rather than residing in the provider's state of licensure? Is licensure relevant to online clinical work? For whom? Should there be specialty licensing for online practitioners?

6. What is *your* vision of online therapy or counseling? What is the potential? What are the risks? Given that the field is blossoming in popularity and providers are already meeting the growing demand, what would be best practice in your profession were you to engage clients using the Internet?

7. What questions would you ask an online counselor about their theoretical orientation and services? Which would you want to be asked? What would an ideal intake process look like?

Now read the rest of this book! See what questions arise and what sorts of research and practice issues you would like to see systematically explored and presented to students and practitioners. Then take part in it. There is still a lot of room at the leading edge. I leave you with a number of our most respected and well-known pioneers among the growing body of researchers, educators, and clinicians immersed in the experience of online counseling.

REFERENCES

Baker, A. (2008). Down the rabbit hole: The role of place in the initiation and development of online relationships. In A. Barak (Ed.), *Psychological aspects of cyberspace: Theory, research, applications* (pp. 163–184). New York, NY: Cambridge University Press.

Barak, A. (2001, November). *SAHAR: An Internet-based emotional support service for suicidal people.* Paper presented at a conference of The British Psychological Society, "Psychology and the Internet: A European Perspective," Farnborough, UK.

Barak, A., & Suler, J. (2008). Reflections on the psychology and social science of cyberspace. In A. Barak (Ed.), *Psychological aspects of cyberspace: Theory, research, applications* (pp. 1–12). New York, NY: Cambridge University Press.

Bellak, L., & Small, L. (1978). *Emergency psychotherapy and brief psychotherapy.* Larchmont, NY: Grune & Stratton.

Fenichel, M. (1997). "Internet addiction": Addictive behavior, transference or more? Retrieved 27 July 2010 from http://www.fenichel.com/addiction.shtml

Fenichel, M. (2000). Online psychotherapy: Technical difficulties, formulations and processes. Retrieved 27 July 2010 from http://www.fenichel.com/technical.shtml

Fenichel, M. (2002). The here and now of cyberspace. Retrieved 27 July 2010 from http://www.fenichel.com/herenow.shtml

Fenichel, M. (2009). Facebook addiction disorder: The latest "Fad"? Retrieved 27 July 2010 from http://www.fenichel.com/facebook

Fenichel, M, Jones, G, Meunier, V, Munro, K, & Walker-Schmucker, W. (2005). ISMHO Clinical Case Study Group: Half a decade of online case study. Retrieved 27 July 2010 from http://fenichel.com/csg6.shtml

Fenichel, M., Suler, J., Barak, A., Zelvin, E., Jones, G., Munro, K., et al. (2002). Myths and realities of online clinical work. *Cyberpsychology and Behavior, 5*(5). Retrieved 27 July 2010 from http://www.fenichel.com/myths

LaRose, R., Eastin, M. S., & Gregg, J. (2001). Reformulating the Internet paradox: Social cognitive explanations of Internet use and depression. *Journal of Online Behavior, 1*(2). Retrieved 27 July 2010 from http://www.behavior.net/JOB/v1n1/paradox.html

Malan, D. (1976). *The frontier of brief psychotherapy: An example of the convergence of research and clinical practice.* New York, NY: Plenum Publishing.

Morrison, C. M., & Gore, H. (2010). The relationship between excessive Internet use and depression: A questionnaire-based study of 1,319 young people and adults. *Psychopathology, 43,* 121–126.

Pew Internet and American Life Project (2002, March 3). Getting serious online: As Americans gain experience, they use the web more at work, write Emails with more significant content, perform more online transactions, and pursue more serious activities. Retrieved August 11, 2010 from http://www.pewinternet.org/Reports/2002/Getting-Serious-Online-As-Americans-Gain-Experience-They-Pursue-More-Serious-Activities.aspx

Pew Internet and American Life Project (2010, February 3). Social media and young adults. Retrieved 27 July 2010 from http://www.pewinternet.org/Reports/2010/Social-Media-and-Young-Adults.aspx

Robert, J. D. (2002). *Online Therapy Goes Mainstream.* New York, NY: The Wall Street Journal, p. D6.

Suler, J. R. (1997). Psychological dynamics of online synchronous conversations in text-driven chat environments. Retrieved 22 October 2010 from http://www-usr.rider.edu/~suler/psycyber/texttalk.html

Suler, J. R. (2000). Psychotherapy in cyberspace: A 5-dimensional model of online and computer-mediated psychotherapy. *Cyberpsychology and Behavior, 3,* 151−159.

Suler, J. R. (2002). The online disinhibition effect. Retrieved 27 July 2010 from http://www.rider.edu/users/suler/psycyber/disinhibit.html

Suler, J. R., Barak, A., Chechele, P., Fenichel, M., Hsiung, R., Maguire, J., et al. (2001). Assessing a person's suitability for online therapy. *Cyberpsychology and Behavior, 4,* 675−679 (See Correction, 2002, *Cyberpsychology and Behavior, 5,* 93).

FURTHER READING

Bai, Y. M., Lin, C. C., Chen, J. Y., & Liu, W. C. (2001). Virtual psychiatric clinics. *The American Journal of Psychiatry, 158,* 1160−1161.

Barak, A. (2002). Psychological applications on the Internet: A discipline on the threshold of a new millennium. Retrieved July 27 2010 from http://construct.haifa.ac.il/~azy/app-r.htm

Bouchard, S., Payeur, R., Rivard, V., Allard, M., Paquin, B., Renaud, P., et al. (2000). Cognitive behavior therapy for panic disorder with agoraphobia in videoconference: Preliminary results. *Cyberpsychology and Behavior, 3,* 999−1007.

Fenichel, M. (1996). Current topics in psychology. Retrieved September 16, 2010 from http://www.fenichel.com/Current.shtml

Fenichel, M. (2002). Online therapy. Retrieved September 16, 2010 from http://fenichel.com/OnlineTherapy.shtml

Grohol, J. M. (1998). Future clinical directions: Professional development, pathology, and psychotherapy on-line. In J. Gackenbach (Ed.), *Psychology and the Internet, intrapersonal, interpersonal, and transpersonal implications* (pp. 111−140). San Diego, CA: Academic Press.

Holmes, L. G. (1998). Delivering mental health services on-line: Current issues. *Cyberpsychology and Behavior, 1,* 19−24.

Hsiung, R. C. (2000). The best of both worlds: An online self-help group hosted by a mental health professional. *Cyberpsychology and Behavior, 3,* 935−950.

International Society for Mental Health Online (ISMHO). (2000). ISMHO/PSI suggested principles for the online provision of mental health services. Retrieved October 19, 2002 from http://ismho.org/suggestions.html

Kanz, J. E. (2001). Clinical-supervision.com: Issues in the provision of online supervision. *Professional Psychology: Research and Practice, 32,* 415−420.

King, S. A., & Moreggi, D. (1998). Internet therapy and self-help groups − The pros and cons. In J. Gackenbach (Ed.), *Psychology and the Internet, intrapersonal, interpersonal, and transpersonal implications* (pp. 77−109). San Diego, CA: Academic Press.

Klein, B., & Richards, J. C. (2001). A brief Internet-based treatment for panic disorder. *Behavioural and Cognitive Psychotherapy, 29,* 113−117.

Maheu, M. M., & Gordon, B. L. (2000). Counseling and therapy on the Internet. *Professional Psychology: Research and Practice, 31,* 484−489.

Murphy, L. J., & Mitchell, D. L. (1998). When writing helps to heal: E-mail as therapy. *British Journal of Guidance and Counseling, 26,* 21−32.

National Board for Certified Counselors. (2001). The practice of online counseling. Retrieved May 19, 2002 from http://www.nbcc.org/ethics/webethics.htm

Ookita, S. Y., & Tokuda, H. (2001). A virtual therapeutic environment with user projective agents. *Cyberpsychology and Behavior, 4,* 155−167.

Oravec, J. A. (2000). Online counselling and the Internet. Perspectives for mental health care supervision and education. *Journal of Mental Health, 9,* 121−135.

Rheingold, H. (2002). The virtual community. Retrieved October 19, 2002 from http://www.rheingold.com/vc/book/intro.html

Robinson, P. H., & Serfaty, M. A. (2001). The use of e-mail in the identification of bulimia nervosa and its treatment. *European Eating Disorders Review, 9,* 182−193.

Stofle, G. S. (2001). *Choosing an online therapist: A step-by-step guide to finding professional help on the Web.* Harrisburg, PA: White Hat Communications.

Suler, J., & Fenichel, M. (2000). The online clinical case study group of the International Society for Mental Health Online: A report from the Millennium Group. Retrieved May 19, 2002 from http:/ismho.org/casestudy/ccsgmg.htm

Suler, J. (2001). The online clinical case study group: An e-mail model. *Cyberpsychology and Behavior, 4,* 711−722.

Suler, J. (2002). The psychology of cyberspace. Retrieved October 19, 2002 from http://www.rider.edu/users/suler/psycyber/psycyber.html

Wiederhold, B. K., & Wiederhold, M. D. (1998). A review of virtual reality as a psychotherapeutic tool. *Cyberpsychology and Behavior, 1,* 45−52.

Chapter two

The Psychology of Text Relationships

John Suler, PhD

Psychology Department, Rider University, Lawrenceville, NJ

Editors' note: Most online interactions take place via the exchange of text messages, either in real-time chat or asynchronous emails. In text-based communication, perhaps more than in any other setting, there is a crucial relationship between what is said and how it is said. In this chapter, the author explains the nature of text-based communication.

I will begin this chapter by pointing out the obvious: text communication is as old as recorded history; hence, the psychology of text

21

Online Counseling. DOI: 10.1016/B978-0-12-378596-1.00002-2

communication dates just as far back. Letter writing and the creation of postal systems enabled more people to interact more personally via text. However, the advent of computer networks made the exchange of text more accessible, more efficient, and faster than ever before in history. Online text communication offers unprecedented opportunities to create numerous psychological spaces in which human interactions can unfold. We truly have entered a new age: the age of "text relationships."

This chapter will explore the psychology of these relationships while pointing out the implications for online clinical work. Many of the psychological dimensions of text communication in general apply across the board to the various types of text communication tool in particular — chat, email, message boards, instant messaging, blogs, and others more esoteric or yet to be invented. These different modalities differ in sometimes obvious, sometimes subtle, ways that make each a unique psychological environment — a fact the online clinician might keep in mind when choosing a communication tool for working with a particular client. Because email is the most widely used, much of my discussion will pertain to that modality, although I also will address important issues concerning the other modalities. I believe that a true understanding of the therapeutic value of any particular online communication tool rests on a wider appreciation of how it compares to and contrasts with the others. Online clinicians might strive to specialize in a particular type of text medium while recognizing its pros and cons vis-à-vis others.

Before I proceed to discussing the unique aspects of text relationships, I would like to point out that text is but one dimension of online communication. To encourage a wider view of the whole horizon of possibilities for online clinical work, I refer the reader to my conceptual model for understanding the larger set of dimensions that shape the various psychological environments of cyberspace: asynchronous versus synchronous communication, imaginary versus realistic environments, automated versus interpersonal interactions, being invisible versus being present, and the extent to which communication is text-driven or sensory-rich with sight, sound, even smells (Suler, 2000). All these dimensions interact with text to create a fascinating variety of therapeutic interventions. Clinicians can combine and sequence these different modalities to address the needs of a particular client.

LET'S TEXT: WRITING SKILLS, STYLES, ATTITUDES

"Text talk" is a skill and an art, not unlike speaking and yet different from speaking in important ways. Proficiency in one does not guarantee success in the other. Some truly great authors and poets might sound bumbling or shallow during in-person conversation. A person's ability to communicate effectively in text talk obviously depends highly on writing abilities. People who hate to write or are poor typists probably will not be drawn to text-based therapy. Self-selection is at work. Others report that they prefer writing as a way to express themselves. They take delight in words, sentence structure, and the creative opportunity to subtly craft exactly how they wish to articulate their thoughts and moods. In asynchronous communication, such as email and message boards, they may enjoy the "zone of reflection," where they can ponder on how to express themselves. In those cases, asynchronous text may be a less spontaneous form of communication than speech and online synchronous communication, such as chat. Unlike verbal conversation, in which words issue forth and immediately evaporate, writing also places one's thoughts in a more visible, permanent, concrete, and objective format. An email message is a tiny packet of self-representation that is launched off into cyberspace. Some people experience it as a piece of themselves, a creative work, a gift sent to their online companion. They hope or expect it to be treated with understanding and respect. Clinicians might look for how these skills and preferences for writing versus speaking might be associated with important differences in personality and cognitive style.

The quality of the text relationship rests on these writing skills. The better people can express themselves through writing, the more the relationship can develop and deepen. Poor writing can result in misunderstandings and possibly conflicts. In the absence of an accurate perception of what the other is trying to say, people tend to project their own expectations, anxieties, and fantasies onto the other. A disparity in writing ability between people can be problematic. The equivalent in f2f encounters would be one person who is very eloquent and forthcoming talking to another who speaks awkwardly and minimally. The loquacious one eventually may resent putting so much effort into the relationship and taking all the risks of self-disclosure. The quiet one may feel controlled, ignored, and misunderstood. As in f2f clinical work, therapists might modify their writing techniques — even basic elements of grammar and composition — to interact more effectively and empathically with the client.

We might tend to think of writing abilities as a fixed skill — a tool for expressing oneself that is either sophisticated, unsophisticated, or something in between. It is also possible that the quality of one's writing interacts with the quality of the relationship with the other. As a text relationship deepens and trust develops, people may open up to more expressive writing. They become more willing to experiment and take risks — not just in what specific thoughts or emotions they express but also in the words and composition used. Composition can advance when people feel safe to explore; it regresses when they feel threatened, hurt, or angry. These changes reflect the developmental changes in the relationship. Writing is not just a tool for developing the text relationship. Writing affects the relationship and the relationship affects the quality of the writing.

This same reciprocal influence exists between the text relationship and writing style. Concrete, emotional, and abstract expression; complexity of vocabulary and sentence structure; the organization and flow of thought — all reflect one's cognitive/personality style and influence how the other reacts. People who are compulsive may strive for well-organized, logically constructed, intellectualized messages with sparse emotion and few, if any, spelling or grammatical errors. Those with a histrionic flair may offer a more dramatic presentation, where neatness plays a back seat to the expressive use of spacing, caps, unique keyboard characters, and colorful language. Narcissistic people may write extremely long, rambling blocks of paragraphs. People with schizoid tendencies may be pithy, whereas those who are more impulsive may dash off a disorganized, spelling-challenged message with emotional phrases highlighted in shouted caps. Different writing/personality styles may be compatible with, incompatible with, or complementary to other styles.

One's attitude about writing also plays an important role. Composition conjures up memories from the school years of one's past. Self-concept and self-esteem may ride on those memories. In the course of an email relationship, those issues from the past may be stirred up.

The ISMHO Clinical Case Study Group (2001) suggests that the clinician, as part of the initial phase of counseling, assess the client's skills, attitudes, and past experiences regarding both reading and writing. A person's reading, writing, and typing skills may not be equivalent, but all are necessary for a text relationship. Some may prefer reading over writing, or vice versa. What do reading and writing mean to the person? What needs do these activities fulfill? Are there any known physical or cognitive problems that will limit the ability to read and write? The clinician might find it helpful to discuss how the person's attitudes and skills regarding in-person communication compare to those regarding text communication. When assessing the person's suitability for text communication, the clinician should remember that developing and enhancing the person's reading and writing skills may be intrinsic to the therapeutic process. Because synchronous text talk (chat, instant messaging) is quite different from asynchronous text talk (email, discussion boards), the clinician might also determine the client's skills and preferences regarding each. How does the person feel about the spontaneous, in-the-moment communication of chat as opposed to the opportunity to compose, edit, and reflect, as in email?

Our skills in text-based clinical work will deepen as we continue to explore the benefits of simply *writing*. Encouraging clients to express themselves in prose may help them to tap and strengthen a variety of therapeutic processes. It may encourage an observing ego, insight, working through, a reinforcing of positive mental resources, and, especially in asynchronous text, the therapeutic construction of a personal narrative, as in journal writing and bibliotherapy.

THE ABSENCE OF FACE-TO-FACE (F2F) CUES

As we will see throughout this chapter and book, the absence of f2f cues has a major impact on the experience of a text relationship. You cannot see other people's faces or hear them speak, meaning that all those subtle voice and body-language cues are lost, which makes the nuances of communicating more difficult. But humans are creative beings. Avid text communicators develop all sorts of innovative strategies for expressing themselves through typed text — in addition to the obvious fact that a skilled writer can communicate considerable depth and subtlety in the written word. Despite the lack of f2f cues, conversing via text has evolved into a sophisticated, expressive art form. The effective text clinician understands and attempts to master this art.

The lack of f2f cues may create ambiguity. Without hearing a person's voice or seeing body language and facial expressions, you may not be sure what the person means. This ambiguity activates the imagination, stirs up fantasies, and enhances the tendency to project your own expectations, wishes, and anxieties onto the somewhat shadowy figure sitting at the other end of the online connection. When in doubt, we fall back on our old expectations about how people relate to us, expectations that formed in our early relationships with our parents and siblings — what psychoanalytic clinicians would call a "transference reaction." As a text relationship develops over time, these reactions toward the other person may ebb and flow. When you first communicate via text, transference might be minimal because you do not know the other person well and have yet to develop a strong psychological investment in the relationship. Transference reactions more readily surface when emotional attachments begin to form but you still do not have a good "feel" for the person because of that lack of f2f cues. Other peak moments occur when emotional topics come up but you are unable to pinpoint exactly where the other person stands on the issue.

Under ideal conditions, as we spend more and more time conversing with a person via text, we begin to understand and work through those transference reactions so that we can see the other person as he or she really is. However, even under the best of circumstances, some aspect of our mental image of the other person rests more on our own expectations and needs than on the reality of the other person. With online communication, our mental image of the other person may be affected by what we think he might look like or how her voice might sound. We may not even be consciously aware that we have formed that impression until we meet the person f2f or talk to her on the phone, only to discover, much to our surprise, that she is in some important way very different from what we expected. In general, transference reactions are unconscious. We do not see them coming and do not fully realize how they are steering our behavior. That is why they can lead us astray, and sometimes into trouble.

In online therapy the client is not alone in this susceptibility to misperceptions, projections, and transference. Faced with those silent words scrolling down the screen, the clinician may develop countertransference: the ability to catch oneself possibly misinterpreting and projecting, to always entertain the possibility that one might be in the midst of a text transference, and to suspend final judgments about the client until more data comes in are key to effective online therapy. Helping clients to also develop this self-correcting awareness and helping them to explore and understand their text-based transference as it interacts with the therapist's countertransference may be a crucial component of their therapy, especially in the psychodynamic varieties.

Some incoming email or discussion board posts may be prepackaged with transference even though the person is a complete stranger to us. If you have a professional or personal website or other information about you is available on the Internet, people can form inaccurate impressions that they launch your way via an "out-of-the-blue" message. They may idealize you, detest you, or anything in between. These kinds of transference reaction often are deeply ingrained, prepared responses in the person that are ready to leap out at any opportune moment. On a fairly regular basis, I receive emails from people whom I call "spoon-feeders." There is no greeting, no sign-off line or name — just a terse request, or should I say *demand*, for something. Another common transference reaction is the "chip-on-my-shoulder" email. People who have antagonistic conflicts with authority figures may feel free to send a flaming email to someone they perceive as a parental figure. The bottom line with these kinds of unrequested email is this: you may not have a relationship with them, but they think they have a relationship with you. When beginning work with new clients, an online therapist might encourage them to discuss their impressions of the therapist as a result of seeing the website or other online information about the therapist.

The absence of f2f cues will have different effects on different people. For some, the lack of physical presence may reduce the sense of intimacy, trust, and commitment in the therapeutic relationship. Typed text may feel formal, distant, unemotional, or to be lacking a supportive and empathic tone. Some people want and need those in-person cues. Others will be attracted to the silent, less visually stimulating, nontactile quality of text relationships — which may be true for some people struggling to contain the overstimulation of past trauma. A person's ambivalence about intimacy may be expressed in text communication because the format is a paradoxical blend of allowing people to be honest and feel close while also maintaining their distance. People suffering with social anxiety or issues regarding shame and guilt may be drawn to text relationships because they cannot be seen. Some people even prefer text because it enables them to avoid the issue of physical appearance, which they find distracting or irrelevant to the relationship. Without the distraction of in-person cues, they feel they can connect more directly to the mind and soul of the other person. Text becomes a transitional space, an extension of their mind that blends with the extension of the other person's mind. Consider this woman's experience with her online lover:

> Through our closeness, we are easily able to gauge each other's moods, and often type the same things at the same time. We are able to almost read each other's thoughts in a way I have rarely found even in ftf [face-to-face] relationships (only my sister and I have a similar relationship in this respect) [. . .] It is in the cybersexual relationship where the most interesting aspects have developed. We are now able to actually "feel" each other, and I am often able to tell what he is wearing, even though we live more than 6000 miles away. I can "feel" his skin and smell and taste senses have also developed during sexual episodes. I have only seen one very small and blurred picture of this person so I have no idea what he really looks like, but I'm able to accurately describe him. He is able to "feel" me too. I'm sure that in the main it is just fantasizing, but to actually and accurately describe the clothing and color and texture of skin is really something I have never experienced before.

Although we may be skeptical about the validity of such reports — or not fully agree with the idea that physical presence is irrelevant — we clinicians should take seriously this subjective experience some people have of connecting more directly to the online companion's psyche. If a client experiences the clinician in this way, how might that determine a diagnosis and the therapeutic plan for that person?

Even though in this section I have been underplaying the sensory component of text relationships, I should emphasize that important visual components are present. As I will discuss later, creative keyboarding techniques (emoticons, spacing, caps, font color, size, etc.) offer a wide visual range of possibilities for presenting ideas and optimizing self-expression, often in ways that mimic f2f cues. As human factor engineers will tell us, the visual interface of our communication software also affects how we think, perceive, and express ourselves. Clinicians might be wise to make comparisons before choosing software for their work.

TEMPORAL FLUIDITY: SYNCHRONICITY AND ASYNCHRONICITY

Unlike in-person encounters, cyberspace offers the choice of meeting in or out of real time. In *asynchronous* communication, such as email and message boards, people do not have to be sitting at their computers at the same time. Usually this means there is a stretching of the time frame in which the interaction occurs, or no sense of a time boundary at all. You have hours, days, or even weeks to respond. Cyberspace creates a flexible temporal space where the ongoing, interactive time together can be stretched out or shortened, as needed. The perception of a temporally locked "meeting" disappears, although sitting down to read a message may subjectively feel as if one has entered a fluid temporal space with the other person, a more subjective sense of here and now. The opportunity to send a message to the therapist at any time can create a comforting feeling that the therapist is always there, always present, which eases feelings of separation and allows clients to articulate their thoughts and feelings in the ongoing stream of their lives, immediately during or after some important event, rather than having to wait for the next appointment.

This asynchronous communication does not require you to respond on-the-spot to what the other has said. You have time to think, evaluate, and compose your reply. This "zone of reflection" comes in very handy for those awkward or emotional situations in a relationship. Some people take advantage of this zone. Others, perhaps acting more spontaneously or at times impulsively, do not. When people receive a message that stirs them up emotionally, they might apply what I call the "24-hour rule." They may compose a reply without sending it (or write nothing), wait 24 hours, then go back to reread the other person's message and their unsent reply. "Sleeping on it" may help to process the situation on a deeper, more insightful level. The next day, from that new temporal perspective, they may interpret the other person's message differently, sometimes less emotionally. The reply they do send may be very different — hopefully much more rational and mature — from the one they would have sent the day before. The "stop and think" rule of thumb can save people from unnecessary misunderstandings and arguments. A wait-and-revise strategy helps to avert impulsiveness, embarrassment, and regret. In online therapy, clinicians can experiment with creative ways of encouraging clients to use this zone of reflection, to take advantage of the opportunity to self-reflect before responding to the clinician's message, perhaps as a way to stimulate an observing ego or enhance the process of working through an issue. In other cases, the clinician may suggest that clients *not* delay their response to encourage a more spontaneous, uncensored reply. For the therapist, the zone of reflection allows interventions to be more carefully planned and countertransference reactions to be managed more effectively.

Because email and other asynchronous forms of communication have this adjustable conversing speed, the pacing of message exchanges will vary over the course of a text relationship. There will be a changing rhythm of freely spontaneous and carefully planned messages that parallels the ebb and flow of the relationship itself. Significant changes in cadence may indicate a significant change in feelings, attitudes, or commitment. The initial excitement of making contact may lead to frequent messages. Some people may even unconsciously experience the interaction as if it is an f2f encounter and therefore expect an almost immediate reply. Later in the relationship, the pacing may level off to a rate of exchange that feels comfortable to both partners. As a general rule, the more frequently people email each other, the more important and intimate the relationship feels to them. Some people email each other every day, or several times a day. Bursts in the intensity of the pace occur when hot topics are being discussed or when recent events in one's life need to be explained. These bursts may reflect a sudden deepening of the intimacy in the relationship. Declines in the pace may indicate a temporary or long-term weakening of the bonds between the couple — either due to a lagging interest in the relationship or distractions from other sectors of one's life. Drastic drops in the pace, or an apparent failure of the partner to respond at all, throws you into a "black hole experience." The partner's silence may be a sign of anger, indifference, stubborn withdrawal, punishment, laziness, or preoccupation with other things. But you do not know for sure. The ambiguity inherent in the no-reply can easily become a blank screen onto which we project our own expectations, emotions, and anxieties.

Some clients will be avid text communicators. The computer will be a major feature of their interpersonal and professional life. They email all day long. Other clients will be novices in the online world. They log on only once or twice a week. To effectively adjust the pacing of their work, the clinician needs to take such differences into consideration.

Asynchronicity presents potential problems. Spontaneity and a sense of commitment to the relationship may decline without that in-the-moment contact. Without being together in real time, some clients may experience the therapist as less "present." Although time zones seem irrelevant, clinicians need to sensitize themselves to the fact that the client's temporal experience of the therapeutic encounter may not match that of the clinician. I "see" the client in the morning, but the client "sees" me at night. Pauses in the conversation, coming late to a session, and no-shows are lost as psychologically significant cues. Although we eliminate the scheduling difficulties associated with an "appointment," we also lose the professional boundaries of that specific, time-limited appointment. In our culture we are not used to interacting with a professional in an asynchronous time frame. Because online therapists run the risk of being overwhelmed with messages from the client or having the client drift away, they must be careful to create guidelines for an effective, reliable, manageable pacing of messages.

In *synchronous* communication, such as chat and instant messaging, the client and therapist are sitting at their computer at the same time, interacting with each other in that moment. Text chat includes the more common message-by-message exchanges in which a button is clicked to transmit the composed and perhaps edited message, as well as chat conversations where everything that both parties type can be seen as it is being typed, including typos, backspacing, and deletions, which enhances the synchronicity, spontaneity, and meaning of the experience. In all types of chat the act of typing does slow down the pace, thus making the conversation a little asynchronous compared to f2f meetings. Technical factors, especially transmission speeds, also determine just how closely a chat meeting approaches the tempo of an in-person encounter. In text-only chat, for example, "lag" due to busy networks may slow down the conversation between the client and therapist, resulting in temporal hiccups of several or even dozens of seconds between exchanges. This creates a small zone of reflection, which can be useful. However, it is not easy knowing when to wait to see if someone will continue to type, when to reply, or when to change the topic of discussion. A conversation may accidentally become crisscrossed until both partners get "in sync." Users skilled in online chat create incomplete sentences or use dot trailers at the end of a sentence fragment. . . that lead the companion into the next message. To allow the other user to express a complex idea, you may need to sit back into a listener mode. Some users will even type "listening" to indicate this posture to others. Some people have a greater intuitive sense of how to pace the conversation: when to talk, when to wait and listen. They possess an empathic understanding of the synchronous text relationship and of the particular person with whom they are conversing.

The temporal pros and cons of synchronous communication are the mirror image of those for synchronous communication. Synchronous communication provides the opportunity to schedule sessions defined by a specific, limited period of time — the culturally familiar "appointment." It can create a point-by-point connectedness that enhances feelings of intimacy, presence, interpersonal impact, and "arriving together" at ideas. People may be more spontaneous, revealing, or uncensored in their self-disclosures. Pauses in the conversation, coming late to a session, and no-shows are not lost as temporal cues that reveal important psychological meanings.

On the down side, the zone of reflection diminishes. Clients may lose the opportunity to compose their message, to say exactly what they want to say. In fact, some people feel they can create a stronger presence in asynchronous communication because they have more opportunity to express complexity and subtlety in what they write about themselves. They present themselves more fully. In synchronous communication, clients also may associate "therapy" specifically with the appointment rather than experiencing it as a process that generalizes to their outside life.

DISINHIBITION

It is well known that people say and do things in cyberspace that they ordinarily would not in the f2f world. They loosen up, feel more uninhibited, and express themselves more openly. Researchers call this the "disinhibition effect." It is a double-edged sword. Sometimes people share very personal things about themselves. They reveal secret emotions, fears, and wishes and show unusual acts of kindness and generosity, and as a result intimacy develops. Clinicians dare to make important interventions that they would have withheld f2f. On the other hand, the disinhibition effect may not be so benign. Out spills rude language, harsh criticisms, anger, hatred, even threats. People act out in all ways imaginable. Intimacy develops too rapidly resulting in regret, anxiety, and a hasty termination of the relationship. Clinicians say something better left unsaid. On the positive side, disinhibition indicates an attempt to understand and explore oneself, to work through problems and find better ways of relating to others. And sometimes it is simply a blind catharsis, an acting out of unsavory needs and wishes without any personal growth at all. Earlier in this chapter I cited an email in which a woman, a complete stranger to me, intimately described her relationship with her online lover. Consider also this email from another stranger:

> i am so suicidal every day that i have to tell somebody i would die and it would be all my parents fault for beating me every day and my classmates faults for making my life miserable every day and my dealers fault for going out of town and my fault for being manic depressive and suicidal and it would all be yalls fault cause your fuckin site is to god damn confusing and i couldnt talk to anybody. *thank you for your time* please feel just fucking free to email me back

What causes this online disinhibition? What is it about cyberspace that loosens the psychological barriers that normally block the release of these inner feelings and needs? Several factors are operating, many of them driven by the qualities of text communication that I have described previously. For some people, one or two of these factors produce the lion's share of the disinhibition effect. In most cases these factors interact with each other and supplement each other, resulting in a more complex, amplified effect.

Anonymity (You Don't Know Me)

As you move around the Internet, most of the people you encounter cannot easily tell who you are. People only know what you tell them about yourself. If you wish, you can keep your identity hidden. As the word "anonymous" indicates, you can have no name — at least not your real name. That anonymity works wonders for the disinhibition effect. When people have the opportunity to separate their actions from their real world and identity, they feel less vulnerable about opening up. Whatever they say or do cannot be directly linked to the rest of their lives. They do not have to own their behavior by acknowledging it within the full context of who they "really" are. When acting-out hostile feelings, the person does not have to take responsibility for those actions. In fact, people might even convince themselves that those behaviors "aren't me at all." This is what many clinicians would call "dissociation."

Invisibility (You Can't See Me)

In many online environments, other people cannot see you. They may not even know that you are present. Invisibility gives people the courage to do things that they otherwise would not. This power to be concealed overlaps with anonymity because anonymity is the concealment of identity. But there are some important differences. In text communication others may know a great deal about who you are. However, they still cannot see or hear you — and you cannot see or hear them. Even with everyone's identity visible, the opportunity to be "physically" invisible amplifies the disinhibition effect. You do not have to worry about how you look or sound when you type something. You do not have to worry about how others look or sound. Seeing a frown, a shaking head, a sigh, a bored expression, and many other subtle and not-so-subtle signs of disapproval or indifference can slam the breaks on what people are willing to express. The psychoanalyst sits behind the patient to remain a physically ambiguous figure, without revealing any body language or facial expression, so that the patient has free range to discuss whatever he or she wants without feeling inhibited by how the analyst physically reacts. In everyday relationships, people sometimes avert their eyes when discussing something personal and emotional. It is easier not to look into the other's face. Text communication offers a built-in opportunity to keep one's eyes averted.

Delayed Reactions (See You Later)

In asynchronous relationships, people may take minutes, hours, days, or even months to reply to something you say. Not having to deal with someone's immediate reaction can be disinhibiting. The equivalent in real life might be saying something to someone, magically suspending time before that person can reply, and then returning to the conversation when you are willing and able to hear the response. Immediate, real-time feedback from others tends to have a powerful effect on the ongoing flow of how much people express. In email and message boards, where there are delays in that feedback, people's trains of thought may progress more steadily and quickly toward deeper expression of what they are thinking and feeling. Some people may even experience asynchronous communication as running away after posting a message that is personal, emotional, or hostile. It feels safe putting it out there where it can be left behind. Kali Munro, an online clinician, aptly calls this an "emotional hit and run."

Solipsistic Introjection (It's All in My Head)

As described earlier, people sometimes feel online that their mind has merged with the mind of the other person. Reading another person's message might be experienced as a voice within one's head, as if that person magically has been inserted or introjected into one's psyche. Of course, we may not know what the other person's voice actually sounds like, so in our head we assign a voice to that person. In fact, consciously or unconsciously, we may even assign a visual image to what we think that person looks like and how that person behaves. The online companion now becomes a character within our intrapsychic world, a character shaped partly by how the person actually presents him- or herself via text communication and partly by our expectations, wishes, and needs. Because the person may remind us of other people we know, we fill in the image of that character with memories of those other acquaintances. As the character now becomes more elaborate and "real" within our minds, we may start to think, perhaps without being fully aware of it, that the typed-text conversation is all taking place within our heads, as if it is a dialog between us and this character in our imagination — as if we are authors typing out a play or a novel. Even when it does not involve online relationships, many people carry on these kinds of conversation in their imagination throughout the day. People fantasize about flirting, arguing with a boss, or very honestly confronting a friend about what they feel. In their imagination, where it is safe, people feel free to say and do all sorts of things that they would not in reality. At that moment, reality *is* one's imagination. Online text communication can serve as the psychological tapestry in which a person's mind weaves these fantasy role-plays, usually unconsciously and with considerable disinhibition.

When reading another's message, it is also possible that you "hear" that person's words using your own voice. We may be sub-vocalizing as we read, thereby projecting the sound of our voice into the other person's message. Perhaps unconsciously, it feels as if I am talking to/with myself. When we talk to ourselves, we say all sorts of things that we would not say to others.

Neutralizing of Status (We're Equals)

In text communication, we do not see the trappings of status and power — the fancy office, expensive clothes, diplomas on the walls, and books on the shelves. In addition, a long-standing attitude on the Internet is that everyone should be equal, everyone should share, everyone should have equivalent access and influence. Respect comes from your skill in communicating (including writing skills), your persistence, the quality of your ideas, your technical know-how. Everyone, regardless of status, wealth, race, and gender, starts off on a level playing field. These factors combined tend to reduce the perception of authority. Usually people are reluctant to say what they really think as they stand before an authority figure. A fear of disapproval and punishment from on high dampens the spirit. But, online, in what feels more like a peer relationship, people are much more willing to speak out or misbehave.

Of course, the online disinhibition effect is not the only factor that determines how much people open up or act out in cyberspace. The strength of underlying feelings, needs, and drive level has a big influence on how people behave. Personalities also vary greatly in the strength of defense mechanisms and tendencies toward inhibition or expression. People with histrionic styles tend to be very open and emotional. Compulsive people are more restrained. The online disinhibition effect interacts with these personality variables, in some cases resulting in a small deviation from the person's offline behavior and in other cases causing dramatic changes.

FLUID AND TRANSCENDED SPACE

In text relationships, geographical distance poses no barrier to accessing other people online. Despite hundreds or thousands of miles of distance, the connection is always seconds away, always available, always on. The therapist can reach into the client's environment, intervening *in vivo*, in ways not possible during f2f counseling. In return, clients may experience the therapist as "here" (e.g., immediately present in their life space). Issues of separation and individuation take on a new meaning, which may be an advantage or disadvantage, depending on the client and the therapeutic circumstances.

A much more subjective, psychological sense of space replaces the physical or geographical sense of space. As mentioned earlier, people may experience text relationships as an intermediate zone between self and other, an interpersonal space that is part self, part other. Sitting down at one's computer and opening up the communication software activates the feeling that one is entering that space. However, the very nature of text relationships — reading, writing, thinking, and feeling, all inside our head as we sit quietly at the keyboard — encourages us to continue carrying that internalized interpersonal space with us throughout the day. How often do we compose email messages in our heads as we wash dishes and drive the car?

Although text relationships transcend geographical distance, they do not transcend the cultural differences associated with geography. People around the world have different customs for conversing and developing relationships, including text relationships. Some of the ideas discussed in this chapter will be culture-bound. A good rule of thumb in conversing with people from other lands is to be appropriately polite and friendly and as clear as possible in what you write. Stretch your email empathy muscles. Unless you are very sure of your relationship with the person, avoid colloquialisms, slang, humor, innuendoes, and, especially, subtle attempts at cynicism and sarcasm, which are difficult to convey in text even under the best of circumstances. Starting off polite and later loosening up as the relationship develops is safer than inadvertently committing a faux pas and then trying to patch up the damage.

SOCIAL MULTIPLICITY

Spatial fluidity contributes to another important feature of cyberspace: social multiplicity. With relative ease, a person can contact hundreds or thousands of people from all walks of life, from all over the world. By posting a message on bulletin boards read by countless numbers of users, people can draw to themselves others who match even their most esoteric interests. Using a web search engine, they can scan through millions of pages in order to zoom their attention onto particular people and groups. The Internet will get more powerful as tools for searching, filtering, and contacting specific people and groups become more effective.

But why do we choose only some people to connect with and not others? A person will act on unconscious motivations — as well as conscious preferences and choices — in selecting friends, lovers, and enemies with whom to establish text relationships. Transference guides them toward specific types of people who address their underlying emotions and needs. Pressed by hidden expectations, wishes, and fears, this unconscious filtering mechanism has at its disposal an almost infinite candy store of online alternatives from which to choose. As one experienced online user once said to me, "Everywhere I go in cyberspace, I keep running into the same kinds of people!" Carrying that insight one step further, another said, "Everywhere I go, I find... ME!"

As I mentioned earlier, online clinicians might keep in mind that a person who contacts them for counseling may already have seen their website or learned a substantial amount about them. The client-to-be may have been shopping around the Internet for a therapist who seemed right for him or her. Knowing how and why the client came to you, what precontact impressions the client formed, and why the client decided against other online therapists all may be important issues to discuss. The therapist might also keep in mind that the client knows those other online clinicians are still waiting off in the wings. Ending one relationship and beginning another involves just a few clicks. Online social multiplicity may magnify the factors contributing to early termination, such as counterdependence, flights into health, a fear of intimacy and vulnerability, and other forms of resistance. Clinicians with a prominent online presence may also receive many unsolicited contacts from strangers with varying degrees of transference reactions and a wide variety of requests for help, advice, and information. They will need to develop strategies for deciding when and how to respond to such contacts from strangers whose motivations and needs may not be obvious.

Social multiplicity creates opportunities for a fascinating variety of group work. People experiencing similar problems, even unusual problems, easily can join together with a clinician in an email or message board group, regardless of their geographical location. In addition to this ability to form unique, topic-focused groups, online social multiplicity creates opportunities for group formats and processes not always possible in f2f meetings. Using layered interactions, a group can function on two different levels using two different channels of communication, with one channel perhaps functioning as a metadiscussion of the other, a computer-mediated enhancement of the "self-reflective loop." The group process becomes layered, with perhaps a core, spontaneous, synchronous experience and a superimposed asynchronous metadiscussion. In a nested group, people can communicate with each other while also being able to invisibly communicate with one or more people within that group. Although such private messaging can create subgrouping and conflict, it also can be useful in enabling group members and the therapist to offer hidden coaching and support that ultimately enhances the whole group. In overlapping groups, individuals or subgroups within one group can communicate with individuals or subgroups from a sister group, which enables a comparison of experiences across groups. Some online clinicians also use a metagroup that silently observes a meeting and then offers its feedback to the whole group or privately to individuals during or after the online meeting. In a wheel group, the clinician might multiconverse with several clients at the same time, as in chat or instant messaging, essentially serving as the hub of the group with all lines of communication directed at the clinician. The clients may not even know that other clients are present or that a "group" even exists.

RECORDABILITY: ARCHIVES AND QUOTED TEXT

Most text communication, including email and chat sessions, can be recorded and saved. Unlike real-world interactions, we have the opportunity to keep a permanent record of what was said, to whom, and when. Most email programs enable users to create filters and a special folder to direct and store messages from a particular person or group, thereby creating a distinct space or "room" for those relationships. If we have only known certain people via text, we may even go so far as to say that our relationships with them *are* the messages we exchanged, that these relationships can be permanently recorded in their entirety, perfectly preserved in bits and bytes. Stored email communication is not unlike a novel, which is not a record of characters and plot but rather *is* the characters and plot.

At your leisure, you can review what you and your partner said, cherish important moments in the relationship, re-examine misunderstandings and conflicts, or refresh a faulty memory. The archive offers clinicians an excellent opportunity to examine nuances of the therapeutic relationship and the progress of their work with the client. Clinicians also might encourage clients to create their own archives, as well as invent a variety of therapeutic exercises that have specific objectives in guiding the client's reviews of that stored text.

Left to their own design, people differ in terms of how much of a text relationship they save. The person who saves less — or maybe none at all — may have a lower investment in the relationship. Or, they may not be as self-reflective about relationships as people who wish to reread and think about what was said. On the other hand, that person may simply have less of a need to capture, preserve, or control the relationship. Some people like to "live in the moment." They may not feel a need to store away what was said, which does not necessarily indicate less of an emotional attachment.

When people save only some of the text, they usually choose those chunks of the relationship that are especially meaningful to them — emotional high points, moments of intimacy, important personal information, or other milestones in the relationship. Comparing the text saved by one person to that saved by the partner could reveal similarities and discrepancies in what each finds most important about the relationship. One person might savor humor, practical information, personal self-disclosures, emotional recollections, or intellectual debate, whereas the other may not. Saving mostly one's own messages, or mostly the other person's messages, may reflect a difference in focus on either self or other. The area of significant overlap in saved messages reflects the common ground of interest and attitude that holds the relationship together.

Unless you are simply searching for practical information (e.g., phone number, address), what prompts you to go back and read old text may indicate something significant happening in the relationship or your reaction to it. Doubt, worry, confusion, anger, nostalgia? What motivates you to search your archive? The curious thing about rereading old text (even if it is just a few days old) is that it sounds different from how it did the first time you read it. You see the previous communication in a new light or from a new perspective, or you notice nuances that you did not see before. You might discover that the emotions and meanings you previously detected were really your own projections and nothing that the sender put there (i.e., your transference reaction). You might realize that your own feelings have distorted your recollection of the history of the relationship.

We are tempted to think that a text archive is a factual record of what was said. In some ways it is. But saved text also is a container into which we pour our own psyche. We invest it with all sorts of meanings and emotions, depending on our state of mind at the moment. Herein lies the therapeutic potential of encouraging clients to reread previous conversations as well as an opportunity for the therapist to understand countertransference reactions.

An advantage of email over f2f conversations is the ability to quote part or all of what the other person said in the previous message. Hitting "reply" and then tacking your response to the top or bottom of the quoted email is a quick and easy rejoinder. In some cases it's a very appropriate strategy – especially when the other person's message was short, which makes it obvious what you are replying to. However, inserting a reply at the top or bottom of a long quoted message may be perceived by the other person as laziness or indifference on your part – as if you simply hit the reply button, typed your response, and clicked on "send." The person may not be sure exactly what part of the message you are responding to and also may feel annoyed at having to download an unnecessarily long file. Sticking a reply at the end of the lengthy quoted message can be particularly annoying because it forces the person to scroll and scroll and scroll, looking for the reply. All in all, quoting the entirety of a hefty message may not come across as a considerate and personal response. The impersonal tone may be exacerbated by those email programs that automatically preface a block of quoted text with a standardized notice such as, "On Saturday, May 28, Joe Smith said:" Whereas this automated notation may work fine for formal, businesslike relationships, or on email lists where multiple conversations are taking place, it may leave a bad taste in the mouth during more personal relationships.

The alternative to quoting the whole message is to select out and respond individually to segments of it. It takes more time and effort to quote segments rather than the whole message, but there are several advantages. People may appreciate the fact that you put that time and effort into your response. It makes your message clearer, more to the point, and easier to read. It may convey to your partner a kind of empathic attentiveness because you are responding to specific things that he or she said. Applying Rogerian reflection, you are letting the person know exactly from what text the importance of their communication seemed to originate. Replying to several segments can create an intriguingly rich email in which several threads of conversation occur at the same time, each with a different content and emotional tone. In one multilevel email, you may be joking, explaining, questioning, recalling a past event, and anticipating a future one. To establish continuity over several back-and-forth exchanges, you can create embedded layers of quoted segments, with each layer containing text from an earlier message. However, too many layers result in a confusing message in which it is unclear who said what and when. Messages with multiple quoted segments need to be formatted clearly.

Usually, one quotes lines from the most recent message received from the email partner. If you have an email archive, you also can quote lines from earlier messages, including messages from long ago. This may have a dramatic impact on your partner. On the positive side, people may be pleased to realize that you are saving their messages — in a sense, holding them in your memory, even cherishing their words. On the negative side, they may feel uncomfortable seeing their words revived from the distant past — especially when they do not quite remember when or in what context they were said. It is a reminder that you have a record of them. The situation can be even more unnerving when they do not have a record of the message themselves, so they cannot verify the accuracy of the quote. A slightly paranoid feeling seeps in. "Am I being deceived, held hostage? Why didn't *I* save that message?" Of course, all of these negative reactions are amplified when people use old quoted text in an accusatory or hostile manner.

Quoting segments can create other problems too. Divvying up the other person's message into numerous quotes, with your comments interspersed, may be experienced by other people as impatient, interruptive, or unempathically disrespectful of the integrity of their message. In flame wars you often see people citing more and more of what the opponent said, using it as ammunition to launch counterattacks. A series of point-by-point retorts becomes a verbal slicing up of the foe, almost as if it reflects an unconscious wish to tear up the person by dissecting his or her message. Often attackers want to legitimize their arguments by citing the opponent's exact words, as if the citation stands as concrete, unquestionable evidence. "This is precisely what you said." However, it's very easy to take sentences out of context, completely misread their emotional tone, or juxtapose several segments extracted from different parts of the other person's emails in order to draw a false conclusion from that forced composite of ideas. It's an attempt to create a contrived reality that Michael Fenichel has aptly called a "cut and paste reality."

MEDIA DISRUPTION

With the exception of such things as laryngitis and noisy heating systems, we take for granted the accuracy and stability of the communication channel during f2f conversations. Online, we need to be more cognizant of possible communication disruptions. There will be moments when software and hardware do not work properly, when noise intrudes into the communication, or when connections break. Busy servers result in lag that drastically slows down a chat conversation. A server may crash, preventing everyone from getting to the message board. Our email that we carefully constructed with special indentations and different fonts of different colors may lose all that formatting as it passes through mail servers that do not notice our creative keyboarding — essentially, a problem in translation. There will even be moments in a text relationship when we receive no reply and no error message at all, leaving us wondering whether the problem is technical or interpersonal. That lack of response opens the door for us to project all sorts of worries, anxieties, and fantasies into this black hole experience.

Some computer-mediated environments are more robust than others, a fact online clinicians need to take into consideration when choosing their tools. Even in stable channels, therapists might take measures to confirm that the mechanical translation of the message is accurate ("Can you see this font?") and to create backup communication procedures if the primary channel fails.

THE MESSAGE BODY

In email and message boards, the body of the message contains the meat of the communication. I like the metaphor of "the body" because it captures the connotation of the physical self — how people appear and move, their sound and tone, their body language, and even the elusive and rather mysterious dimensions of "presence." The message body is the most complex component of the communication. Messages can vary widely in length; organization; flow of ideas; spelling errors; grammar sophistication; spacing of paragraphs; use of quoted text, caps, tabs, emoticons, and other unique keyboard characters; and in the overall visual "feel" of the message. As mentioned earlier in this chapter, the structure of the email body reflects the cognitive and personality style of the individual who creates it.

One interesting feature of the message body — not unlike the physical body — is the extent to which it is planned and controlled or spontaneous and free. Carefully constructed text, even when intended to be empathic, may lack spontaneity. It is possible to overthink and micromanage the message to the point where it sounds contrived. Nevertheless, despite conscious attempts to present oneself exactly as one wishes, hidden elements of one's personality unconsciously may surface. On the other hand, completely freeform, loosely constructed text may confuse or annoy people. The most effective message is one that strikes a balance between spontaneity and carefully planned organization. Short messages with a few obvious spelling errors, glitches, or a slightly chaotic visual appearance can be a sincere expression of affection and friendship — as if the person is willing to let you see how they look hanging around the house, wearing an old t-shirt and jeans. Or, such a message can be a genuine expression of the person's state of mind at that moment: "I'm in a hurry, but I wanted to dash this off to you!" In the course of an ongoing text relationship, there will be an engaging rhythm of spontaneous and carefully-thought-out messages that parallels the ebb and flow of the relationship itself. Composition can become more casual, detailed, and expressive as the relationship develops and people feel safe to explore; it regresses when they feel threatened, hurt, or angry. In some cases, chaotic, regressed text may indicate decompensation and psychosis.

Text construction reflects an important personality trait — text empathy. Is there just the right measure of organization so the reader understands, along with the right measure of spontaneity so the reader appreciates, the writer's genuineness? Does the sender pay attention to and anticipate the needs of the recipient? Empathic people specifically respond to what their text partners have said. They ask their partners questions about themselves and their lives. They also construct their messages anticipating what it will be like for the recipient to read it. They write in a style that is both engaging and readily understood. With appropriate use of spacing, paragraph breaks, and various keyboard characters (...///**) to serve as highlights and dividers, they visually construct the message so that it is easy and pleasing to read. They estimate just how long is too long. Essentially, they are good writers who pay attention to the needs of their reader. This is quite unlike people with narcissistic tendencies who have difficulty putting themselves into the shoes of the recipient. They may produce lengthy blocks of unbroken text, expecting that their partner will sustain an interest in scrolling and reading for seemingly endless screens of long-winded descriptions of what the sender thinks and feels. Paradoxically, the narcissistic person's need to be heard and admired may result in the recipient hitting the delete key out of frustration or boredom.

Text empathy includes an intuitive feeling for what others might be feeling and thinking. Curiously, it is reported that, even in the stripped-down sensory world of text relationships — even in the bare bones of chat communication — others sometimes sense what's on your mind, even when you didn't say anything to that effect. Did they detect your state of mind from subtle clues in what or how you typed? Are they picking up on some seemingly minor change in how you typically express yourself? Or does their empathy reach beyond your words appearing on the screen? Obviously, this intuitive insight into the message body is a skill crucial to the success of an online clinician. It is a skill that may be different from intuition in f2f communication.

Humans are curious creatures. When faced with barriers, they find all sorts of creative ways to work around them, especially when those barriers involve communication. Despite the auditory and visual limitations of text relating, experienced onliners have developed a variety of keyboard techniques to overcome some of the limitations of typed text — techniques that lend a vocal, kinesthetic quality to the message and that indeed create a metaphorical message "body." They attempt to make text conversations less like postal letters and more like an f2f encounter. In addition to the expressive use of fonts, colors, spacing, and indentations, some of these creative keyboarding strategies include the following:

- *Emoticons* like the smiley, winky, and frown, which are seemingly simple character sets that nevertheless capture very subtle nuances of meaning and emotion. The smiley often is used to clarify a friendly feeling when otherwise the tone of the sentence might be ambiguous. It also can reflect benign assertiveness, an attempt to undo hostility, subtle denial or sarcasm, self-consciousness, and apologetic anxiety. The winky is like elbowing your email partner, implying that you both know something that does not need to be said out loud. It often is used to express sarcasm. The frown is used to express personal displeasure or sadness, or to show sympathy for an email partner who is unhappy.
- *Parenthetical expressions* that convey body language or "subvocal" thoughts and feelings (sigh, feeling unsure here). They are an intentional effort to convey some underlying mood or state of mind, almost implicitly saying, "Hey, if there is something hidden or unconscious going on inside me, this is probably it!"
- *Voice accentuation* via the use of caps, asterisks, and other keyboard characters in order to place vocal *EMPHASIS* on a particular word or phrase.
- *Trailers* to indicate a pause in thinking... or a transition in one's stream of thought. Combined with such vocal expressions as... uh... um..., trailers can mimic the cadence of in-person speech, perhaps simulating hesitation or confusion.
- *LOL*, the acronym for "laughing out loud," which serves as a handy tool for responding to something funny without having to actually say "Oh, that's funny!" It feels more natural and spontaneous — more like the way you would respond in an f2f situation.
- *Exclamation points*, which tend to lighten up the mood of otherwise bland or serious-sounding text. Text peppered lightly with exclamations, at just the right spots, provides a varying texture of energy that highlights mood and enthusiasm. Too many exclamation points may result in text that seems contrived, shallow, or even uncomfortably manic.
- *Expressive acronyms*, such as imo (in my opinion) and jk (just kidding), used as shorthand expressions.

As with all things, practice makes perfect, so people tend to fine-tune and enhance their text expressiveness over time. As a relationship develops, the partners also become more sensitive to the nuances of each other's typed expression. Together they develop their own emoticons, acronyms, and unique communication techniques not immediately obvious to an outsider. They develop a private language that solidifies their relationship and the distinctness of their identity together. Usually, that language crystallizes around issues that are discussed frequently and therefore are personally important to them. To understand and enhance the therapeutic relationship, clinicians might pay attention to — and even encourage — the development of this private language with the client.

MESSAGE PERIPHERALS

Important features of interpersonal communication surround the message body in discussion board posts and especially email. Sometimes we overlook these peripheral features and head directly for the meat of the message. Nevertheless, as experienced online clinicians well know, these message peripherals can yield sometimes obvious, sometimes subtle, but always useful insights into the psychology of the other person and our relationship with that person. As seemingly insignificant aspects of the exchange, they often become small gems of communication, deceptively packed with meaning. When they change over time, they serve as signposts indicating changes in the relationship.

The Username

The username people choose reflects the identity that they wish to present online. The name chosen may be one's real name, a pseudonym, or a combination thereof. Using one's real name indicates a wish to simply be oneself. It is a straightforward presentation. Pseudonyms can be more mysterious, playful, revealing approaches. They may express some hidden aspect of the person's self-concept. They may reveal unconscious motivating fantasies and wishes (or fears) about one's identity. A change in username may reflect an important change in how a person wishes to relate to others and be perceived by others. Moving from a pseudonym to one's real name may express the wish to drop the "mask" (albeit a meaningful mask).

The Subject Line

The subject line is a tiny microcosm unto itself. Often people use it to simply summarize or introduce the major idea(s) contained in the text body. Experienced onliners understand the more subtle techniques for communicating meaning and emotion in the titles they bestow to their text. The subject line can lead into, highlight, or elaborate a particular idea in the text body. It can ask a definitive question, shoot back a terse answer, joke, tease, prod, berate, shout, whisper, or emote. Sometimes its meaning may blatantly or discreetly contradict the sentiment expressed in the text body. Creative application of caps, commas, slashes, parentheses, and other keyboard characters adds emphasis and complexity to the thoughts and emotions expressed in the subject line. Here are some examples illustrating these ideas:

the solution is. . .
loved it!
Jim! help, Help, HELP!!
I'm so impressed (yawn)
Have To Do This
Things afoot. . .
Even more/sorry
????
OK folks, settle down
&**%$#))(*@#%%$
Bob/battles/techniques/bullshit
sigh. . .

In an email archive, examining the list of subject lines across the development of the relationship is like perusing the headlines of a newspaper over the course of months or years. That list of titles reflects the flow of important themes in the history of the email encounter. These patterns or trends over time might reveal subtle or unconscious elements in the relationship. Even if online clinicians are reluctant to devote much time to rereading old messages, they can gain considerable insight into the progress of therapy by creating pithy subject titles, paying attention to the titles created by the client, and periodically scrolling through their archives to peruse those titles.

The use of "re:" versus creating a new subject title reflects an interesting dynamic interchange between text partners. Creating a new title means taking the lead in the relationship by introducing a new caption for the interaction. It is an attempt to conceptualize, summarize, and highlight what the person perceives as the most important feature of the conversation. Creating a new title calls into play the "observing ego" – that ability to step back and reflect on what is happening. It also reveals a sense of responsibility and ownership for the dialog – in some cases maybe even an attempt to control the dialog. In this fashion, some text partners "duel" with each other via the subject line. Simply clicking on reply without creating a new title may indicate less of an observing ego and more of a spontaneous reaction. It suggests a "I want to reply to what you said" mode of operation. Some people chronically fail to create a new title and persistently use "re:" They may be a bit passive in the relationship, indifferent, lazy. They may not feel that sense of responsibility, ownership, or control. Even if none of this is true, their partner may still perceive them as being that way. Online clinicians might pay special attention to when and how they create new titles versus using "re:" to maintain the captioned continuity of the discussion.

The Greeting

Similarly to writing letters or meeting someone on the street, the text conversation usually begins with the greeting. Different greetings convey slightly different emotional tones and levels of intimacy. They set the mood for the rest of the message — and sometimes may contradict the tone of the message. Starting with "Dear Jane" is somewhat formal, reminiscent of writing letters, and rarely used among experienced text communicators. "Hello Jane" is more casual, but still polite as compared to the looser "Hi Jane." The more enthusiastic "Hi Jane!" or "Hi there!" may have quite a significant impact on the reader when it appears for the first time, as well as when later it defaults to a plain "Hi Jane," perhaps indicating indifference, anger, or depression. "Jane!!" conveys an even higher level of enthusiasm, surprise, or delight. On the contrary, a simple "Jane" as a greeting tends to be a very matter-of-fact, "let's get to the point" opening, sometimes suggesting an almost ominous tone, as if the sender is trying to get your attention in preparation for some unpleasant discussion. Of course, adding the person's name to the greeting, as in "Hi Jane" rather than simply "Hi," always indicates a deeper level of intimacy — or, at the very least, the fact that the person made the small extra effort to personalize the message. Over the course of a batch of messages, the back-and-forth changes in the greeting become a revealing little dance — sometimes playful, sometimes competitive. Who is being polite, friendly, intimate, enthusiastic, emotional?

No greeting at all is an interesting phenomenon that cuts two ways. In some cases, it may reveal that the sender is lazy or passive, or that he or she lacks any personal connection to you or any desire for a personal connection. In some messages I have received of this type, I felt almost as if the sender perceived me as a computer program ready to respond to his or her needs — with no identity or needs of my own. On the other hand, no greeting may indicate the exact opposite motive. The sender indeed feels connected to you — so much so that a greeting is not required. She assumes you know that it is you who is on her mind. Or, he never felt like he left the conversation and the psychological "space" he inhabits with you, so why inject a greeting into the message? In an ongoing back-and-forth dialog, there may be no greetings at all throughout a string of exchanged text. In the f2f world, you do not say "hello" in the midst of an energetic discussion. In cyberspace, the same principle holds. Although each email message looks like a letter that, according to tradition, should start off with a greeting, it isn't. It is a segment of an ongoing conversation.

The Sign-off Line

Whereas the greeting is the way people say hello and "sign in," the sign-off line is the way they exit from their message. As with the greeting, the sign-off is a fingerprint revealing the status of the person's mood and state of mind — sometimes obvious, sometimes subtle: "Here's where I'm at as I say goodbye." A contrast between the greeting and the sign-off may be significant, as if writing the message altered the person's attitudes and feelings. Across a series of messages, the sign-off lines may be a string of repartees between the partners that amplifies, highlights, or adds nuance to their dialog in the message bodies. The progression of exchanged sign-off lines may itself become an encapsulated, Morse-code dialog between the partners. "Sincerely," "Regards," or other similar sign-offs are rather safe, all-purpose tools borrowed from the world of postal mail. They are formal, polite ways to exit. Some avid email users employ them sparingly because they suggest a snail-mail mentality and a lack of appreciation for the creatively conversational quality of email. Here are some examples of sign-off lines that are a bit more revealing of the person's state of mind and his or her relationship to the email partner:

HUGZZ,
an unusually annoyed,
just my 2 cents,
stay cool,
still confused,
sheesh...

Almost invariably, the person's name follows the sign-off line, which demonstrates how intrinsically connected the sign-off line is with his or her identity. Simply typing one's real name is the easiest, most straightforward tactic. Some people creatively play with the sign-off name as a way to express their state of mind, some aspect of their identity, or their relationship to the text partner. Usually, this type of play only feels appropriate with friends; otherwise, it indicates that one wishes to be friendly, loose, and imaginative.

Leaving out the sign-off line and/or name may be an omission with meaning. It might suggest a curt, efficient, formal, impersonal, or even angry attitude about the conversation. The ending could appear especially bureaucratic or impersonal if the person inserts his signature block and nothing else. On the other hand, friends may leave out a sign-off line and name as a gesture of informality and familiarity: "You know it's me." They may assume that the conversation is ongoing as in an f2f talk, so there is no need to type anything that suggests a goodbye.

Many email programs offer the option of creating a signature block that is automatically placed at the bottom of the message unless that feature is turned off. People usually place factual or identifying information into that file — such as their full name, title, email address, institutional affiliation, phone number, etc. It is a prepackaged stamp indicating "who, what, and where I am." What a person puts into that file reflects what they hold dear to their public identity. Some programs offer the feature of writing alternative signature files, which gives the person the opportunity to create several different fingerprints, each one tailored for a specific purpose. For example, one block may be formal and factual, another more casual and playful. Each one is a slightly different slice of the person's identity. Because all signature blocks have a nonspontaneous, prepackaged feeling to them, friends often make a conscious effort to turn this feature off when writing to someone who knows them well. In a sense, they are dropping their formal status and title. The message in which the signature block first disappears may reflect the sender's move toward feeling more friendly and casual in the relationship. As with the sign-off line and name, a change in a person's signature block reflects a shift in his or her identity or in how he or she wishes to present his or her identity.

Some email users place an ASCII drawing or a quote into their signature block. Sometimes the quotes are serious, humorous, intellectual, tongue-in-cheek, famous, or homespun. What people use can reveal an important slice of their personality, lifestyle, or philosophy of life. In online counseling, the clinician might consider talking with the client about the meaning of the drawing or quote and any changes the client makes to them.

TEXT TALK IN REAL TIME

The synchronous forms of text communication — as in instant messaging and chat — have evolved into a style of relating that is quite different from the asynchronous methods. The exchange of text usually involves only short sentences and phrases; what I like to call "staccato speak." Some people find that experience too sparse. They feel disoriented in that screen of silently scrolling dialog. Other people enjoy that minimalist style. They love to see how people creatively express themselves despite the limitations. They love to immerse themselves in the quiet flow of words that feels like a more direct, in the moment, intimate connection between one's mind and the minds of others. Some clinicians also prefer this point-by-point exchange of ideas. They feel it creates a greater sense of presence and a more full interpersonal influence "in the here and now."

Staccato speak influences communication in a variety of ways. The terse style works well for witty social banter and sometimes elicits that type of relating. Conversations may involve very short, superficial exchanges or very honest and to-the-point discussions of personal issues. One does not have the verbose luxury of gradually leading the conversation to a serious topic, so self-disclosures sometimes are sudden and very revealing. To make conversations more efficient, experienced synchronous communicators develop a complex collection of acronyms, which accelerates the development of a private language. In public chat settings, when people are meeting for the first time, they often quickly test the waters to determine the characteristics of the users around them and whom they want to engage. Questions that would be considered less than tactful in f2f encounters are a bit more socially acceptable here. Terse inquiries tossed out to a fellow user, or the entire room, might include "Age?," "M/F?," "Married?"

Synchronous communication in groups is considerably more challenging than one-on-one discussions — a fact that the clinician interested in group work might consider. Chat room banter can seem quite chaotic, especially when many people are talking or you have just entered a room and attempt to dive into the ongoing flow of overlapping conversations. There are no visual cues indicating what pairs or groups of people are huddled together in conversation, so the lines of scrolling dialog seem disconnected. If people do not preface their message with the other user's name, it's not easy to tell who is reacting to whom or if someone is speaking to the whole group. Messages appear on your screen in an intermixed, slightly nonsequential order. The net result is a group free association where temporality is suspended, ideas bounce off each other, and the owner and recipient of the ideas become secondary.

You have to sit back and follow the flow of the text to decipher the themes of conversation and who is talking with whom. Consciously and unconsciously, you set up mental filters and points of focus that help you screen out noise and zoom your concentration in on particular people or topics of discussion. Often, you become immersed in one or two strings of dialog and filter out the others. With experience, you develop an eye for efficiently reading the scrolling text. Some people may be better at this specific cognitive-perceptual task than others.

Saved transcripts of chat sessions often are more difficult to read after the fact than when you are there at the time the chat occurs. In part, this is because during a post hoc reading of a log you read at the pace you usually read any written material — which is quickly, but much too quickly to absorb the chat conversation. While online, the lag created by people typing and by thousands of miles of busy Internet wires forces the conversation into a slower pace. So, you sit back, read, wait, scan backward and forward in the dialog (something you cannot do in f2f conversation), and think about what to say next. There is more time for those perceptual/cognitive filters to operate. There is also more time for a psychological/emotional context to evolve in your mind — a context that helps you to follow and shape the nuances of meaning that develop in the conversation.

Quite unlike f2f encounters, people can send private messages to others in a chat room — a message that no one else in the room can see. There may be very few or no messages appearing on your screen but people may be very busy conversing. In f2f encounters the equivalent would be a silent room filled with telepaths! If you are engaged in one of those private discussions, as well as conversing with people out loud, you are placed in the peculiar situation of carrying on dual social roles — an intimate you and a public you, simultaneously. Even more complex is when you attempt to conduct two or more private conversations, perhaps in addition to public ones. You may be joking privately with Harold, conducting a serious personal discussion with Elizabeth, while engaging in simple chitchat out loud with the rest of the room. This complex social maneuver requires the psychological mechanism of dissociation — the ability to separate and direct the components of your mind in more than one direction at the same time. It takes a great deal of online experience, mental concentration, and keyboarding skill (eye–hand coordination) to pull it off. A clinician needs to be aware of how these complex communication patterns might be affecting the group's dynamics, as well as to hone the skills of conducting public and private conversations simultaneously. Most important is the ability to coordinate efforts with a co-therapist via private messaging while also speaking to the group.

INTEGRATION: CROSSING THE TEXT BOUNDARY

If there are any universally valid principles in psychology, one of them is the importance of integration: the fitting together and balancing of the various elements of the psyche to make a complete, harmonious whole. A faulty or pathological psychic system often is described with terms connoting division and fragmentation, such as "repression," "dissociation," and "splitting." Health, on the other hand, is usually specified with terms that imply integration and union, such as "insight," "assimilation," and "self-actualization." Integration — like commerce — creates synergy. It leads to development and prosperity. The exchange enriches both sides of the trade.

Even though I have devoted this chapter to a discussion of text relationships, I cannot emphasize enough the importance of the clinician considering the therapeutic possibilities of moving beyond the text relationship, of crossing the text boundary into other modes of communication. People learn by reading and writing, but they learn more by combining reading and writing with seeing, hearing, speaking, and doing. The integration of different modes of communication accelerates the process of understanding, working through, and assimilating psychological change. The clinician might consider the therapeutic possibilities of embedding graphics, audio, and video files into the text relationship. He or she might also consider whether, when, and how speaking with the client on the phone or in person might enhance the progress of therapy.

The developmental path in most online relationships leads toward becoming more and more real to the other person — a process accelerated by bringing the relationship into new channels of communication. At first the companions may converse only via email or chat. If they try chat in addition to email, or vice versa, they often experience that move as a deepening of the relationship. Crossing any communication boundary often is perceived as reaching out to the other in a new way, as a gesture of intimacy. The big moves of crossing the text boundary into phone and, later, in-person contact often become important turning points in the relationship.

Hearing the other's voice on the phone and, especially, meeting f2f give the opportunity to test out the image of the other person that you had created in your mind. While conversing via text, how did you accurately perceive this person and where did your perceptions go astray? By answering those questions, you may come to understand how your own mind-set shaped your online impressions. You may have wanted or needed the person to be a certain way. Steered by your past intimate relationships, you may have expected them to be a certain way. You may have completely overlooked something in the text relationship that could not be ignored in the real-world encounter. Afterward, you may together discuss, assimilate, reminisce, and build on the encounter. You can share the ways in which the meeting confirmed and altered your perceptions of each other. But, the in-person meeting does not always enhance the relationship for some people. They may be disappointed after the meeting. The other person was not what they had hoped. This unfortunate outcome may indicate that their online wishes were strong but unrealistic.

Some people choose not to phone or meet their email companion in person, even though such meetings could be arranged. They prefer to limit the relationship to cyberspace. Perhaps they fear that their expectations and hopes will be dashed, or they feel more safe and comfortable with the relative anonymity of email contact. They may be relishing the online fantasy they have created for themselves. Or, they simply enjoy the text relationship as it is and have no desire to develop the relationship any further. In all cases, choosing not to increase f2f contact with the text companion is a choice not to make the relationship more intimate, well-rounded, or reality-based.

The implications of these ideas for online counseling and psychotherapy can be profound. Although therapists sometimes may choose to communicate with a client only via text – given the needs of that client or perhaps of the therapist – they might keep in mind the therapeutic possibilities of using different modes of communication and, especially, of crossing the text boundary. Combining different modes, or progressing from one mode to another, offers opportunities for a more robust understanding of the other person, for deepening intimacy and trust, and for exploring transference and countertransference reactions.

An important dimension of what I call the "integration principle" is the process of bringing together one's online lifestyle with one's in-person lifestyle. Encourage clients to discuss and translate their f2f behaviors within the text relationship. Encourage them to take whatever new, productive behaviors they are learning via text and apply them to their in-person lifestyle. Encourage them to talk to trusted friends and family members about their online text relationships, including their therapy. If you are working with someone via text and in person, help them to discuss the text relationship when meeting in person and the in-person relationship when online. This will prevent a dual relationship in which certain issues are isolated to one channel of communication (probably text) and never fully worked through. Encourage clients to communicate via online text with their in-person family members and friends, while also encouraging (but not forcing) them to meet the people they know online in person or via phone.

If a goal of life is to "know thyself," as Socrates suggested, it must entail knowing how the various elements of thyself fit together to make that big self that is you. Reaching that goal means understanding and taming the barriers between the sectors of self. Barriers are erected out of the need to protect or out of fear. Those barriers and anxieties too are a component of one's identity. Sequencing, combining, and integrating different modalities of communication help us to explore the different dimensions of self that are expressed in those modalities and also helps us to understand our resistances to communicating in new and perhaps growth-promoting ways.

SUMMARY

The Internet makes text relationships more accessible than ever before in history. The unique aspects of text relationships open up new possibilities for online clinical work: reading and writing skills shape the communication; there are minimal visual and auditory cues; communication is temporally fluid; a subjective sense of interpersonal space replaces the importance of geographical space; people can converse with almost anyone online and with multiple partners simultaneously; conversations can be saved and later re-examined; and the environment is more susceptible to disruption. Several of these factors cause social disinhibition. Although we tend to focus on the body of the message, the peripheral components of a text communication — such as the username and message title — also enhance meaning. As effective as text work can be, we should not overlook the therapeutic possibilities of moving outside text and integrating other communication modalities into our work.

DISCUSSION QUESTIONS

1. What makes text relationships unique compared to in-person relationships?
2. How do writing skills and styles interact with the text relationship?
3. What are the pros and cons of absent f2f cues?

4. What are the factors that contribute to the disinhibition effect?
5. How can clinicians therapeutically use temporal fluidity, spatial fluidity, and recordability?
6. What are the basic creative keyboarding techniques?
7. How do message peripherals add to the meaning of text communication?
8. How can crossing the text boundary and integrating communication modalities be therapeutic?

KEY TERMS

24-hour rule The principle indicating the value of waiting one day before sending a message related to an emotional situation.

Anonymity The partial or complete invisibility of one's identity.

Black hole experience A situation in cyberspace when one receives no response from either a computer or a person.

Creative keyboarding The use of keyboard characters to convey emotion, body language, and subvocal thinking.

Cut-and-paste reality A term coined by Michael Fenichel that refers to the distortion of the meaning of a person's text message by quoting excerpts of it out of context or by inappropriately juxtaposing excerpts.

Delayed reactions In asynchronous communication, the postponing of a reply to someone's text message.

Disinhibition effect The tendency for people to do or say things in cyberspace that they normally would not say or do in their f2f life.

Dissociation The process of isolating components of one's self or identity from each other.

Dual relationship Somehow relating to someone differently online as compared to the in-person relationship with that person.

Emoticons Keyboard characters that mimic facial expressions, such as the smiley, winky, and frown.

Integration principle A principle stating the salutary effects of bringing together one's online and offline lifestyles.

Invisibility Also known as "lurking," the condition of being unnoticed or unseen in an online environment.

Media disruption A situation in which technical problems interfere with effective communication in an online environment.

Message body The actual message written by a person in an email.

Message peripherals The additional features of an email surrounding the message body, such as the subject, username, greeting, and signature block.

Parenthetical expressions In text messages, expressions in parentheses that indicate body language and underlying thoughts and feelings.

Presence The sensation of actually being present in an online environment or of another person being present in an online environment.

Private language The idiosyncratic patterns of conversing that develop over time between people in text communication.

Recordability The ability to save text messages.

Social multiplicity The ability in cyberspace to establish relationships with numerous and different types of people.

Solipsistic introjection In text relationships, the tendency to perceive the other person as a character or voice within one's own internal psychological world.

Staccato speak The terse style of communicating in chat and instant messaging.

Subject line The title of an email message or discussion board post.

Synchronicity/asynchronicity Online communication that occurs in real time, as in chat and instant messaging, or outside of real time, as in email and discussion boards.

Temporal fluidity The flexible quality of when to respond to other people in asynchronous communication.

Text empathy The intuitive ability to sense another person's thoughts and feelings in text communication.

Trailers A string of periods to indicate a pause in speech or a transition of thought in text communication.

Transference reactions The distorted perception of a person based on one's wishes, needs, and emotions stemming from past relationships with other people.

Voice accentuation The use of capital letters and asterisks to emphasize words in a text message.

Zone of reflection The period of time during which one can reflect on a message before replying to it.

REFERENCES

International Society for Mental Health Online (ISMHO) Clinical Case Study Group (2001). Assessing a person's suitability for online therapy. *Cyberpsychology and Behavior, 4*, 675−680.

Suler, J. R. (2000). Psychotherapy in cyberspace: A 5-dimensional model of online and computer-mediated psychotherapy. *Cyberpsychology and Behavior, 3*, 151−159.

Chapter | three

Online Counseling: Does It Work? Research Findings to Date

Ron Kraus
Editor, EthicsCode.com

IS ONLINE COUNSELING EFFECTIVE? DOES IT REALLY WORK?

The few visionary pioneers who first considered online counseling in the last decade of the past millennium had no legal, ethical, or research findings to rely on as guidelines. A couple of years after the Internet was first introduced to the public in the 1990s, the concept of online counseling was still very new, unregulated, and mostly unfamiliar.

Most people tend to fear the unknown and yet are intrigued by it at the same time. When it came to dealing with the unfamiliar issue of online counseling, the American Psychological Association (APA) demonstrated a similar attitude, combining interest with caution. As the field emerged, the APA released two statements relating to "services by telephone, teleconferencing and Internet," first in 1995 and again in 1997

55

Online Counseling. DOI: 10.1016/B978-0-12-378596-1.00003-4

(see http://www.apa.org/ethics/education/telephone-statement.aspx). The fact that statements on the subject were issued at all suggests clearly that interest in the clinical community existed. Unfortunately, these statements only said that not enough evidence had been gathered from research to decide whether the practice was effective, and caution was strongly advised.

Naturally, the majority of clinicians who sought the APA's advice on the matter were discouraged from consulting clients online. And so, while a few brave pioneers kept investing time, effort, and resources in researching and developing the new modality, most clinicians remained cautious and hesitant about online counseling.

Quite understandably, the first and most basic question professionals were concerned about related to the issue of efficacy. Does online counseling work? To many in the therapeutic community, the very idea of text relations replacing the intimate f2f office consult was unimaginable. How would the therapist know how the client feels if he or she could not see and hear them? Can empathy or support be expressed and felt via text alone? Clinical research results were scarce at that time and so, while public use of the Internet spread like wildfire in the years following its introduction, lack of sufficient research and doubts about the efficacy of online counseling lingered in the clinical community.

During the past few years, the efficacy of online counseling has been studied quite thoroughly (a comprehensive list of all articles related to online counseling can be found on Azy Barak's site at the University of Haifa: http://construct.haifa.ac.il/~azy/refthrp.htm). The general conclusion drawn from many studies and several meta-analysis reviews is that online counseling can be as effective as f2f sessions. This chapter will review some of these studies.

WHAT DO WE KNOW ABOUT THE EFFICACY OF ONLINE COUNSELING VIA TEXT?

Most early studies concluded that online counseling has potential, but authors were often careful not to suggest that the modality was well understood. Mallen et al. (2005), for example, wrote at the conclusion of their review of the literature that evidence exists to indicate that online counseling is a viable option but that questions about appropriateness and efficacy still remain.

As hesitation and doubt characterized the clinical community's initial approach to the subject, Griffiths and Christensen (2006) even acknowledged the surprise some felt when online counseling was found to be effective:

> The internet is playing an increasingly important role in the delivery of self-help treatments for mental disorders. But are such programs

effective? Somewhat surprisingly, the answer would appear to be yes [. . .] we found consistent evidence that internet programs are efficacious

Griffiths and Christensen, 2006, pp. 16–29

Others also have seen potential in the online modality but suggest caution. In their conclusions, Postel et al. (2008) wrote,

Two reviews independently assessed the methodological quality of randomized controlled studies concerning e-therapy for mental health problems. Fourteen reports (papers) were found. Although inconclusive, e-therapy may play a role but requires additional work

Postel et al., 2008, pp. 707–14

Abbott et al. (2008) seemed confident about the efficacy of the modality when they wrote that it has been found to be effective in treating a range of psychological disorders.

In 2008, a meta-analysis of online counseling research to date was published by Barak et al. The study was conclusive in supporting the efficacy of online counseling. The authors based their conclusions on a review of 92 studies reported in 64 papers, collectively examining the effectiveness of therapeutic interventions done with some 9764 clients (Barak et al., 2008).

More recent studies support the findings reported in the above-mentioned meta-analysis. Perini et al. found that their results are consistent with previous literature indicating that Internet-based programs for depression and other mental disorders can be clinically effective (2009).

When the Global Assessment of Functioning (GAF) and client satisfaction were investigated, it was again demonstrated that clients can benefit from online consultations. In a study by Murphy et al. (2009), GAF and Client Satisfaction Survey scores for clients receiving either f2f or online counseling were investigated. Results indicated that no significant differences were found for degree of change in GAF between assessment and closing between the two modalities (Murphy et al., 2009).

Further support for the usefulness of text-based online counseling comes from Richards' 2009 study (2009). He wrote that users have reported satisfaction with online counseling and that the service's impact within the community of users is complementary (Richards, 2009).

When reviewing studies measuring the equivalence of online counseling to other approaches, it is important to remember the Dodo bird effect, which generally shows the equivalence of any techniques being compared. Still, from the studies reviewed so far we can see quite clearly that most research results have found online counseling to be as effective as f2f meetings. In fact, the existence of CPT code 98969 (known in the US as CPT code 0074T until it was replaced by the new code in 2008) suggests that the efficacy of the modality is now officially recognized by the medical establishment. The practical implication of this is that clinicians can bill the client's insurance for online service using the new code.

Interestingly enough, even though evidence now exists to support the practice, most clinicians are still hesitant about and many are unfamiliar with the potential of online counseling. A 2007 survey found that only about two percent of active clinicians offer counseling online (Horgan et al., 2007), which is an indication that doubt and ignorance may still exist in the professional community.

Now that the efficacy of the modality has been established, it will be interesting to see how clinicians' attitudes toward online practice change over time. With the spread of technology and better understanding of the field, it is expected that resistance to online counseling will gradually dwindle in the coming years.

IS VIDEOCONFERENCING EFFECTIVE FOR CLINICAL WORK?

It is interesting to note that the hesitation of the professional community concerning online counseling is not only due to the mistaken belief that therapeutic text relations are less effective than traditional ones. Apparently, negative prejudice seems to exist even when the consults are done via teleconferencing.

In a study from 2005 it was demonstrated that psychologists believe that the therapeutic alliance created via teleconferencing will be less meaningful than that which is formed in an f2f encounter. Results showed that the psychologists were wrong (Rees & Stone, 2005). In fact, most studies investigating the efficacy of online counseling conducted via teleconferencing found that the practice is basically as effective for clients as f2f meetings.

In a 2005 review and meta-analysis investigating whether telepsychiatry can replace in-person assessments, Hyler et al. concluded that psychiatric consultation and short-term follow-up can be as effective when delivered by telepsychiatry as when provided f2f.

Morgan et al. (2008) stated similar conclusions after investigating the usefulness of telemental health in the corrections system. Results indicated no significant differences in inmates' perceptions of the work alliance with the mental health professional, post-session mood, or overall satisfaction with services when telemental health and f2f modalities were compared within each type of mental health service (Morgan et al., 2008).

Not all studies are fully comfortable with the new modality, and some reviews of the subject mention the need for more and better research. Simpson (2009) agreed that a number of case studies and case series have suggested that videoconferencing can be clinically effective and acceptable to patients, though feeling that there is a lack of methodologically rigorous studies with adequate sample sizes from which we can draw conclusions that can be generalized.

In a comprehensive 2008 review of the effectiveness of video, text, and telephone consults for various mental health conditions by Hailey et al., several areas were identified as promising, though more research was recommended. The authors reviewed 72 papers that described 65 clinical studies. Evidence of success with telemental health was reported in the areas of child psychiatry, depression, dementia, schizophrenia, suicide prevention, post-traumatic stress, panic disorders, substance abuse, eating disorders, and smoking prevention. Evidence of success for general telemental health programs and in the management of obsessive-compulsive disorder were less convincing. The authors conclude that the evidence of benefits from telemental health applications is encouraging, though still limited (Hailey et al., 2008).

From the few examples provided above it is easy to see that videoconferencing has the potential to successfully supplement f2f meetings for various mental health conditions. As use of videoconferencing grows more widespread in the coming years, it is likely to become a more acceptable treatment modality.

EXPANSION OF ONLINE COUNSELING RESEARCH

Early studies of online counseling mostly focused on the question of efficacy. In recent years, researchers began looking beyond that basic question, investigating how online counseling can be applied to various mental health conditions and populations.

One area that seems to draw much attention is online Cognitive Behavioral Therapy (CBT) and its applications to various mental health conditions. Andersson (2009) agrees that online CBT counseling works as well as f2f sessions but also complains that most studies so far relate to efficacy:

> In some studies, Internet-delivered treatment can achieve similar outcomes as in face-to-face CBT, but the literature thus far is restricted mainly to efficacy trials.
>
> **Andersson, 2009, pp. 175–80**

Berger et al. (2009) discuss the potential of online counseling to treat social phobia. Their study results support the hypothesis that Internet-delivered interventions with minimal therapist contact are a promising treatment approach to social phobia (Berger et al., 2009).

Other studies have also concluded that phobias can be successfully treated online. In preliminary data from a study by Botella et al. (2008) regarding the efficacy and effectiveness of online treatment in a series of 12 cases, participants showed an improvement in all clinical measures at post-treatment, and the therapeutic gains were maintained at a three-month follow-up (pp. 659–64).

Bergström et al. (2009) showed online CBT to be effective in the treatment of panic disorder. The study results supported earlier efficacy data on Internet-based CBT for panic disorder and indicated that it is also effective within a regular psychiatric setting (Bergström et al., 2009). Similar conclusions supporting the efficacy of Internet-based CBT were also reached by Klein et al. (2006).

In a meta-analytic review of the subject, Cuijpers et al. (2009) seem optimistic about the future of CBT online. Their work reviews the use of the Internet for delivery of CBT and concludes that Internet treatment is likely to become an option for suitable patients in the future (Cuijpers et al., 2009). Similar conclusions were voiced by Kessler et al. (2009); in their study, CBT was found to be effective when delivered online in real time by a therapist, with benefits maintained over eight months. The writers believe that online delivery could broaden access to CBT (Kessler et al., 2009).

March et al. (2009) examined the efficacy of CBT online for the treatment of child anxiety. In their conclusions, they wrote that Internet delivery of CBT for child anxiety offers promise as a way of increasing access to treatment for this population (March et al., 2009).

In a 2009 meta-analysis study looking into the efficacy of online CBT for the treatment of anxiety, Reger and Gahm claimed that Internet- or computer-based CBT was superior to waiting list and placebo and equal to therapist-delivered treatment of anxiety.

When it comes to treating addictions, such as alcoholism, evidence for efficacy is less consistent. In the conclusion of their 2008 systematic review, Bewick et al. wrote that the current review provides inconsistent evidence on the effectiveness of online screening and brief intervention for alcohol use. According to Bewick and colleagues (2008), research suggests that web-based interventions are generally well received, but further controlled trials are needed to fully investigate their specific efficacy.

So, even though it may have some limits and research is still ongoing, online counseling via videoconferencing is here to stay.

SUMMARY AND CONCLUSIONS

Thus far, hesitation combined with lack of familiarity with research findings and ignorance about the clinical potential of online counseling have limited widespread use. As long as universities are not offering education and training in online counseling, progress will probably continue to be slow. In 2007, Horgan et al. found that Internet use for health care information and online counseling was still meager. The survey found that health plans frequently used the Internet to provide information but used it less often to provide clinical services directly. Most services offered online provider directories and educational information. Two-thirds offered behavioral health self-assessment tools, and almost one-half provided online referral. According to this study, only two percent offered interactive online counseling (Horgan et al., 2007). Miller and West (2009) also wondered where the revolution was, as their results indicated that only a few people use online resources to get information or communicate with a health professional.

A somewhat more optimistic perspective is found in the results of the 2008 APA Health Service Provider Survey, which found that, from 2000 to 2008, the number of clinicians using online communications to provide services such as counseling, consulting, and supervision gradually increased (APA, 2010).

When online counseling is taught at the graduate level in clinical programs, the revolution that started over a decade ago will be complete. It seems that, by now, enough research findings exist to justify adding online counseling to the arsenal of strategies, modalities, and techniques that are currently taught. After all, if a CPT code for billing online service exists, why should professional schools not teach the subject?

From a review of the current literature relating to online counseling, a few conclusions can be drawn. First, it is now quite clear that sufficient empirical evidence exists to prove the efficacy of online counseling. In addition, it seems that various forms and applications of online counseling are now developing. Current research goes beyond the question of efficacy and continues to reveal the promise of online counseling for various mental health conditions.

It is quite likely that widespread use of the new modality is simply a question of time. Once clinicians overcome their initial resistance and fear of the unknown, recognize online counseling as an effective tool, backed by research findings, and receive training in the new modality, the online revolution will be complete.

KEY TERMS

Chat A form of immediate text communication online.
CPT codes 0074T and 98969 The original and current codes used for billing online counseling services.
Efficacy A term used when examining the effectiveness of a procedure.
E-therapy One of the terms used to describe online counseling.
Face-to-face (f2f) An in-office therapy session.
Global Assessment of Functioning (GAF) An assessment measure used by clinicians to determine a patient's current and past levels of psychosocial functioning.
Meta-analysis A systematic form of comparative analysis that generates general conclusions from a review of several studies on a subject.
Telepsychiatry and telepsychology Additional terms used to describe mental health counseling online.
Videoconferencing A form of interaction online that allows the parties to see and hear each other.

REFERENCES

A comprehensive list of all articles related to online counseling can be found on Azy Barak's site at the University of Haifa: http://construct.haifa.ac.il/~azy/refthrp.htm.

Abbott, J-A. M., Klein, B., & Ciechomski, L. (2008). Best practices in online therapy. *Journal of Technology in Human Services, 26*, 360–375.

American Psychological Association (APA). (2010). Telepsychology is on the rise. *Monitor on Psychology, 41*(3), 11.

Andersson, G. (2009). Using the Internet to provide cognitive behaviour therapy. *Behaviour Research and Therapy, 47*, 175–180.

Barak, A., Hen, L., Boniel-Nissim, M., & Shapira, N. (2008). A comprehensive review and a meta-analysis of the effectiveness of Internet-based psychotherapeutic interventions. *Journal of Technology in Human Services, 26*, 109–160.

Berger, T., Hohl, E., & Caspar, F. (2009). Internet based treatment for social phobia: A randomized controlled trial. *Journal of Clinical Psychology, 65*, 1021–1035.

Bergström, J., Andersson, G., Karlsson, A., Andréewitch, S., Rück, C., Carlbring, P., et al. (2009). An open study of the effectiveness of Internet treatment for panic disorder delivered in a psychiatric setting. *Nordic Journal of Psychiatry, 63*, 44–50.

Bewick, B. M., Trusler, K., Barkham, M., Hill, A. J., Cahill, J., & Mulhern, B. (2008). The effectiveness of web-based interventions designed to decrease alcohol consumption – a systematic review. *Preventive Medicine, 47*, 17–26.

Botella, C., Quero, S., Banos, R. M., Garcia-Palacios, A., Breton-Lopez, J., Alcaniz, M., & Fabregat, S. (2008). Telepsychology and self-help: The treatment of phobias using the Internet. *Cyberpsychology and Behavior, 11*(6), 659–664. doi:10.1089/cp.b.2008.0012.

Cuijpers, P., Marks, I. M., van Straten, A., Cavanagh, K., Gega, L., & Andersson, G. (2009). Computer-aided psychotherapy for anxiety disorders: A meta-analytic review. *Cognitive Behaviour Therapy, 37*, 66–82.

Griffiths, K. M., & Christensen, H. (2006). Review of randomized controlled trials of Internet interventions for mental disorders and related conditions. *Clinical Psychologist, 10*, 16–29.

Hailey, D., Roine, R., & Ohinmaa, A. (2008). The effectiveness of telemental health applications: A review. *The Canadian Journal of Psychiatry, 53*, 769–778.

Horgan, C. M., Merrick, E. L., Reif, S., & Stewart, M. (2007). Internet-based behavioral health services in health plans. *Psychiatric Services, 58*, 307.

Hyler, S. E., Gangure, D. P., & Batchelder, S. T. (2005). Can telepsychiatry replace in-person psychiatric assessments? A review and meta-analysis of comparison studies. *CNS Spectrums, 10*, 403–413.

Kessler, D., Lewis, G., Kaur, S., Wiles, N., King, M., Weich, S., et al. (2009). Therapist-delivered Internet psychotherapy for depression in primary care: A randomized controlled trial. *Lancet, 374*, 628–634.

Klein, B., Richards, J. C., & Austin, D. W. (2006). Efficacy of Internet therapy for panic disorder. *Journal of Behavior Therapy and Experimental Psychiatry, 37*, 213–238.

Mallen, M. J., Vogel, D. L., Rochlen, A. B., & Day, S. X. (2005). Online counseling: Reviewing the literature from a counseling psychology framework. *The Counseling Psychologist, 33*, 819–871.

March, S., Spence, S. H., & Donovan, C. L. (2009). The efficacy of an Internet-based cognitive-behavioral therapy intervention for child anxiety disorders. *Journal of Pediatric Psychology, 34*, 474–487.

Miller, E. A., & West, D. M. (2009). Where's the revolution? Digital technology and health care in the Internet age. *Journal of Health Politics, Policy and Law, 34*, 261–284.

Morgan, R. D., Patrick, A. R., & Magaletta, P. R. (2008). Does the use of telemental health alter the treatment experience? Inmates' perceptions of telemental health versus face-to-face treatment modalities. *Journal of Consulting and Clinical Psychology, 76,* 158–162.

Murphy, L., Parnass, P., Mitchell, D. L., Hallett, R., Cayley, P., & Seagram, S. (2009). Client satisfaction and outcome comparisons of online and face-to-face counselling methods. *British Journal of Social Work, 39,* 627–640.

Perini, S., Titov, N., & Andrews, G. (2009). Clinician-assisted Internet-based treatment is effective for depression: Randomized controlled trial. *Australian and New Zealand Journal of Psychiatry, 43,* 571–578.

Postel, M. G., de Haan, H. A., & De Jong, C. A. (2008). E-therapy for mental health problems: A systematic review. *Telemedicine and e-Health, 14,* 707–714.

Rees, C. S., & Stone, S. (2005). Therapeutic alliance in face-to-face versus videoconferenced psychotherapy. *Professional Psychology: Research and Practice, 36,* 649–653.

Reger, M. A., & Gahm, G. A. (2009). A meta-analysis of the effects of Internet- and computer-based cognitive-behavioral treatments for anxiety. *Journal of Clinical Psychology, 65,* 53–75.

Richards, D. (2009). Features and benefits of online counselling: Trinity College online mental health community. *British Journal of Guidance & Counselling, 37,* 231–242.

Simpson, S. (2009). Psychotherapy via videoconferencing: A review. *British Journal of Guidance & Counselling, 37,* 271–286.

PRACTICAL ASPECTS OF ONLINE COUNSELING

Chapter four

The Technology of Online Counseling

Jason S Zack, PhD, JD

Patterson Belknap Webb & Tyler LLP — New York, New York, USA[1]

INTRODUCTION

This chapter discusses the technological underpinnings of online counseling, namely the hardware, software, and networking infrastructure that allow counselors and clients to communicate and conduct business via the Internet. The previous edition of this chapter, drafted nearly seven years ago, took pains to accommodate the computer or Internet

---

[1] Although the author is affiliated with the named law firm, this paper represents the author's own opinions and was not written in connection with any of the author's duties as an employee of the firm.

67

Online Counseling. DOI: 10.1016/B978-0-12-378596-1.00004-6

neophyte. Although many of us were computer literate then, it is hard to imagine any mental health professional or potential client today who would need an introduction to basics such as establishing an email account or using the basic functionality of a web browser. However, those who feel fairly confident with the fundamentals may still have important questions related to setting up a website, using technology to keep communications secure, or taking advantage of new social media tools to enhance one's practice.

GENERAL CONSIDERATIONS

Other chapters in this book will discuss theoretical issues, but one that bears mentioning here is that *online practice cannot be divorced from technology*. Although Internet service providers (ISP) and applications such as Skype and iChat have become much more reliable over recent years, glitches are still inevitable and must be expected. Like aviation, online counseling remains a technology-dependent pursuit, and the hardware and software you choose will have an important impact on the phenomenology of your work (and quite possibly its effectiveness).

Clients and counselors vary in their levels of patience and understanding. Some clients may personalize the technology as an interloper in your relationship, or you could become implicated in technical problems, whether culpable or not (e.g., "my therapist sent me a virus!"). For some, especially before establishing a regular session protocol, there remains a sense of fragility in online counseling interactions. Imagine conducting sessions in a conventional office with a nagging fear that the roof will cave in or the legs of your sofa will give way unexpectedly, possibly just after you or the client says something *really important*. Online counseling can be like that. . . at least the first few times. Although theoretical constructs associated with online counseling such as disinhibition and hyper-personalization are important, theory will not help if technology gets in the way. The most competent online counselors will be those who take technological limitations in their stride. Familiarity with the technology and calm in the face of technical problems are your keys to success and sanity.

GETTING STARTED: THE BASICS

You are a mental health professional sitting in your office. Maybe your office is in a building; maybe it is at your house or on a university campus. It dawns upon you that online counseling might be a good fit for your needs and interests and you want to give it a whirl. What do you need? At minimum, you will need a computer, an Internet connection (high-speed, ideally), and a web browser. That's really it. Beyond that, you may wish to consider:

1. A stand-alone email application
2. A stand-alone chat application

3. A videoconferencing program and webcam
4. A domain name (yourname.com)
5. A website (www.yourname.com)
6. A webhosting account (to store a website)
7. Security software/hardware
8. Social media accounts (e.g., Facebook, Twitter)
9. A virtual world account (e.g., on Second Life)

Computer

For the purposes of online counseling, you need a computer that is reliable (does not crash or quit unexpectedly) and that ably runs the latest Internet software. Mac or Windows operating systems are both fine, depending on your comfort level. The latest Mac OS and Windows operating systems make it very easy to use the Internet and network with other computers. Any new computer will have Internet functionality (Ethernet ports or wireless cards built in). One of the best features of online counseling is that you can bring your practice with you, conducting your business from a hotel room as easily as the office. In fact, online counselors may get their start by providing distance-based services as a stopgap measure while they are temporarily out of town. These days, affordable laptops can easily substitute for desktop machines and are completely sufficient for online counseling purposes.

Internet Connection

Next, you need a reliable Internet connection. Internet connections are provided by ISPs. In most cases, you will use a high-speed, full-time Internet connection supplied by your local telephone company, cable provider, workplace, or hotel. Most ISPs offer Internet connections at varying "bandwidths" (related to the speed of uploading and downloading data). Your ISP's basic dedicated connection should be fast enough for online counseling, certainly for text-based online counseling modalities (email or chat), but you may prefer a faster connection if you plan to use bandwidth-demanding modalities such as videoconferencing or virtual worlds.

Wireless Access

Today, many hotels, university campuses, and coffee shops provide free wireless (often used synonymously with "Wi-Fi") Internet access. Wireless technology is built into most new computers or is easily added and allows you to access the Internet nearly as fast as most ordinary wired connections. If you have more than one computer in your office or home, you can also use a Wi-Fi base station to share the same wired Internet connection among them. Wi-Fi is also great if you would like to work while sitting on a sofa or in a café (but note privacy considerations, discussed below).

Web Browser

Every computer today comes with a web browser — the program you use to access the World Wide Web. You will need a copy of the latest version of Firefox, Safari, or Internet Explorer installed and running on your computer, depending on your preference. They can be downloaded for free.

Email Account

As an online counselor, you may prefer to use a special email address that you only use for your online counseling work and that you can access via a web browser. If you have your own domain and webhosting account (see below), you can easily create multiple email addresses for different purposes (e.g., DrJoe@joetherapist.com, DrBob@joetherapist.com, info@joetherapist.com, billing@joetherapist.com, etc.). You can also get free email accounts from Google (http://gmail.google.com) and other websites. For online counseling purposes, you may prefer to use an encrypted email service such as Hushmail (http://www.hushmail.com), which will ensure your communications are kept secure.

Email Program

If you want to have more control over your emails, with the ability to review offline, archive on a CD/DVD or storage drive, organize by client, add complex formatting, etc., then you really need an email program. Most new computers come with some sort of free email program (e.g., Microsoft Outlook Express or Apple's Mail; Thunderbird is a free yet fully featured email client available from the makers of Firefox: http://www.mozillamessaging.com). Many email programs, especially commercial ones such as Microsoft Outlook, may be integrated with calendar programs, which may also be helpful in managing your online counseling practice. Online counselors may wish to use their email program's signature functionality to set up a standard message about confidentiality and emergency contact information.

Chat Program

If you plan to offer real-time text chat counseling services, you may wish to acquire or familiarize yourself with chat software, which allows you to communicate dynamically and interactively with other people, comment by comment. Although you can chat using web applications such as Google Talk, free-standing chat programs offer additional functionality such as the ability to save session transcripts. Chat programs are usually free to download and good ones are produced by Apple (iChat), Skype, AOL (AIM), Yahoo!, Microsoft (Messenger), and other developers.

Videoconferencing Program and Webcam

Videoconferencing programs send and receive dynamic (moving) images between computers across the Internet. Videoconferencing requires a high-speed Internet connection and a webcam on at least one end of the conversation. Webcams are small video cameras that are built in or attached to your computer, typically via a USB port. The most popular videoconferencing programs today are iChat and Skype, although Google has now added web-based video functionality to its Google Talk service.

Website

If you operate an independent or small group online practice or wish to promote your services, you will want to set up a website. There are a variety of ways in which to do this. Some options are cheap and easy, whereas others are more budget and labor intensive. You can design and maintain a simple, attractive website purely through a web-based site template or "turnkey" virtual office services, or you can use specialized web design software (e.g., Adobe Dreamweaver) to make a rich and complex site. Of course, you can also hire a web designer to create and maintain your site for you. Which option you choose will depend on whether you plan to use your website purely as a multimedia brochure (providing static information) or as a dynamic clinic with built-in tools to facilitate submission of forms and interactive communication. Having a website will allow you to set the tone for your practice (professional or high-tech flashy versus low-budget; personal or amateurish) and ultimately customize your clients' experiences with you.

Domain Name

If you have a website, you will probably want to acquire a domain name. Then, instead of directing potential clients to somewhere like http://sites.google.com/site/joetherapist/, you can simply send them to http://www.joetherapist.com. In this case, "joetherapist.com" is the domain name.

Domain names are distributed by domain registrars – companies such as GoDaddy and NetworkSolutions. A domain name is like a signpost that points to the address of your website. Through your registrar account, you set the registrar's domain name to point to the location where your website files are being stored. Most registrars also offer a domain forwarding service that automatically directs visitors to the actual location of the website. However, if you have a webhosting service (described below), you can attach the domain name directly to the site location.

Webhosting Service

Websites are no more or less than a series of files (text, images, code that dynamically generates content or visitor-supplied information, etc.) that are made available to the public over the Internet and that can be interpreted by a web browser. These files need to be stored on a server. Given that commercial servers have large and fast storage drives, redundant systems, firewall protection, 24-hour uptime, etc. most small businesses outsource their web storage to a webhosting service (GoDaddy is a popular webhosting service). For a monthly fee, a webhosting service gives you a large chunk of storage space with always-on access to the Internet. The webhosting account can be used for many purposes, from websites to file-sharing to streaming media to email. If you have a website, a webhosting account is preferable because it gives you more control over the files than free websites provided with many ISP accounts. With a webhosting account, you can easily set your domain name to receive emails at joe@joetherapist.com, and you can distribute the web space and email accounts among multiple users.

Security Software/Hardware

Internet security features are built into today's operating systems, but you may also wish to add firewall software, such as Norton Internet Security or ZoneAlarm. A firewall blocks certain types of information from being transmitted or received by your computer. If you prefer a hardware option, you might also wish to purchase a router (which can connect to your DSL or cable modem account and be accessed by multiple computers in your home/office); firewall functionality is built into most routers. You may also wish to purchase email encryption software, such as PGP (Pretty Good Protection), which allows you to encode your private client files and emails.

In the end, you must balance security with accessibility — only implement as much security as you can tolerate using without it seriously impinging upon your ability to practice (10 deadbolts on your front door make it hard to get out in a fire). The easiest solution is probably to use your operating system's built-in firewall capabilities, a web-based private email service, and an inexpensive program for encrypting client records stored on your machine (don't forget to backup!).

Security issues are discussed more thoroughly later in this chapter.

Social Networking

Setting up free accounts with social networking and social bookmarking sites such as Facebook, LinkedIn, Twitter, and Digg can be a great way to promote your services and create awareness about mental health issues. These sites, which have now become central to net culture, make it easy to post information that others might find interesting and equally easy for others to pass along what you post. Just be careful to set privacy controls so that information intended only for close friends does not get transmitted to business associates and curious clients searching for you in the public domain. Be aware that a list of all your Facebook friends may be visible to each of them or to the general public.

Virtual Worlds

Finally, some online counselors are providing innovative services on so-called "virtual worlds" such as Second Life (http://www.secondlife.com). In virtual worlds, counselors and clients can create personalized graphical representations of themselves called "avatars" and interact in a visually stunning, three-dimensional environment where anything is possible. Second Life accounts are free, as is the viewer software needed to participate. For a fee, Second Life users can acquire virtual land — property on which one might construct an online clinic, for example, replete with a waiting room, library of mental health information, or whatever you can imagine. Several books have been written that provide great introductions to Second Life; see, for example, Rymaszewski et al. (2008). More and more mainstream businesses are creating virtual outposts in Second Life, which keeps getting better and will continue to improve over time with advances in technology. Online counselors have long characterized their sessions as clients visiting their virtual office. With virtual worlds, this characterization is more literal than ever. And that online office has the potential to be more equipped and well-designed than the one you might have in the "real" world.

UNDERSTANDING THE INTERNET

The Internet is probably the most complex system ever devised by humans. As such, it can be daunting to comprehend. Most of us would rather not think about what happens between the sending and receiving of an email, or between typing in a web address and the information appearing on the screen. Fortunately, virtually everything that takes place on the Internet relies on a few simple principles that have changed little since the net's inception.

At its most basic, the Internet is a collection of thousands of computer networks, all of which have to cooperate and allow data to move among them using defined communication protocols. It is important to understand that the Internet is not a giant computer run by a giant corporation. In fact, nobody "runs" the Internet or owns it. The Internet is completely decentralized, and it was designed that way from the beginning. It was not always meant to be available to the public, however. The Internet had its genesis in the US military, which wanted to create a computer network that would remain stable even in the event of a catastrophe such as a nuclear attack against key communication centers.

The Internet Protocol (IP) routes information using "IP addresses." These addresses are expressed as four numbers separated by periods.

An example IP address might be 192.168.70.3. These being difficult to remember, something called a "domain name" was created. Special computers called "domain name servers" translate the domain names into IP addresses so that, when you send something to apple.com, for instance, your computer knows that it should really go to 17.254.3.183. Domain names are a system of dividing Internet addresses into discrete groups based on their topic area. These areas are reflected in the last several letters of a domain name. The oldest and most common domain names end with .com (for commercial entities), .org (for organizations), .gov (for government entities), .edu (for educational institutions), and .net (for Internet-related entities). Other less commonly used domains have been created as well, including .biz, .tv, .usa, .uk, and many more.

Client–Server Architecture

The software used for the Internet, and used by individuals to interact via the Internet, operates by something called "client–server architecture." Because the terms "client" and "server" are often used in discussing Internet-enabled software, it is important to understand what they mean in your work as an online counselor. Programs that reside on your own computer and that use the Internet, such as a web browser or email program, are called "clients." Your ISP's computer is called the "server," and software that resides on that computer and delivers website content and emails to individual users on demand is called "server software." What is special about client–server architecture is that the Internet does not care what kind of data it is transmitting or what programs will be using it. All that matters is that it gets from the server to the client — they will know what to do with it.

UNDERSTANDING THE WEB

So what is the World Wide Web? Is it the same thing as the Internet? In a word, no. Although the web uses the Internet and the terms are often used synonymously (e.g., "I found it on the Internet"), they are quite different. The World Wide Web consists of millions of electronic documents linked to one another and accessed via the Internet Protocol. The individual documents are called "web pages" and collections of web pages residing on the same server are called "websites."

Web pages are simple text files incorporating special codes and commands (or "syntax") that a web browser program understands. The text of a web page document tells a web browser where to show images, how to display text, and what to do when a user uses the mouse to point to, scroll, or click on a particular part of the page. The core system used to write web pages is called HyperText Markup Language (HTML). Many books have been written on designing effective websites and writing web pages with HTML and web-editing programs.[2] Special code like java-script and CSS can also be added to HTML pages (or kept in separate files) to improve site appearance, make the site more interactive, or generate dynamic content.

If you do create your own private website, you will want to make sure that it appears listed in many of the popular web search engines such as Google and Yahoo! Most of these websites have forms to submit your URL for "spidering." Search engines have developed automated programs ("spiders") that will crawl around web (get the name?) and examine the contents of websites so that users can be directed to information that is useful to them. You can embed keywords and a description in the code of your web pages to facilitate this process.[3]

UNDERSTANDING EMAIL

Email (asynchronous text messaging) is the standard mode of communication on the Internet. Most people in the developed nations have exchanged emails. There are two types of email transmission commonly used for online counseling. We will call them "standard email" and "webmail."

Standard Email

Here is a simplified sample itinerary for a typical email. Let's say therapist123@verizon.net sends an email to joe2345@comcast.net. First, the message is encoded and split into packets. The packets are transmitted to the ISP's (Verizon's) server. The ISP's DNS (domain name server) translates the domain "comcast.net" into its IP address (76.96.54.12) and Verizon's SMTP (simple mail transfer protocol) software sends the packets on their way. The packets arrive at comcast's mailserver (mail.comcast.net), which reassembles the packets and deposits the message in the mailbox file in the recipient's account (joe2345). The email remains in that mailbox on the comcast.net server until Joe tells his email program to get new mail, at which point it is retrieved, deleted from the server, and placed in the mail database on Joe's computer.

The key points to understand for the purposes of online counseling are that (1) the mail is not transmitted directly from one computer to the other; (2) the mail is not removed from the recipient's server until it

---

[2] For a comprehensive reference on web design, see Niederst (2006). Castro (2006) provides a straightforward yet comprehensive guide to HTML and other related coding languages that are readable by modern web browsers.

[3] A complete discussion of search engine optimization is beyond the scope of this chapter, but a number of books have been written on the subject. Google also has a popular program called AdWords that can help direct web traffic to your site. AdWords participants bid on different search terms and costs are limited to a level that you set ahead of time. For details, see http://adwords.google.com.

is retrieved (and then only if the mail client tells the server to delete retrieved messages, which is usually the default setting); and (3) the email is transmitted in plain text and is readable to anyone who has access to the server mailboxes or who cares to snoop on the packets as they travel across intermediate servers. Computer criminals have been known to use "packet sniffer" programs to do this very thing.

If you are curious about the path an email took to arrive to you, select a message in your email client program and choose "view header." You will see a variety of information, including IP addresses and domain names of each server involved in the transmission of the message. The header also displays the "reply to" address, which is set by the sender and is the address to which your email will be sent if you click "reply" in your email program. The "reply to" address is arbitrary and not necessarily the same address as the account that sent the message. Always double-check the recipient's address before clicking "send" on an email.

Webmail

Webmail works similarly to standard email, but it does not require an email client program. Rather, all email is retrieved and read via a password-protected website. Most ISPs and free email providers (e.g., gmail) allow you to check your email via a web interface. An advantage of this is that you can check your email from any computer in the world equipped with a web browser. Secure webmail services do not actually send your message anywhere. They require both parties (sender and recipient) to be registered with the service. Then, when you send your message, it is made available to the recipient, who has an account on the same server. Because they do not require the installation of any encryption software (they use the encryption built into all modern web browsers), secure webmail services are an attractive and commonly used option for online counseling. Examples include safe-mail.net (http://www.safe-mail.net) and Hushmail (http://www.hushmail.com). When a new message is received, the recipient gets a standard email simply announcing that a new message has arrived. To see the message, the recipient must log on to his or her secure webmail account.

A Precautionary Message

By now, most of us have become aware of the risks of email, often by witnessing a horrible mistake made by someone who clicked "send" too quickly and emailed unintended recipients, with consequences ranging from simple embarrassment to job loss and divorce. You should always read a message twice before sending and double-check the list of recipients. If you need to send a message to many recipients simultaneously, email is a great tool, but be sure to put your list of recipients in the "bcc:" field of the email. If you put your entire list in the "To:" or "cc:" fields, every recipient will have access to your entire mailing list.

UNDERSTANDING TEXT CHAT

Text chat allows you to communicate with somebody in real time via the Internet. Whereas email requires you to send a message in a big chunk, text-chat communications proceed line-by-line, with counselor and client(s) communicating synchronously. Chat is one of the older technologies of the Internet. As an online counselor, you will likely use chat in one of two ways. Online counselors may chat with clients via web-based chat rooms (including those in virtual worlds) or via a separate chat client.

Chat can be facilitated by web-based instant messenger applications or free-standing instant messaging programs. Numerous systems have been developed to allow instant messaging (chat). Google Talk, iChat, Skype, AOL Instant Messenger (AIM), and Microsoft Messenger are some of the most common IM services.

Here's how it works. When you run your chat program and sign on using your screen name and password (e.g., using AIM), the AOL server makes a note of your online status and your IP address. Anyone else registered with AIM can add your screen name to their "buddy list." While you are signed on, the server constantly monitors the status of individuals on your buddy list so that AIM will tell you when one or more of your buddies is online and available to chat. While logged into your chat program, you can set your status to reflect whether you are available for a conversation. Ordinarily, chats take place between individuals and nobody is able to barge into your conversation. However, some IM services allow you to set up password-protected virtual chat rooms so that you can have chat sessions with multiple individuals, allowing for group counseling sessions.

Emoticons are frequently used in chat sessions so that participants can indicate emotional tone. One advantage of using emoticons in chat sessions is that most IM programs support graphical "smilies." That is, typing ":-)" will show up in the text log as "☺". Chat client software typically support a large number of graphical emoticons.

UNDERSTANDING VIDEOCONFERENCING

Videoconferencing is like using text chat, in that communication is conducted in real time. However, instead of line-by-line text messages, video images are transmitted.

Videoconferencing usually requires each participant to use client software (e.g., Skype or iChat) and, generally, all participants need to be using the same software unless the software conforms to a standard protocol. Today's videoconferencing software is just as easy to use as text-chat software and works the same way. To participate in a videoconferencing session, webcam and microphone accessories are needed. Most webcams and laptop computers have microphones built into them. The latest video-conferencing software allows you to send text-chat messages while you see full motion video on the screen. Further, the software typically allows you to see video images of all participants (including yourself).

UNDERSTANDING FORMS AND DOCUMENT SHARING

As an online counselor, you may wish to collect data from your clients using web-based forms and allow clients to download worksheets and other self-help material as part of the counseling process. The Internet makes it so easy to share data that many f2f counselors use it to collect and share information with their clients as well.

On the Internet, the standard way to share proprietary documents is to use the portable document format (PDF). You can certainly create a web page with psychoeducation about anxiety, depression, or coping with anger, for example, but plain web pages are easy to copy, may not be formatted properly, and may not print well. PDFs allow you to prepare a document so that it looks and prints exactly right every time. Further, you can lock a PDF so that it cannot be edited or printed if you are concerned about copyright issues. When you want to collect information from your clients, web forms are a good way to do it. Forms are most often used for client-intake questionnaires and other brief assessment measures. Forms are built into HTML and, using a basic HTML editor, you can easily create web pages with edit fields, check boxes, selection menus, and choice (radio) buttons. However, you must provide instructions that tell the web server what to do when the "submit" button is clicked.

There are a few other options for data collection. For example, some sites will help you set up forms and collect data via free web-based survey services (e.g., http://www.surveymonkey.com). Data submitted by surveys is not secure without SSL (secure socket layer) encryption, so you may wish to consider using a secure form-processing service such as FormsStack (http://www.formsstack.com). Another alternative would be to send the client a blank text-version of your form via email. They could then edit it in their reply and return it using a secure mail system.

UNDERSTANDING SECURITY

With privacy and confidentiality being so crucial in counseling, it is important to understand how to use technology to protect your clients' information. In this section we will discuss security risks and countermeasures.

Debates about online counseling invariably turn to the importance of privacy and the risk of "hackers" having access to client disclosures. Granted, f2f counseling measures are generally not that secure. Most counselors close their doors during sessions, but how many use sound-proofing? Most counselors lock their office doors at night, but how many files are left in plain view on a desk? What would happen in the event of a burglary? We would suggest that, rather than constituting an added liability for online counseling, security features are one of the main *benefits* of online counseling. Technology allows us to store records easily and safely. With the use of a few simple and inexpensive precautions, Internet communications are arguably *more* secure than f2f conversations – nobody can eavesdrop and you do not need a full-time security guard to patrol your office.

Without taking the necessary simple security steps, there are some serious risks, but if you understand how the technology works then you will not have a problem. It is analogous to knowing that you probably should not conduct a private counseling session in a café. The problem is that most net novices do not know when they are in a private room and when they are in public.

The Internet was not originally designed to be particularly secure. Since its inception, however, steps have been taken to improve the Internet for the purpose of activities such as electronic commerce and storing medical records.

Risk Points

Figure 4.1 is, remarkably, still as accurate today as it was when it was created nearly 10 years ago. It is a basic layout depicting potential risk

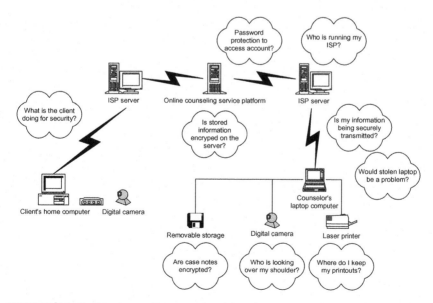

FIGURE 4.1 Online counseling security risk points.

points in online counseling. As previously described, when information is transmitted online, it is broken up into pieces (packets) and the pieces travel from server to server until they reach their final destination. To use an email as an example, it is like taking a postcard and giving it to a postal worker, who then rips it up into a few pieces and hands each piece to whatever postal worker happens to be walking by. Each piece gets handed from postal worker to postal worker (whomever may be headed in the direction of the recipient) until they all finally arrive at the individual's mailbox, whereupon they are reassembled and the recipient can read the postcard. In this case, there is no envelope disguising the message, nor is anyone particularly concerned who handles the pieces as long as the handlers are wearing a postal-worker uniform. Clearly, there are some risks.

Let's consider a typical email, traveling from an online counselor to a client. The counselor writes the email on her notebook computer using a standard email program, such as Outlook. The message is sent. First, the message is transmitted to the counselor's ISP. Then (in packet form) it is routed across the Internet from server to server to its final destination, the client's ISP. The message (now reassembled) sits on the ISP's server until the client retrieves it, whereupon it is downloaded to the client's computer. The message stays on the client's computer until it is filed or deleted. After it is deleted, the message remains on the computer's hard drive until it is overwritten.

See if you can identify all of the potential risk points.

- **The counselor's laptop**. Is the counselor working in private? How is the sent message stored? What if the laptop is stolen?
- **The message, *en route***. Who has access to the message as it travels? Could somebody capture all the packets and store them before sending them along their way?
- **The client's ISP**. Who has access to the client's email box on the server? What form does the message take as it waits to be retrieved?
- **The client's computer**. Who can download the messages? Who else uses the computer? How does the message appear in the client's email inbox? How is the message stored?

Being aware of the risk points gives you the power to effectively implement countermeasures and adopt best practices for secure Internet-based communications.

Countermeasures and Best Practices

There are a number of security protocols you can adopt to improve the privacy of your communications.

PASSWORD PROTECTION

Your computer should have some sort of password protection. Every modern operating system allows you to set your computer to require the entry of a password at startup. This is a simple precaution you can use. In addition, you should set your screensaver to turn on automatically after a brief idle period and require a password to resume activity. It is best not to share your computer with others if you are using it for online counseling, but, if you do, be sure to set up a separate password-protected account. Windows, Mac, and Linux operating systems allow you to do this with ease.

When choosing a password, you should use a short unfamiliar phrase that is at least eight characters long, including both upper and lowercase letters and at least one numeral or non-alphanumeric character. For ultimate security, you should avoid writing your password down; however, in order that client records be accessible in the event that you are incapacitated, we recommend you write your passwords down and store them in a safe deposit box. Provide instructions to a colleague on what to do in case of emergency.

ENCRYPTION

It is a good idea to encrypt documents that are private. Cryptography is a complex science involving number theory and mathematical operations that are well beyond the scope of this book but have been discussed extensively elsewhere (e.g., Garfinkel, 2002). It is not difficult to implement encryption into your everyday routine, whether you are transmitting or storing confidential information.

There are two basic encryption strategies that you should know about: "symmetric" encryption and "public key" encryption. Symmetric encryption is best used for storing documents privately on your computer. The same key is used to encrypt and decrypt the document. It is the most secure method because, without the key, anyone intercepting the message will have no idea what the file is — it will just look like a jumble of random characters. There are many symmetric encryption programs available and they are even built into most computer operating systems.

With public key encryption, you generate a "keypair" — a set of two keys, one private and one public. You can give your public key to everyone — even post it on your website. Anyone who wants to send you a private message then uses the public key to encrypt the document. Since you have the private key, you are the only one who can decrypt the file. Encryption keys are very different from passwords. They are generally very long strings of randomly generated characters. When you hear about a 128-bit key, that means that there are 2^{128} possible keys that could decode the file. Even if all the computers in the world cooperated, it would take longer than the age of the universe to try all the possible keys (Free Software Foundation, 1999). Naturally, you do not have to memorize or type in these keys. They are stored on your computer in a key database. You can post your public key on your website, email it in plain text to your colleagues and clients, or list it with a public keyserver;

that is, directory of keys. Anyone with the key can use it to send you an encrypted message that only you can open. Access to your private key is protected on your own computer by a typical password of your choosing.

As it turns out, public key encryption is the method built into all modern web browsers to allow secure communications between your computer and a website. When your browser shows a lock or key in the lower left corner (on Netscape and Internet Explorer), you have a secure connection. Basically, the server (e.g., Amazon.com) has sent you its 128-bit public key and your browser then uses that public key to encrypt data (e.g., your credit card number) that you transmit to the server. If that data is intercepted along the way, it will be undecipherable to the third party because they do not have the secret key. This process is called SSL encryption (see Garfinkel, 2002, for more detail about communications layers and other aspects of security).

Webmail systems such as gmail use SSL to allow users to exchange private messages without using any extra security software. Because the messages never leave the server (e.g., Safe-Mail.net), it is sufficient for both parties to enter and read messages by means of their browsers. It is important to log out of your account and close your browser when you finish with the mail so that nobody else can see the messages in your account.

WIPING

As mentioned above, private information that you delete off your computer remains on its hard drive until it is overwritten. Recovery software can easily restore files from a discarded drive (consider this before selling your used computer). This problem is easily remedied using wiping software, which writes a random series of ones and zeros over data to be erased. The drive formatting tools built into most operating systems allow you to securely erase a drive that you no longer need.

WEAKEST LINK

Remember that your security procedures are only as strong as their weakest point. You can encrypt all of your data, but if your password is on a sticky note tacked to your monitor you have a serious limitation. Similarly, you can do everything possible on your end as a counselor, but if your client sends you an unencrypted message there is nothing you can do about it.

FIREWALLS

Today, most of us have computers that are constantly connected to the Internet. Moreover, many of our computers are connected to large or small networks of multiple computers. Given the proper expertise, sophisticated users can spy on other network computers if the proper precautions are not taken. As briefly mentioned earlier, we recommend that you set up a firewall. A firewall can be software or a hardware device that blocks certain types of information from coming to or leaving your computer. For example, a firewall can be set up to only allow websites, email, and chat data to travel to and from your machine. You can protect yourself from unauthorized intrusions easily and inexpensively by using software such as Norton Internet Security or the firewall built into your computer's operating system. Alternatively, if your network has a router between your computer and your cable/DSL modem, you can set up your router to only allow certain types of data to travel between the Internet and your computer. Ordinarily, operating systems and routers have default settings set to limit risk, but if you are concerned you could check out some third-party firewall software or consider adding a router to your network.

TECHNOLOGY TRENDS IN ONLINE COUNSELING

Technology is ever-changing. We predicted that the first edition of this chapter would be outdated within a few years and, for the most part, that was correct. It remains wise to stay abreast of new technological innovations.

Increasingly portable, faster computers and faster Internet connections will allow online counselors to offer videoconferencing services with ease, and new generations of wireless Internet access will remove any limits on accessibility. Counselors can make themselves as available as they like. Fortunately, powerful computing platforms have made their way to the masses and web applications have largely eliminated the early obstacle of getting counselors and clients onto the same operating system, using the same specialized software.

Virtual worlds such as Second Life are increasing in popularity and sophistication so that counseling via avatar no longer seems to be a matter of science fiction. The rise of social networking has revolutionized the way we think about interacting with one another and has created a new laboratory for our clients to explore their interpersonal relationships (not to mention new opportunities for intervention).

A great way to keep up with new trends in technology is to read computer magazines such as *PC World* and *MacWorld*, and, for a broader view of things to come, we recommend a digital lifestyle magazine such as *Wired*. Finally, a more scholarly approach to online counseling trends and research can be found in journals such as *Cyberpsychology, Behavior, and Social Networking*.

CONCLUSION

Online counselors need to be familiar with the "tools of the trade" — namely, the technological underpinnings of online counseling. Having a general idea of how everything works behind the scenes will allow you to be a better online counselor and respond appropriately when there are technical issues to address. Clearly, this discussion is not exhaustive; indeed, volumes have been written on each of the above topics (many of which require a computer-science background). We hope you will use this chapter as a starting point from which to incorporate new technologies into your work so that you can provide the most efficient online counseling services.

DISCUSSION QUESTIONS

1. What is the difference between the Internet and the web?
2. Who owns the Internet?
3. What are some security risks in online counseling?
4. What is the difference between symmetric encryption and public-key encryption?
5. What are the advantages of PDF documents?

REFERENCES

Castro, E. (2006). *HTML, XHTML & CSS: Visual quickstart guide* (6th ed). Berkeley, CA: Peachpit Press.

Free Software Foundation. (1999). *The GNU privacy handbook*. Retrieved August 15, 2010 from http://www.gnupg.org/gph/en/manual.html

Garfinkel, S. (2002). *Web security, privacy, and commerce* (2nd ed). Sebastopol, CA: O'Reilly & Associates.

Niederst, J. (2006). *Web design in a nutshell* (3rd ed). Sebastopol, CA: O'Reilly & Associates.

Rymaszewski, M., Au, W. J., Wallace, M., Winters, C., Ondrejka, C., & Batstone-Cunningham, B. (2008). *Second Life: The official guide* (2nd ed). Indianapolis, IN: Wiley Publishing, Inc.

Chapter five

Ethical Issues in Online Counseling

Ron Kraus
Editor, EthicsCode.com

INTRODUCTION

This chapter is written for students, clinicians, and organizations that wish to understand the ethical guidelines for professional online practice.

In the US, health care practitioners must be licensed by their state before they are allowed to offer professional services to the public.

85

Online Counseling. DOI: 10.1016/B978-0-12-378596-1.00005-8

While people may consult whomever they can reach or afford, the medical insurance companies will not honor claims for health care services unless these were provided by licensed professionals.

The state license requirement is valuable as it ensures that the public is served only by professionals who meet certain educational and training standards. Once licensed or certified, clinicians need to work under the terms and limits of their state license, and the relevant state board monitors any reported violations. As a result of this format, most professional schools in the US teach their graduates the ethical regulations in their field. Licensed clinicians can review the relevant rules, standards, and/or ethical considerations on their state's website. Consequently, most professionals as well as graduate students are usually familiar with their ethical obligations to clients.

In addition to learning about ethics in graduate school or on the state board's website, many professional organizations, such as the APA, National Association of Social Workers, and the like, publish their own ethical codes for members. Unlike state board regulations, which are like laws, professional groups' ethics codes only relate to members of the specific organization. The consequence of ethics violation may be the removal of the member from the professional organization. In other words, professional organizations may publish ethics regulations but these are not state laws but rather the required standards for members. Obviously, if a serious ethical violation is reported, professional organizations may take further action and/or direct the complaint to the state board or police.

As the ethics of online counseling is new and thus is not yet being taught in professional graduate schools, many clinicians are still unfamiliar with the requirements related to the modality. This chapter is written specifically to clarify current ethical standards that relate to mental health care delivery online. To maintain quality of service, avoid potential complications, and serve the community safely, professionals who practice online should know the limits of online consults and understand various ethical as well as legal considerations that apply to this type of work.

THE COMMUNICATION REVOLUTION: A BRIEF REVIEW

With the introduction of the Internet in the 1990s and the following spread of portable devices, a communications revolution has begun. Never before in history have so many people been able to communicate, access information, or find resources with such ease and speed, regardless of geographical distance. Information today is accessible from everywhere and at all times. Today, graduate students are comfortable with the Internet, use search engines and portable communication devices, and have immediate access online, as these technologies have been in existence since their childhood. But, for the older generation, this is not the case.

When the parents of today's graduate students were in school, just searching for a bibliography in the library was a challenge in itself. Usually, index cards with publication title and/or author pointed to either books or articles on the subject, and these titles would (or would not) be found on a shelf somewhere. Often, the information on the index card did not include a full abstract, and so only reading the publication, once found, would reveal whether the resource was at all useful.

In the more distant past, scholars needed to work very hard just to access information. Prior to the days of telegraph, telephone, and Internet, weeks, months, and even years could pass before mail arrived from a colleague. When Darwin went sailing around the world, exploring the origins of species and making amazing discoveries, his findings and adventures were not shown on television and online that very evening to viewers all over the world. Today, live f2f videoconferencing consults and immediate information exchanges can be done with ease over the Internet. A search for resources and information nowadays is so much easier when just entering a few keywords into an Internet search engine produces results within milliseconds.

We live in the age of information, and it is immediate, easily accessible, abundant, and often overwhelming. Immediate and free public access to knowledge has many dramatic implications. In the age of constant contact, one may wonder how the story would have ended if only Romeo and Juliet had been able to text-message each other. Would anyone have thought of running the Marathon if the victorious Greek commander could have simply used email or his cell phone to contact headquarters? Information is power, and it is available today to more people than ever before in history. The communications revolution is still changing our world.

In 1999, the Harris poll found that the public was already showing enormous interest in obtaining information online. This was particularly true when it came to searching for health- and mental-health-related information (Taylor, 1999). But now that we have the ability to research, consult, and exchange information like never before, are we actually communicating better? Has understanding between people, groups, or nations improved with the communications revolution?

WHAT ARE THE ETHICAL REGULATIONS FOR ONLINE COUNSELING?

Very soon after the introduction of the Internet, health-care-related information, services, and resources started appearing online. A few brave pioneers who believed in the potential of online counseling began to build websites offering information and interactive services to the public. At the same time, cautionary statements by the APA relating to emerging technologies (see ethics statements from 1995, 1997, and 2010: http://www.apa.org/ethics/education/telephone-statement.aspx), lack of regulations, and the absence of sufficient research data kept most clinicians wary of the new practice. Responsible clinicians who wanted to practice online ethically were frustrated when they found that no guidelines were available. As a result, several attempts were made to define the do's and don'ts of online counseling.

Interestingly enough, private initiatives to define the ethical regulations for online practice were published before state and professional organizations established formal rules for the emerging field. The Health on the Net Foundation (HON) (http://www.hon.ch) was among the first non-governmental operations to establish rules for health care websites. The specific recommendations made by the HON code can be found at http://www.hon.ch/HONcode/Conduct.html.

While the recommendations and requirements of the HON Code are very solid, the main focus is on medical websites, services, and information. Among other efforts, several leading online health information providers, such as America Online, Healthwise, Medscape, iHealthCoalition, and WebMd, formed the Hi-Ethics Alliance to create consensus on a code of ethics for the medical sector. Perhaps a good example to demonstrate how unregulated the Internet health care field was during its infancy is the fact that the above-mentioned initiative was begun after the sector had been criticized for lax standards in providing medical advice and in filling out prescriptions online.

In 2000, an attempt was made to organize several US agencies in order to collaboratively work out a set of rules and regulations for clinicians who work online (Rippen & Risk, 2000). More about aspects of this early ethics initiatives relating to online health care practice can be found in Eysenbach (2000).

Among the first to write about ethical issues related to mental health counseling online was the former head of the APA's Ethics Committee, George Stricker. In his visionary 1996 article titled "Psychotherapy in Cyberspace," Stricker provides a good review of some of the main concerns that online practitioners should pay attention to. Among the issues discussed are the establishment of a therapeutic relationship and the responsibilities it carries, the need to know the true identity of the client, the case of emergency, and the need to consider in-office care. Also discussed are the privacy of online communication, the limits of text-based communication as a treatment modality, and the need to give clients the means for dispute resolution.

In 1999, OnlineClinics.com was born. The group's president and the distinguished members of its Advisory Board agreed that definition of the ethical guidelines for the emerging field would necessarily be the first step before interactive mental health services could be offered. As a result, two former heads of the APA Ethics Committee, a psychologist and attorney specializing in health care law, and one optimistic visionary composed and published EthicsCode.com in 1999. At first, the code was meant to guide members of OnlineClinics but, as the value of the principles for the global mental health community became recognized, EthicsCode.com was published for public use. At that point and perhaps for the first time ever, specific guidelines for mental health practice online were published. Over 10 years have passed since the publication, but the simple 10 principles of EthicsCode.com are still valid and useful today.

WHAT IS ETHICAL? WHAT IS MORAL? WHY IS ETHICAL BEHAVIOR IMPORTANT?

When uncertain about the exact meaning of a new term, my father used to say, "get a dictionary definition." Following his good advice, this section will start with definitions of the terms involved. The *Oxford Dictionary* (Hornby et al., 1971), defines "ethic" as "science of morals, rules of conduct," and "ethical" as "of morals or moral questions." The word "moral," according to the same dictionary, means that which concerns principles of right and wrong. It thus seems that the term ethics relates to principles of appropriate, correct, and just behavior among members of the human family. Yet, now that the terms are perhaps clearer, how does one distinguish between right and wrong? What is the source of our moral and ethical codes? And why would it be wise to follow these principles, anyway?

Ethics: The Philosophical and Religious Foundation

Concepts of ethics and morality have appeared in many cultures throughout recorded history. Even though the various moral codes of different cultures are often separated by time, language, religion, and/or geography, it seems that some basic rules of conduct are common to all members of the human family. The oldest and most common source for moral guidance usually comes from a culture's religious scripts. A review of Jewish, Christian, Eastern, and Muslim cultures reveals that the fundamental rule of conduct taught by Buddha, Jesus, Mohammad, Moses, and others is that people should treat each other as they would like to be treated themselves. The old saying "Love thy neighbor as thyself" is a message that repeatedly emerges in various scriptures as the most basic religious/spiritual/moral commandment, calling us to behave ethically. The philosopher Immanuel Kant seems to have arrived at similar conclusions. The tenet is often called the "Golden Rule"; following are some examples of its expression by various cultures, taken from Godin (1996).

Hurt not others in ways that you yourself would find hurtful.

Buddhist; Udana-Varga 5:18

Surely it is the maxim of loving kindness: Do not unto others what you would have not done unto you.

Confucian; Analects 15:23

Always treat others as you would like them to treat you: that is the law and the prophets.

Christian; from "The Sermon on the Mount," Matthew 7:12

No one of you is a believer until he desires for his brother that which he desires for himself.

Islamic; from Muhammad's last sermon, Sunnah

What is hateful to you, do not to your fellow man. That is the entire Law: all the rest is commentary.

Jewish; Talmud, Shabbat 31a

Thousands of years later, it is still helpful to keep the Golden Rule in mind in ethical questions related to treatment and service issues online. The question one should ask oneself when uncertain about an ethical issue is simple: How would I view events were I the other person? The imaginary shift of oneself into the place of the other — indeed, not always an easy task — is one way to better understand the impact of our actions and how these may be perceived.

Ethics: The Legal Side

Licensed clinicians, regardless of training, theoretical background, personal philosophies, or cultural or religious beliefs, are still obligated to follow laws and regulations that govern their profession. In most cases, the agency that issues and regulates a professional license is the clinician's state. To keep a license in good standing, a clinician must know and follow the ethics regulations of his or her state's governing agency when providing professional services to the public. In addition to respecting the state license, including the responsibilities it carries, some practitioners are members of a local, state, national, or international professional association. As in the case of the state license, professionals who are certified members of an association have to be familiar with, as well as adhere to, the organization's ethics code. Although a professional organization, such as the APA or the National Association of Social Workers (in the US), may deal with a member's ethical violations internally or even take further action if need be, such an association has no authority to revoke a clinician's state license. Simply put, licensed clinicians have to know the regulations of their state and their professional associations in order to avoid potential violations and legal risks.

The Psychology of Business: The Value of Trust

Psychology has come a long way since Freud first introduced his revolutionary ideas, including those relating to what he named "the pleasure principle." Many years later, some of Freud's concepts still seem valid today. In essence, Freud's pleasure principle explains that we are largely motivated by a wish for the gratification of our needs as well as the wish to avoid pain. Borrowing Freud's pleasure principle to explain consumer behavior in the modern era, we can understand why customers prefer products and services that are not only gratifying but also reliable. Trust, it seems, is good for business and sales. Consumer trust in a reliable product or service is a good way to ensure, maintain, and increase revenues. The link between trust and sales is a known fact that motivates not only politicians during an election but also the business and advertising communities. Such groups invest enormous amounts of money attempting to convince the public that their product or service is reliable and worthy. Indeed, once quality and reputation are established, brand name is created in the public's mind. People prefer the brand name that is associated with a valued and trusted product/service. Keeping ethical principles in mind when serving clients is a good way to create and maintain their trust. Clients, who are satisfied with the quality of the product/service they get, will also help to promote the good reputation and future business success of the product/service provider. Recommendations regarding the business aspects of online counseling are discussed in more detail in Chapter 7.

To summarize, justification for ethical/moral conduct comes from various sources, including religious, philosophical, legal, psychological, and business considerations. Regardless of personal philosophy, online professionals need to be familiar with their state's (and/or province's or country's) and, if applicable, their professional association's ethics code(s) and carefully adhere to their principles.

WHAT IS PSYCHOTHERAPY?

In most cases, the term "therapy" relates to the process of healing or recovering. Psychotherapy is an interpersonal and personal process that aims to help people better understand and cope with situations, emotions, or perceptions. In essence, psychotherapy is a process of communication and dialogue. The therapeutic dialogue may focus on both intrapersonal and interpersonal issues. For some, psychotherapy may enhance the ability to cope, help identify obstacles to personal fulfillment, allow a search for better alternatives, and/or enable personal growth. Still, it is important to remember that psychotherapy does not produce the same results for everyone.

While mental health professionals strongly believe that there are benefits to psychotherapy, results are not guaranteed and depend on various factors, among which are the individual's motivation and willingness to "work it through," and the feeling that both the process and the selected therapist can really help. Among other important predictors of the success of psychotherapy are the skill, approach, experience, and ability of the therapist, as well as a good match between client and therapist. The question of whether psychotherapy is an effective process has been thoroughly researched (see http://www.apa.org/pubs/journals/releases/amp-65-2-shedler.pdf) and apparently answered. In spite of the debate and after much investigation over the years, psychotherapy, which includes a wide variety of treatment techniques, methods, and approaches (all of which are not necessarily similar or equally effective), is now considered an acceptable form of treatment for emotional and behavioral problems in Western culture.

It is important to explain clearly the process of evaluation and psychotherapy to a new client, as well as to discuss the effectiveness, limits, and available alternatives to treatment. It is considered unethical to promise a client results that one cannot ensure. In the same way, clinicians should not tell a client that one method of treatment is superior to another if such a claim cannot be supported by current research and scientific evidence.

IS IT ETHICAL TO PROVIDE PSYCHOTHERAPY ONLINE?

The question of whether online communications are ethical at all as a form of service mostly stem from the concern that remote communications, such as text and telephone, may be insufficient or less effective than f2f, in-office encounters.

Most psychotherapists believe that nonverbal communication is important to understanding the total message. Nonverbal communication is our body language and everything we communicate besides the spoken word: posture, gestures, dress and appearance, facial expressions, and the like. Nonverbal communication is considered important for us to correctly "read" and understand each other. Since videoconferencing is not yet widely available to the average consumer, the current way in which most people communicate online is through the written word and over the telephone. As a result, the therapist's ability to "read" a client's nonverbal communication online (consisting of only text or voice) is limited.

Indeed, it may be true that office visits are preferable in some ways to online consults, because the clinician can better assess the nonverbal cues listed above, and can also offer immediate, concrete help if such is required. Still, initial research seems to indicate that there may not be a significant difference either in the outcome of the treatment or clients' satisfaction when online work is compared to f2f encounters (see Chapter 4). We also know that telephone hotlines have been serving the community successfully for decades, preventing clients from harm in critical times. It seems that to deny people the ability to locate and communicate with providers of professional help through the Internet may itself be unethical, especially as we already accept and use hotline services very effectively. While possibly limited when compared to in-office consults, Internet and telephone communications may be helpful to those who require service but cannot or dare not communicate through other means. With the core philosophy of the helping professions in mind, we believe that it is better to ensure that services are offered responsibly and with all ethical considerations rather than not at all. Being familiar with the contents of this book will allow clinicians and organizations to provide responsible, professional service while avoiding potential hazards.

WHAT CONSTITUTES TREATMENT OR THERAPY?

A therapist–client relationship is usually established when a clinician is contracted to diagnose a condition and recommend treatment. Because of its special nature, not all contacts and communications online fit the definition of psychotherapy, even when they take place between an expert and a consumer. It is important for online practitioners to understand clearly what constitutes therapy as opposed to an educational consult, such as expert opinion. Legally, the responsibility that a therapist has toward the client differs according to the nature of their relationship. A therapist conducting traditional, in-office treatment is usually also expected to act as the "case manager," responsible for assessing the general safety and wellbeing of the patient in treatment. However, such responsibilities are not required if the professional was contracted, for example, only to conduct an evaluation, give psychological testing, or provide an expert opinion. Clinicians who work online can serve the community in several ways. A passive website, for example, can provide information, educate, and/or recommend techniques, strategies, and/or links for people to use as a source for self-help. An interactive site offers clients means of communication with a clinician, such as by email, chat room, telephone, or videoconferencing. Even when initial contact is made and a client communicates online with a professional, a therapeutic relationship may not yet be established. Clinicians have to decide what type of service they wish to provide online and clearly explain it to potential customers.

ETHICAL CONSIDERATIONS FOR ONLINE PRACTICE

A New Medium: Know the Potential, Recognize Limits, and Inform Clients

The Internet and mobile communications revolution provides people with new ways to interact with each other. Today, people around the globe can communicate easily, directly, and immediately via text, voice, and even videoconferencing. Within the past several years, visitors to health and mental health websites have been able to locate and even communicate with various professionals online. Yet, when an individual practitioner or organization is tempted to simply go online and offer professional service to the global community, it is crucial that they remember that not all clients and/or situations can or should be dealt with online. Some situations require in-office treatment or assessment. For example, it may be inappropriate to use the online modality with a client who poses a risk of danger to self or others. In times of emergency or when there is real threat to a person's wellbeing, online communications are an insufficient treatment modality. Following are some situations in which online consults are not recommended:

• If a client has thoughts of hurting or killing him/herself
• If a client has thoughts of hurting or killing another person
• If a client is in a life-threatening or emergency situation of any kind
• If a client has a recent history of suicidal, violent, or abusive behavior
• If a client holds what others may consider to be unrealistic beliefs (delusions)
• If a client sees or hears things that others do not (hallucinations)
• If a client is actively abusing alcohol or drugs

More about the considerations regarding appropriateness of service online can be found at the website of the ISMHO at http://ismho.org/casestudy/ccsgas.htm (Suler et al., 2001).

It is important for online clinicians to clearly explain the medium's limits to visitors and potential clients and to advise how and where f2f evaluation and/or help can be obtained in times of need. A responsible clinician must become acquainted with the extant professional literature about online counseling, giving particular attention to the effectiveness of treatment and outcome studies. Not only should an ethical clinician know about the medium, current research findings, and limits, but this knowledge must also be shared with clients. Clients should understand the potential risks and benefits of online counseling in order to make an informed decision. Clinicians should discuss with the client the effectiveness, limits, and risks, and point out the availability and effectiveness of alternative treatment. More about the suitability of clients for online services can be found at http://ismho.org/casestudy/ccsgas.htm.

The Possibility of In-office Care and a Contingency Arrangement

When a clinician responds to a request for service online, it is still important to consider the possibility of f2f sessions. Not only could an initial intake (or even continued care) in the actual office potentially be more beneficial, but online clinicians also need to recognize that the f2f modality may be required at some point. Even if a new online client is not experiencing a crisis when making first contact, clinicians should remember that anyone may sometimes experience an emotionally overwhelming situation that requires more intensive care. Thus, clinicians have to assess the suitability of potential clients for online care and also inform the client that in-office services may be required. A responsible therapist should accept a client into his or her care only if

1. Both parties agree that the therapist is within reasonable geographical distance from the client and can thus provide in-office care if the need arises; or
2. Both parties agree upon a contingency referral arrangement for cases when in-office care is required.

Why it is Important to Know the Identity of an Online Client

One characteristic of the Internet medium is that people can use it to communicate with relative anonymity. One can easily register an email identity and begin communicating through an e-identity, an alter-self online that need not reveal the writer's real name. Much like the experience in a confessional booth, some people actually relish the fact that their listener does not see them or know their identity when unloading sensitive information. In fact, by their nature, online contacts are already known to facilitate more direct, less inhibited communications (Suler, 2002) and, due to the safety that is created by physical distance between the parties, may also be helpful for those who find it difficult to openly discuss intimate or sensitive issues (Budman, 2000). Although online communication and fictional names allow for some level of anonymity when requesting service, it would be problematic for clinicians to therapeutically engage with clients whose identity they do not know. The reason behind this requirement needs to be understood by both clinician and client.

There are two main reasons why a responsible clinician should insist on knowing the identity of the online client. The first consideration is the client's safety: it is necessary to enable the clinician to offer concrete intervention if or when such is needed. When a therapeutic relationship exists, clinicians are usually obligated to try to protect their clients from harming self or others. At times, clinicians may even have to take active steps to prevent harm, such as contacting the client at home over the telephone, calling a relative of the client, or consulting with other agencies, such as a hospital or an emergency service. To comply with the need to safeguard their clients, clinicians who work online should know who their clients really are so that they have the ability to establish contact with the client (or his or her emergency contacts) through means other than email in times of crisis or danger. The second reason clinicians online need to know the identity of their clients is to avoid dual relationships. Clinicians are usually advised against entering a therapeutic relationship with a colleague or family member because this dual relationship may interfere with the intimate process of mental health treatment. Dual relationships are prohibited for clinicians and compromise the effectiveness of counseling for the client.

Delivering Clinical Services Across State Jurisdictional Lines

The Internet allows people and organizations to post information and advertise services to the public on the World Wide Web. The ease with which people can access information, get services, and communicate gives many the illusion of proximity. It is almost as if cyberspace were a different dimension in which geographical, national, cultural, and other boundaries disappear, leaving many with the feeling that they are citizens of one interconnected global community. And yet, when it comes to the provision of professional services online, clinicians must respect the limitations of their licenses and malpractice insurance policies. Simply put, online clinicians may provide professional care only to those clients who reside in the state(s) or province(s) in which the practitioner is licensed or certified. The reason for that restriction is a legal one: the governing state agency that issues the professional license can only authorize practice in that particular state. Further, in most cases, the clinician's professional malpractice insurance is valid only if the clinician practices within the scope of his or her license. In other words, providing service to clients from a state where the clinician is not licensed may automatically violate the terms imposed by the insurer. In turn, the professional malpractice insurance company may not be obligated to cover any legal expenses or damages if a clinician were to be found guilty of malpractice while serving residents of states where he or she is not licensed to practice. Though the temptation to accept calls online from anywhere does exist, a responsible clinician should not risk being sued in the client's state, where the regulations might be different from the clinician's state. Traveling to a trial in another state, perhaps hundreds of miles away (where the online client may reside), without the reassuring protection of a malpractice insurance policy is a risk not many would care to take.

So far, recipients of mental health services online in the US have not complained about unsatisfactory practices by mental health providers. This, however, should not be reason to encourage professional service across state lines. As the modality gains recognition, a case involving practice across state lines online may eventually be brought to the attention of a court. In cases where no better, local alternatives exist, such as for residents of very remote or rural areas, a responsible clinician should remember to explain to clients the limits of the medium in general and the inability to have f2f sessions should such be required.

Once clients are made aware of the limits and restrictions, local resources, and alternatives, they still have the right to consult a distant expert, if they so choose and if the practitioner is willing to take the risk. Clinicians and clients should be aware of the difference between communications that are for specific education, referral, or information purposes and those that can be called therapy or treatment.

One legal way for clinicians online to broaden the scope of their practice is to try to obtain a license in neighboring states. In some instances, states do recognize a license issued by another state, a situation often referred to as "reciprocity." Obtaining a license to practice (as well as to be insured) in more than one state may be a solution for some clinicians. There seems to be movement toward making a clinical license transferable and valid throughout the US, but we are not quite there yet. In recent years, much through the efforts of an organization called the National Register of Health Care Providers in Psychology, some provinces and states have adopted a mechanism by which reciprocity is made possible. Unfortunately, it may take years before US clinicians can transfer their professional credentials between all states with the same ease that they can, for example, transfer a driver's license. Until that time, clinicians are recommended to serve clients where they are licensed to practice, or at least recognize the serious risks should they choose not to do so.

UNDERSTANDING THE RISKS TO THE CONFIDENTIALITY OF ONLINE COMMUNICATIONS

The World Wide Web is a network of computers that allows storage and transmission of data (see Chapter 4). One of the benefits of the communications revolution is that the public is able to avoid postage costs when sending messages online. Hard to imagine nowadays, the word "email" was not even a familiar term only a decade ago. However, as convenient as it is, the wonderful world of email is not all that perfect. For one, an email message is not quite like a letter one puts inside an envelope and slips into a regular mailbox. Email is more like a postcard, which many handlers may view. Experience has shown me that no harm has been done to my privacy and good reputation by sending numerous postcards over the years to friends and relatives. However, great embarrassment was caused when a private note to a girl I loved was read by others for whom it was not intended. Similarly, in the world of online communications, email is not always private and people should try to avoid exposing details that may be embarrassing or damaging. Whereas childhood love notes could cause only limited embarrassment in my junior high school class, similar mishaps online could cause greater harm because they could be circulated globally.

One simple and often inexpensive way to protect yourself is to download one of the email encryption software packages. Although security systems are never totally perfect, when the client and clinician both use encryption while communicating, privacy is increased. Another way to guard against privacy violations is to communicate using an online counseling platform, which intrinsically provides an extra measure of privacy for secure chat and email. To maintain ethical service, online clinicians should inform themselves about and advise clients of the potential risks to confidentiality in regard to Internet transmissions.

Although experience shows that many clients do not worry much about confidentiality when using regular email, it is the responsibility of the clinician to explain the limits to the privacy of such communications and offer alternatives. Session notes and other documentation gathered online should not be sent to another account or to a supervisor without using the same protection as that used for the client's privacy. Clinicians who conduct real-time text-based sessions through an existing product should check that the software/network they are using is designed to maintain privacy, that it includes the ability for encryption, and that records of the sessions are not made or shared by a third party.

The last item discussed is important, because some providers/software/systems do, indeed, keep track of all communications that go through them. When evaluating a network's virtual office or considering which communications product to use, clinicians must be careful to ascertain that records of their sessions and communications will not be made and/or kept somewhere on the system so that privacy is maintained. Clinicians can and should take notes as they work with clients. To ensure privacy of records, clinicians also have to protect the records after the session. Thus, notes from online (and other) communications should not be kept on the clinician's computer (hard drive) but on a protected disc that can be safely locked elsewhere according to current regulations.

The Limits of Confidentiality

Confidentiality and its limits are important issues to understand for people considering treatment. In general, professional therapists strictly maintain confidentiality. In fact, therapists are required by law, professional regulations, and ethical codes to maintain their clients' confidentiality. Laws, professional regulations, and ethical codes governing exceptions vary by state and profession, but some general information about the limits of confidentiality that may be useful to potential clients includes:

- In all states, therapists must report to authorities suspected child abuse or neglect (see http://www.reportchildabuse.com for links and instructions).
- In some states, therapists must report to authorities suspected abuse of elders, spousal abuse, and sexual misconduct by other therapists.
- If a client poses an imminent risk to self or others, therapists are required to inform those who can assist in managing the risk, including those put at risk by the client, emergency medical service, and/or appropriate authorities.
- If clients become involved in certain types of legal proceeding, therapists may be required to respond to demands by an attorney or by the courts for otherwise confidential information about such clients.

These proceedings may include, for example, cases where clients place their psychological condition at issue, child custody disputes, civil commitment hearings, lawsuits by a client against the therapist, and court-ordered treatments.

- If clients themselves request information about their treatment or their treatment records, or give consent to the therapist to release that information to others, such as to the health insurance carrier or other treating agencies, therapists generally must comply with their clients' wishes.

Keeping Private Communications and Data Secure

By law, clinicians and organizations are now required to keep clients' private information secure and private (see the HIPAA regulations at http://www.hhs.gov/ocr/privacy; HHS, Office of the Secretary, 2002) when it is maintained or transmitted online. Thus, when considering a venue or product through which to conduct online consultations, clinicians should make sure that it includes a way to protect the security of confidential data transmissions and storage. Sites and products that allow authorized access with a password usually also mention the level of encryption security that is used. Common for adequate security today are products/sites with a 128-bit encryption level, but some already offer a 1024-bit encryption level and higher. The level of security being developed for secure access and transmission of data is expected to continue to rise. Similarly to the need to periodically update psychological testing tools, clinicians online should try to keep their security technology current. Occasionally updating security features for communications and data will help to ensure that privacy is adequately protected. Network-type sites often offer built-in security solutions that include firewall-type protection and other security measures. Good security is usually quite costly, and the price continues to rise in direct correlation with the level of the protective measure's sophistication. Still, experience shows that no security system is completely safe forever, although the security industry is prosperous and works to prove otherwise. An ethical clinician will therefore explain to a client how access to data and communications is protected, as well as acknowledge the limits to even the best security. In general, it may be wise to try to keep as little information as possible in places that may become accessible to others.

WHO COVERS THE COST OF TREATMENT ONLINE?

In October 2001, Medicare (a US federal health program) announced a change to its policy that would allow billing for online videoconferencing consults (even if *not* in real time) at the same rate as for f2f consults (see http://dms.dartmouth.edu/nhtp/pdf/medicare.pdf). Although this was an important move in the right direction, text-based consults are still mostly not considered a reimbursable service by many insurance carriers. As a result, most users of the new medium have to cover the expense of consultation online out of their own pocket, usually with a credit card. Clinicians who provide online consults should clearly explain current reimbursement policies to their clients. Online clinicians should inform potential clients of the current limitations to online care with regard to third-party involvement in, or reimbursement for, online professional services.

It took some time for insurance companies to recognize telephone consults as a billable, integral form of patient care activity. Today, time spent on the phone with a patient, another expert, an agency, or a family member is recognized as a part of the service. It may not be long before more changes are made to alter existing policies of reimbursement. When more agencies add text-based and videoconferencing consults into what is considered an acceptable modality of service, it is estimated that clients will also be able to get insurance-company confirmation for that service, and additionally do the billing directly online.

QUALITY ASSURANCE AND DISPUTE RESOLUTION

The main reason for ethical rules is to protect the public from harm. Because clinicians are licensed by a governing agency, such as a state certification board, it is that agency that clients may contact in the case of a problem. Licensed clinicians must provide accurate information about their credentials, license, training, and/or certification to clients. In the real office, clinicians and agencies often post such documentation for public view. When clinicians work online, clients have the same right to know who the provider is, what his or her credentials are, and where and how to proceed in situations regarding professional conduct. Responsible online clinicians will post information about their professional standing for the public to view, as well as show links to agencies that govern or supervise their work and license. Display of such links and information will allow patients to conduct further inquiries in case a dispute about the quality of service, treatment procedure, diagnosis, billing practices, or any other issue cannot be resolved directly between the clinician and the client. If a clinician is being supervised or consults with another professional or agency, the name of and information about that supervising person/agency should also be available to clients. In cases concerning the quality of care, clients have the right to know where and how to apply for a resolution.

RECORD KEEPING

In most cases, clinicians are mandated to make and keep some treatment records of people in their care. Treatment and medical records of clients are confidential. Clinicians are usually bound by professional regulations to respect the privacy of their clients and adhere to certain precautions when handling and keeping treatment records. There should be no difference between the way in which clinicians keep and safeguard treatment records when communications take place online, over the telephone, or in f2f encounters. Online clinicians maintain records of clients who receive their service online using standard office procedures, (e.g., of such content and detail as are kept in the nonvirtual office).

MASTERY OF THE NEW MEDIUM

In a process similar to that of obtaining a driver's license, therapists must fulfill certain requirements before they can become licensed to run an independent practice. The first requirement of clinicians-to-be is to demonstrate sufficient academic knowledge by successfully graduating from a recognized institution or program. Further, to be independent practitioners in the mental health field, clinicians in most states also have to complete an intensive training program that includes many hours of supervised practice. After completing both the academic and supervised training requirements, clinicians must also pass qualifying tests to be awarded a professional license for independent practice. The long process of education, supervision, and training that therapists are required to complete is designed mainly to ensure that clinicians are well prepared in both theory and practice, and thus qualified to provide responsible service to the public. Even after being licensed, clinicians who face a situation that requires a form of treatment they are not sufficiently trained for are obligated to acquire the needed skill, consult an expert, or refer the client to an expert, so that the best possible treatment is provided.

The new medium of online consulting is similar to a new treatment technique that needs to be mastered. To ensure mastery and understanding of the medium, online clinicians must acquire technical skills, get consultation, or contract to practice under an experienced supervisor prior to providing professional services online.

ISSUES OF PRIVACY: THE HIPAA REGULATIONS

Little or no regulation existed to monitor online operations for some years after the field emerged, but the new HIPAA regulations now regulate the ways in which private patient information should be handled when it is delivered and stored online. In essence, the HIPAA regulations require that practitioners and services that handle or transfer patient data online must observe rules of privacy and also inform their patients about the procedure, safeguards, and risks to privacy that may be involved. As a federal initiative probably crafted by skilled attorneys and other professionals, the HIPAA regulations take a global and conservative approach; the regulations maintain that a local state rule, if it protects the privacy of patients to a level higher than that required by the HIPAA regulations, would supersede the latter. The HIPAA regulations are explained in detail and over hundreds of pages, yet the basic principles of informed consent and observance of the privacy of confidential information are not new concepts for most clinicians. (For more information about the HIPAA regulations, see http://www.hhs.gov/ocr/privacy.)

SUMMARY

Licensed clinicians are obligated to follow their state's and professional association's ethics regulations when serving the public. Consultation online is a new medium and regulations in the field are still forming. Careful adherence to existing rules as well as compliance with the considerations discussed in this chapter will ensure that clinicians and professional organizations serve the community responsibly. In addition to reviewing the manuals of relevant state(s) and professional board(s), exploring some of the following sites may be helpful:

- **The American Counseling Association (ACA).** http://www.counseling.org/Resources/CodeOfEthics/TP/Home/CT2.aspx
- **The American Psychological Association (APA).** http://www.apa.org (ethics page at http://www.apa.org/ethics/code/index.aspx)
- **The American Psychiatric Association.** http://www.psych.org
- **The Ethics Code.** http://www.ethicscode.com
- **The Health on the Net Foundation (HON) Code.** http://www.hon.ch/HONcode/Pro/Conduct.html
- **The International Society for Mental Health Online (ISMHO).** https://www.ismho.org/suggestions.asp
- **The American Association for Marriage and Family Therapy.** http://www.aamft.org (ethics page at http://www.aamft.org/resources/lrm_plan/ethics/ethicscode2001.asp)
- **The National Association of Social Workers.** http://www.socialworkers.org (ethics page at http://www.socialworkers.org/pubs/code/default.asp)
- **The National Board for Certified Counselors (NBCC).** http://www.nbcc.org (ethics statement at http://www.nbcc.org/AssetManagerFiles/ethics/nbcc-codeofethics.pdf)

Because the field is still forming, clinicians would be wise to continue to monitor the relevant regulations related to online counseling as well as to observe updates.

GUIDE FOR FURTHER STUDY AND SOME RECOMMENDATIONS

Understand the Regulations

Online counseling is a relatively new field. State boards, federal institutions, insurance carriers, and professional associations are still evaluating their policies as more data is gathered. Clinicians should therefore understand current regulations as well as occasionally review them, because policies that relate to online consultations are periodically updated. It would be wise to check the regulatory body and/or the professional organization's website for the most updated version of the policies and regulations. Clinicians and organizations should both understand and follow the recommended guidelines related to work online.

Work Carefully and Within Ethical Limits

Clinicians must work within the limits of their license and malpractice insurance. In most cases, this means that clinicians limit their online practice to serving clients who reside within their state. Clinicians also should keep in mind that not all situations can be effectively dealt with online and clients may require in-office care or other forms of intervention at some point. Before launching a practice into cyberspace, it would be wise to first become familiar with the current laws as well as adopt and/or display an ethics policy. Clinicians may elect to adhere to existing guidelines, such as those at http://www.HONCode.org or http://www.ethicscode.com, for example, or display their own policy for the public. If a clinician or organization elects to write their own version of an ethics policy, such principles should reflect current professional guidelines.

Before initiating service, online clinicians should prepare various forms and information for clients geared toward guaranteeing their understanding of the procedure. Some forms that the online clinician should have include: informed consent to treatment, an intake form, patient bill of rights, consent to release of information, treatment plan, understanding limits to treatment and privacy online, and the like.   These forms can be sent or shown to potential clients online to reduce the risk of misunderstanding.

Learn More About the Limits and Benefits of the Online Medium and Educate Clients

Clinicians continuously expand their understanding and the online counseling field is still growing. Clinicians need to follow developments in the field on a regular basis, so that new discoveries, risks, techniques, or regulations do not go unnoticed. Further, clinicians must understand that covering the educational—theoretical component is but the first step in acquiring the skills needed to become proficient in the new medium. Clinicians should review relevant literature and use the links recommended throughout this book for further study. Clinicians should try to stay current with recent research, recommendations, and discoveries. It is also important to explain the limits and risks involved in online counseling to potential clients.

Continue to Educate Self and Others

Reading this book is one good way to become more familiar with the theory and practice of online counseling. Clinicians who believe in the potential of this medium to improve service, availability, and communication with clients should remember that many in the professional community are still unsure about this form of service. Thus, once clinicians are knowledgeable, they may need to educate others, such as colleagues, supervisors, and administrators, about the benefits and risks involved in online counseling. It is quite possible that patients, who already use email and are known to seek health information online, will need little more encouragement to use the new service than, perhaps, the provision of the clinic or clinician's virtual address. Still, clients, too, will need to be informed and educated about the benefits and limits of the medium when such is offered. One of the nice things about working online is that resources are quite easily accessed. The National Institute of Mental Health (http://www.nimh.nih.gov), for example, has a patient education page that may serve as a model for individuals and organizations that aim to set up such a service. For details, see http://www.nimh.nih.gov/health/index.shtml.

Promote Higher Standards of Practice Online

Since the Internet first started to expand in popularity, many have placed web pages online to offer services to the public. Some of these sites were or are still wonderful initiatives; some ended up evaporating and/or gave the professional community a bad reputation. Clinicians need to carefully follow the ethical regulations of their state(s) and professional association(s) when providing service online. More importantly, clinicians need to demonstrate professional practice when working online and promote the same for the community.

KEY TERMS

Case management A term used in the mental health field that means that a clinician has responsibility for assessing, facilitating, and monitoring the patient's overall functioning.

Confidentiality A term referring to people's right to privacy when they are receiving health care services. Confidentiality may be breached by clinicians if clients give written consent to release information, if real danger to self or others exists, or if a clinician is mandated to answer to a court of law.

Diagnosis A term adopted from the medical field, referring to the classification of a condition or disorder. Treatment cannot start before a diagnosis is made.

Dispute resolution The due process by which disagreements are resolved if clients raise grievances against a clinician to a governing agency.

Dual relationship A therapeutic relationship with a colleague or family member, for example, would create an undesired situation in which more than one relationship exists. Dual relationships are prohibited for clinicians because they may compromise the effectiveness of counseling for the client.

Emergency and crisis situations In the mental health field, crisis and risk situations are those in which real danger to self or others exists. In crisis situations, clinicians are mandated to take concrete steps to protect clients and others from harm.

Encryption A way to transfer or keep information after it is coded, usually to increase security and privacy.

Ethics Principles of appropriate, correct, and just behavior among members of the human family.

Ethics regulations A code of professional conduct that organizations require their members to know and follow.

Face-to-face (f2f) Describes a situation where patient and professional meet in the same office and not online.

Firewall A term used in the Internet security industry referring to the protection of a host server from unauthorized entries.

HIPAA regulations Federal regulations that specify how health and mental health should be handled and protected so that patient privacy is maintained.

Informed consent The process by which a person is educated about a suggested procedure is given a fair opportunity to consider it.

Internet A network of computers that are interconnected. This network allows the global community to access, store, process, and transfer vast amounts of data. With the Internet, citizens of the global community have easy, immediate, and almost unlimited access to people, information, products, and services online.

Jurisdiction line A term that defines the physical boundaries of the legal authority to practice.

Nonverbal communication Nonverbal communication is our body language and everything we communicate besides the spoken word: posture, gestures, dress and appearance, facial expressions, and the like. Nonverbal communication is considered important for us to correctly "read" and understand each other. It is important to understanding the total message and does not exist in text-based communications.

Psychotherapy A term used in the mental health field to describe the personal as well as interpersonal process that aims to help people better understand and cope with situations, emotions, or perceptions. Psychotherapy is a process of communication and dialogue that may focus on understanding and better handling of both intrapersonal and interpersonal issues. Psychotherapy may help people enhance their ability to cope, improve their understanding and regulation of emotions, and/or enable personal growth. Still, psychotherapy does not produce the same results for everyone.

State-issued license An official document issued by a state that certifies that an individual has passed all requirements, including education, training, and supervision, and has been found qualified to hold a license to practice the profession.

Supervision In the health and mental health field, clinicians use the experience of senior colleagues while training and when working to monitor their work or enhance skills.

Therapy A broad term that usually relates to the process of healing or recovering.

REFERENCES

American Psychological Association (APA). (1997). APA statement on services by telephone, teleconferencing and Internet. Retrieved November 1, 2002 from http://www.apa.org/ethics/stmnt01.html

Budman, S. H. (2000). Behavioral health care dot-com and beyond: Computer-mediated communications in mental health and substance abuse treatment. *American Psychologist, 55*, 1290−1300.

Department of Health and Human Services (HHS), Office of the Secretary (2002, August 14). Standard of privacy of individually identifiable health information. *Federal Register, 67*(157), Rules and Regulations.

Eysenbach, G. (2000). Towards ethical guidelines for e-health. *Journal of Medical Internet Research, 2*(1), e7.

Godin, S. (1996). *The official rules of life: For those of you who thought you'd mastered life's little instructions and learned everything you needed to know.* New York: Simon & Schuster.

Hornby, A. S., Gatenby, E. V., & Wakefield, H. (1971). *The advanced learner's dictionary of current English.* London: Oxford University Press.

Rippen, H., & Risk, A. (2000). E-health code of ethics: Policy Proposal. *Journal of Medical Internet Research, 2*(1), e2.

Stricker, G. (1996). Psychotherapy in cyberspace. *Ethics and Behavior, 6*(169), 175–177.

Suler, J. (1996/2002). The online disinhibition effect. Retrieved August 28, 2003 from http://www-usr.rider.edu/~suler/psycyber/disinhibit.html

Suler, J. R., Barak, A., Chechele, P., Fenichel, M., Hsiung, R., & Maguire, J., et al. (2001). Assessing a person's suitability for online therapy. *Cyberpsychology and Behavior, 4*, 675–679. (See Correction, 2002, *Cyberpsychology and Behavior, 5*, 93.)

Taylor, H. (1999). Explosive growth of cyberchondriacs continues. Retrieved August 28, 2003 from http://www.harrisinteractive.com/harris_poll/index.asp?PID=117

Chapter six

Legal Issues for Online Counselors

Jason S Zack, PhD, JD

Patterson Belknap Webb & Tyler LLP — New York, New York, USA[1]

CHAPTER OUTLINE

INTRODUCTION

Despite promising process and outcome research, and obvious theoretical and practical appeal, many mental health professionals remain reluctant to offer online counseling services, fearing that such activities might be unethical or illegal (Ragusea & Vandecreek, 2003). In short, therapists wonder whether online counseling is legally "okay." This chapter reviews the key legal issues and state of the law pertaining to online counseling in the US. It is not meant to offer, nor should it be considered, legal advice. What I can do is provide the basic tools to help you and your legal counsel to make an informed decision for yourselves.[2] The pertinent laws are

---

[1] Although the author is affiliated with the named law firm, this paper represents the author's own opinions and was not written in connection with any of the author's duties as an employee of the firm.

[2] This paper is limited to legal issues that arise specifically out of the practice of *online* mental health counseling. For comprehensive information on legal issues related to mental health counseling, readers are urged to consult more general texts on that subject.

Online Counseling. DOI: 10.1016/B978-0-12-378596-1.00006-X

not necessarily an impediment to online counseling but rather are best seen as a set of parameters to help guide your practice based on lessons learned by counselors and clients in other contexts. Knowing what the law says should make you feel *more* confident in your work, not less.

The first section of this chapter explains why the law matters, arguing that existing laws clearly apply to online counseling activities. The next section addresses the question of whose laws apply and how they might be enforced. Finally, specific duties and legal issues that are particularly relevant to online counseling are surveyed.

SCOPE OF PRACTICE: THE LAW MATTERS

At the time of writing, there still appears to be no case law precedent specifically involving online counseling services,[3] but that does not mean that there is no law applicable to online counseling and, therefore, that "anything goes." On the contrary — whenever a novel situation arises in the law, courts interpret existing statutes and precedents from other contexts. Online mental health counseling shares many of the same features as traditional counseling approaches and courts will look to the traditional setting for parallel standards of professional and ethical practice.

Any discussion of legal issues must begin with a comparison of the scope of the law and the activities to which it ostensibly applies. Terminology is a good place to begin.[4] Some suggest the name by which professionals describe their services (e.g., online therapy, cybertherapy, e-therapy, e-counseling, online counseling, life coaching, cyber-consultation, etc.) might affect their legal responsibilities; for example, Grohol (1999) states, "Licensing laws in most areas restrict the practice of psychotherapy, not e-therapy." Although online counselors are using a variety of terms to describe their services, the term a provider adopts for his or her service is likely to be irrelevant in the eyes of the law, because

---

[3] Note that we have begun to see some cases involving telemedicine, including, for example, cases where individuals have been prosecuted by states for prescribing medication (psychiatric meds, no less) over the Internet without a license from the patient's state. See, for example, *Hageseth v. Superior Court of San Mateo County* (2007) (finding there was jurisdiction to prosecute a Colorado physician for practicing medicine without a license in California where he was never physically present in California and the conduct occurred in cyberspace — the patient, who had received a prescription of fluoxetine, committed suicide). See also *Golob v. Arizona Medical Board* (2008) (affirming Arizona medical board's censure, probation and $10 000 civil penalty against an Arizona-licensed physician who had prescribed medication to more than 9000 patients via the Internet without first conducting a physical examination); also *Jones v. N.D. State Bd. of Med. Exam'rs* (2005) (presenting a similar case). These cases are likely to be cited in hypothetical actions that would implicate a counselor for delivering "talk therapy" services online without a license.

[4] I arbitrarily refer to online counseling by different terms, partly for variety yet primarily to emphasize that, under most state laws, there is no real difference as to whether a mental health provider describes his or her work as "counseling" or "therapy," or whether they deliver services to "clients" or "patients."

most statutes define professional practice terminology based on the specific *activities* conducted. Thus, it is disingenuous to simply assert that online counseling is not "real" counseling (e.g., Ainsworth, n.d.; Manhal-Baugus, 2001). The differences between psychotherapy and e-therapy are not self-evident in view of statutory practice definitions, and one cannot simply assert that, because there are no statutes or case law specifically invoking the term "e-therapy", the law as applied to traditional f2f psychotherapy and personal counseling generally does not apply. The applicability of any given behavior-regulating law will depend on exactly what the provider is doing. A court will ask what services the provider offered and compare them to the relevant statutes. What the provider called his or her services is unlikely to matter. For example, in Delaware,

> 'Marriage and family therapy services' includes the diagnosis and treatment of mental and emotional disorders, whether cognitive, affective, or behavioral, within the context of interpersonal relationships, including marriage and family systems, and involves the professional application of psychotherapy, assessment instruments, counseling, consultation, treatment planning, and supervision in the delivery of services to individuals, couples and families.
>
> **Del. Code Ann. Tit. 24, § 3051(d)**

Thus, a Delaware-licensed marriage and family therapist may offer "life coaching" yet the term would not make the law irrelevant if the life coaching involves counseling or consultation, which it almost certainly would. Likewise, omitting one of the cited activities (e.g., treating but not diagnosing mental and emotional disorders) would not render the statute inapplicable.

In most cases, it will probably not suffice to claim that e-therapy is not equivalent to more traditional forms of psychological service. Just as "it will be hard to argue that activities, which can be seen as treatment or diagnosis, even though electronically delivered, do not constitute the practice of medicine" (Blum, 2003, p. 422), it will be hard to argue that mental health evaluation and counseling services provided via the Internet do not constitute psychotherapy, consulting or any of the myriad terms that state laws define as the practice of the various mental health professions.

In fact, some states have already enacted statutes clarifying that psychotherapy includes distance-based services. For example, Arizona's behavioral health statute states,

> Unprofessional conduct includes the following, *whether occurring in this state or elsewhere:* [...] Failing to comply with the laws of the appropriate licensing or credentialing authority to provide *behavioral health* services *by electronic means* in all governmental jurisdictions where the client receiving these services resides.
>
> **Ariz. Rev. Stat. Ann. § 32-3251 (12)(dd), emphasis added**

"Practice of behavioral health" is defined as "the practice of marriage and family therapy, *professional counseling*, social work and substance abuse counseling" (Ariz. Rev. Stat. Ann. § 32-3251 (6), emphasis added). Further, "professional counseling" is broadly defined to mean:

> The professional application of mental health, psychological and human development theories, principles and techniques to:
> (a) Facilitate human development and adjustment throughout the human life span.
> (b) Assess and facilitate career development.
> (c) Treat interpersonal relationship issues and nervous, mental and emotional disorders that are cognitive, affective or behavioral.
> (d) Manage symptoms of mental illness.
> (e) Assess, appraise, evaluate, diagnose and treat individuals, couples, families and groups through the use of psychotherapy.
>
> **Ariz. Rev. Stat. Ann. § 32-3251 (8)**

Thus, in Arizona, online counseling is explicitly covered under the general statutory paradigm for professional counseling. Other states have adopted similar statutes. In Minnesota,

> 'Practice of social work' means working to maintain, restore, or improve behavioral, cognitive, emotional, mental, or social functioning of clients, in a manner that applies accepted professional social work knowledge, skills, and values, including the person-in-environment perspective, by providing in person or through telephone, videoconferencing, or *electronic means* one or more of the social work services described in [the statute, which includes services typically offered by social workers offering online counseling].
>
> **Minn. Stat. Ann. § 148D.010 Subd. 9(a), emphasis added**

WHOSE LAWS APPLY, AND HOW?

It is fine to know that states regulate what online counselors do, but whose laws apply? For example, if a therapist is based in one state and the client is in another, the provider may wonder (1) where must I be licensed?; (2) should I worry if I violate a law in the client's state?; and (3) where can I be sued? What if the client or therapist receives/conducts mental health services from multiple locations (e.g., from a summer home)? In this section, I review what the introduction of the first edition of this book called "perhaps the largest of all legal impediments to be overcome" in online counseling: the question of how to address the legal problem of being in two places at once (Sammons & DeLeon, 2003, p. xxviii).

The General Statutory and Regulatory Legal Scheme

Like everyone, online counselors practicing in the US need to be aware of federal laws (those passed by Congress), state laws (including statutes and common law), and regulations (rules promulgated and enforced by both federal and state agencies).

FEDERAL LAW

Congress creates federal laws under the powers granted to it in the US Constitution. Congress has the authority to pass laws related to telehealth and other businesses that potentially involve interstate commerce (broadly construed) under authority granted in the Commerce Clause (US Const., art. I, § 8). Federal law also determines rules related to federally funded programs and services created under Congress' mandate to promote the general welfare of the US (US Const., art. I, § 8). Agencies, part of the executive branch of the government, are responsible for enforcing laws passed by Congress and for promulgating their own rules within the scope of their authority. Agencies responsible for health care service delivery fall under the HHS. The Health Resources and Services Administration (HRSA), a division of the HHS, administers telehealth and telemedicine projects.[5]

STATE LAW

Most laws related to health care service delivery, however, are enacted by the individual states, which regulate professions under the auspices of the "police powers" left to them by the Tenth Amendment. States establish licensure requirements for mental health professionals and create specialized agencies to oversee professions — generally with the authority to enact rules necessary to enforce the statutes passed by the state legislatures. The regulations promulgated by those agencies (e.g., a state's Board of Psychology) are laws that are just as valid and important to follow as state statutes. State laws may cover anything not pre-empted or otherwise disallowed by federal law (including the Constitution). State law not only determines what are *criminal* offenses (enforced by state and local law enforcement agencies), but also *civil* causes of action; that is, rights of private parties to sue for damages. Thus, it is important for online counselors (and any mental health professionals) to know the exact rules that govern the practice of their profession in the state(s) where they practice.

Procedure

CRIMINAL ACTIONS

If an online counselor violates a statute or regulation (e.g., practicing without a license or revealing a client's confidential information), he or she may be subject to criminal charges or civil sanctions brought by state or federal prosecutors or state professional boards. The matter would

---

[5] See http://www.hrsa.gov/telehealth.

then be adjudicated by a court or agency tribunal (e.g., a hearing before a State Board of Psychology). Prosecutors and agencies vary in the extent to which they pursue alleged offenders. Enforcement patterns may change over time in response to political agendas, levels of complaints filed, relative danger to the public, or a high-profile news event. Penalties are established by statute or agency regulation, and may range from reprimand to license suspension, fines, and imprisonment.

PRIVATE ACTIONS

If an aggrieved online counseling client (or other party) seeks a remedy available to him or her under the relevant law, the plaintiff may file a civil lawsuit against a counselor in state court for any cause of action he or she wishes (under state or federal law). The plaintiff may also file a civil lawsuit in federal court in certain circumstances. The question of which state's law applies in diversity cases is complicated and beyond the scope of this chapter, but, generally, in negligence cases

> the rights and liabilities of the parties [. . .] are determined by the local law of the state which, with respect to the issue, has the most significant relationship to the occurrence and the parties

taking into account

> (a) the place where the injury occurred, (b) the place where the conduct causing the injury occurred, (c) the domicil, residence, nationality, place of incorporation and place of business of the parties, and (d) the place where the relationship, if any, between the parties is centered.
>
> **Rest. 2d Conflict of Laws § 145 (1971)**

This could be a difficult determination in Internet counseling cases.

Personal Jurisdiction in Internet Law Suits

A court must be able to assert personal jurisdiction over a party to a lawsuit in order to try the case. A plaintiff can always sue a defendant in the state where the defendant resides, but plaintiffs often prefer to sue in their home state because it is easier to litigate where they live. Online counselors should know that they are probably subject to lawsuits filed in their clients' states.

The analysis of whether a state can exercise personal jurisdiction over a nonresident defendant involves two steps. First, the court must determine whether the state's "long-arm" statute authorizes the suit. Usually, long-arm statutes authorize actions against defendants for actions related to, among other things, business conducted in the state, contracts executed in the state, real estate held in the state, and torts that harm residents of the state. Second, the court must determine whether the defendant had sufficient "minimal contacts" with the state and exercising jurisdiction would not "offend traditional notions of fair play and substantial justice" (*Int'l Shoe Co. v. Washington*, 1945).

The law is still evolving with regard to how courts resolve jurisdiction in civil cases involving the Internet, especially involving harm allegedly caused by information placed on (and retrieved from) a website that is available to anyone in the world (Kaye, 2000/2007). Cases vary when it comes to which Internet interactions represent sufficient minimum contacts to justify jurisdiction, although there are some general rules. For example, "interactive" websites typically lead to a finding of personal jurisdiction, whereas "passive" websites do not (*Zippo Mfg. Co. v. Zippo Dot Com, Inc.*, 1997). This analysis has been adopted by a number of courts (Halkett, 2003). Thus, even in the absence of a client – therapist relationship, an online counselor's website alone could expose him or her to lawsuits in other states, especially if the site offers more than a static online brochure.

However, the cases most likely to be brought (tort claims) would probably base jurisdiction on traditional notions of minimum contacts, focusing on the harm that allegedly occurred to the client in the state where the lawsuit is brought. When harm results from interstate transactions, personal jurisdiction is generally appropriate in either the defendant's state of residence or the state where the alleged harm occurred to the plaintiff. For example, Pennsylvania law authorizes jurisdiction over nonresidents "causing harm or tortious injury by an act or omission in this Commonwealth" or "causing harm or tortious injury in this Commonwealth by an act or omission *outside* this Commonwealth" (42 Pa. Cons. Stat. Ann. § 5322(a)(3)−(a)(4), emphasis added).

Enforcement of Default Judgments

If the provider's attorney is 100 percent convinced that there is no ground for asserting personal jurisdiction, he or she might simply choose not to appear, but in that case a default judgment would be entered against the therapist after a hearing to determine damages (Hazard et al., 2005). The judgment could then be enforced against the therapist in any state in the country, under the Full Faith and Credit Clause (Hazard et al., 2005; US Const., art. IV, § 1). At that point, the therapist could litigate the issue of whether the out-of-state court had jurisdiction, but would be precluded from raising any substantive issues (Hazard et al., 2005). In other words, if the next court rules that jurisdiction was proper in the first suit, the therapist is liable by default. If there is any doubt about jurisdiction (to be expected in any online counseling case), most states will allow the therapist's attorney to make a special appearance in the out-of-state court solely for the purpose of contesting jurisdiction (Hazard et al., 2005). Thus, online therapists should be aware that, even if they believe that jurisdiction in the client's state is improper, simply the possibility that it is proper means that the therapist should be prepared to be sued in the client's state, at least for the purpose of disputing jurisdiction.

Contractual Provisions for Forum Selection and Choice of Law

In order to avoid disputes about jurisdiction, online counselors may ask clients to sign contracts at the outset of their work together, whereby the client acknowledges that any disputes will be settled under the law and/or litigated in the provider's state. Such "forum selection" clauses generally enjoy presumptive validity (17A Am. Jur. 2d *Contracts* § 259, 2007) but are not airtight. Forum selection clauses may be overridden if

> application of the law of the chosen state would be contrary to a fundamental policy of a state which has a materially greater interest than the chosen state in the determination of the particular issue and which [. . .] would be the state of the applicable law in the absence of an effective choice of law by the parties.
>
> **Rest. (2d) of Conflict of Laws § 187 (2006)**

Beyond that, some states do not recognize forum selection clauses, or merely use them to inform the court's decision as to whether to claim jurisdiction over the matter (17A Am. Jur. 2d *Contracts* § 259 (2007)). Thus, it may be difficult to enforce such clauses if the client's state has laws protecting consumers from negligent online counseling but the therapist's state does not (17A Am. Jur. 2d *Contracts* § 263, 2007). Finally, a plaintiff may dispute the agreement with traditional contract defenses such as fraud, duress, undue influence, incapacity, and unconscionability.

LEGAL ISSUES PARTICULARLY RELEVANT TO ONLINE COUNSELORS

Licensure

Licensure is often one of the first concerns that mental health professionals raise when contemplating offering services online. As discussed earlier, most states regulate the practice of mental health counseling, in all its forms, although the states vary in their definitions. State practice laws generally require that anyone providing mental health services to residents of that state be licensed. New York law, for example, states that

> Only a person licensed or otherwise authorized under this article shall be authorized to practice psychology or to use the title 'psychologist' or to describe his or her services by use of the words 'psychologist,' 'psychology' or 'psychological' in connection with his or her practice.
>
> **N.Y. Educ. § 7601**

The statute further defines "practice" to include

> counseling, psychotherapy, marital or family therapy, psychoanalysis, and other psychological interventions, including verbal, behavioral, or other appropriate means as defined in regulations promulgated by the commissioner.
>
> **N.Y. Educ. § 7601-a.**

Indeed, most states restrict unlicensed individuals from practicing anything that even *looks* like mental health counseling, typically exempting particular occupations such as the clergy and professions that are regulated elsewhere in the statutes, such as nursing. In Florida,

> 'Practice of psychology' means the observations, description, evaluation, interpretation, and modification of human behavior, by the use of scientific and applied psychological principles, methods, and procedures, for the purpose of describing, preventing, alleviating, or eliminating symptomatic, maladaptive, or undesired behavior and of enhancing interpersonal behavioral health and mental or psychological health. The ethical practice of psychology includes, but is not limited to, psychological testing and the evaluation or assessment of personal characteristics such as intelligence, personality, abilities, interests, aptitudes, and neuropsychological functioning, including evaluation of mental competency to manage one's affairs and to participate in legal proceedings; counseling, psychoanalysis, all forms of psychotherapy, sex therapy, hypnosis, biofeedback, and behavioral analysis and therapy; psychoeducational evaluation, therapy, remediation, and consultation; and use of psychological methods to diagnose and treat mental, nervous, psychological, marital, or emotional disorders, illness, or disability, alcoholism and substance abuse, and disorders of habit or conduct, as well as the psychological aspects of physical illness, accident, injury, or disability, including neuropsychological evaluation, diagnosis, prognosis, etiology, and treatment.
>
> **Fla. Stat. § 490.003(4)**

Such a comprehensive definition arguably encompasses just about anything a psychologist is likely to do with a client on or off the Internet (practice definitions of other specialties and the term "psychotherapy" tend to be equally broad). The definitional statute goes on to specify that psychological services may be offered "without regard to place of service" (Fla. Stat. § 490.003(4)(a)). The statute says nothing about an office, a couch, or talking.

Thus, states (1) regulate the practice of mental health services and (2) require anyone providing such services to be licensed. Before the rise of telehealth, these two concepts were a unity, but now they may function to require licensure in both the therapist's state and the client's state. Both the client's state and the therapist's state have an interest in controlling what happens in an online counseling interaction (whether to ensure their practitioners are qualified or to protect their citizens).

Many states offer an exemption for professionals who are licensed in another state and are only practicing temporarily. Depending on how the exemption is written, there may be latitude for occasional or limited work with clients in that state. For example, New York's statute allows for

> The representation as a psychologist and the rendering of services as such in this state for a temporary period of a person who resides outside the state of New York and who engages in practice as a psychologist and conducts the major part of his practice as such outside this state, provided such person has filed with the department evidence that he has been licensed or certified in another state or has been admitted to the examination in this state pursuant to section seventy-six hundred three of this article. Such temporary period shall not exceed ten consecutive business days in any period of ninety consecutive days or in the aggregate exceed more than fifteen business days in any such ninety-day period.
>
> **N.Y. Educ. § 7605(8)**

Other states may not require filing proof of licensure and practitioners could have tremendous latitude, especially for email therapy, if laws are written to allow a certain number of hours per month by unlicensed or elsewhere-licensed individuals (Koocher & Morray, 2000). Online counselors should be familiar with the licensure restrictions and exemptions, both in their states of licensure and in the states in which their clients are located. This puts a burden on practitioners who wish to provide services across state lines (especially those who offer services to individuals to and from many different states), but unfortunately this is the law in the absence of national licensure laws or lenient reciprocity rules. The good news is that the Internet makes this easy to do for the average practitioner. Every state makes its laws available online and generally has a search function or well-structured table of contents. Practice regulations are typically found under a heading such as "Professions." You can also generally find links to the relevant state regulations on the website of a state's licensing board. See, for example, http://www.op.nysed.gov/prof/psych/psychlaw.htm (which provides links to the psychology laws, rules, and regulations in New York). Even if you decide that you do not need (or want) to be licensed in your client's state, you are well-advised to show you made an effort to understand any special requirements that might be imposed by the client's state. In other words, if you decide to expose yourself to being prosecuted for practicing without a license, at least show that you made a reasonable effort to understand the duty of care in that state, in the event that you are subjected to a civil law suit (more on duties below).

It is worth noting that the federal government has expressed some interest in promoting telehealth by addressing the licensure issue. Bills such as the Telehealth Improvement Act of 2004 (S. 2325, 2004) and the Telehealth and Medically Underserved and Advancement Act of 2006, (H.R. 6394, 2006) have been introduced, aiming to explore license portability. Unfortunately, both bills died in committee. As of this writing, a bill has been introduced in Congress (Promoting Health Information Technology Act of 2009) that aims to "Facilitat(e) the provision of telehealth services across state lines," in part by requiring the Secretary of the HHS to "encourage and facilitate the adoption of State reciprocity agreements for practitioner licensure in order to expedite the provision across State lines of telehealth services" (H.R. 1039, 2009).

Unlike contract clauses − which may work to contractually limit the client − therapist relationship, legal duties based on that relationship, and choice of law for civil disputes − it is the *state* that determines whether a license is required for various occupations and their practices. Contracts are made between private parties, and it is unlikely to make a difference to the state whether a client clicks an agreement acknowledging that the counseling takes place in the counselor's state (i.e., that the client is virtually traveling to the counselor's office).

Legal Duties

Psychotherapists have many duties to their clients, which are defined by statute or under common law doctrine (25 Am. Jur. Proof of Facts 3d 117, 2007). Violation of these duties may be grounds for a civil lawsuit (e.g., malpractice) against the professional. The duties most often implicated in online counseling may be grouped into the general categories of competence, consent, and confidentiality.

COMPETENCE AND THE STANDARD OF CARE

The breach of a legal duty potentially results in liability for "negligence." Just as in f2f therapy, an online mental health professional will be liable for negligence if (1) a professional − patient relationship exists, (2) the professional breached a legal duty imposed by virtue of that relationship, (3) the breach of that duty caused injury to the client, and (4) the client suffered damages as a result of that injury (57A Am. Jur. 2d Negligence § 71). The specific cause of action (malpractice, wrongful death, etc.) will depend on the exact circumstances of the case and the exact duties will vary for each type of suit, but these are the general elements of negligence. In other words, the "basic liability issues" are no different from those in f2f settings (Rice, 1997; Sammons & DeLeon, 2003). "In negligence cases, the duty is always the same, to conform to the legal standard of reasonable conduct in light of the apparent risk" (*Darling v. Charleston Cmty. Hosp.*, 1965, p. 257). In the medical context, the standard is generally "what a reasonable physician in the same specialty would do in a similar circumstance, regardless of where the care was provided" (Johnson, 2003; Rannefeld, 2004). Still, it remains true that, unlike f2f mental health counseling, "standards of care for distance service provision have not been firmly established" (Sammons & DeLeon, 2003, p. xxix) and litigation will be necessary to flesh out the standards of care for online counseling. For example, just how much effort must a counselor make in order to provide for the client's safety in the event he or she believes the client to be a danger to himself or to others? Could the duty be less than (or different from) that established for f2f counselors (Koocher & Morray, 2000)? Online counselors might argue that the benefits of making services available to clients via the Internet weigh in favor of relaxing the burden upon them to act in an emergency. Conversely, a state might argue that the safety of its citizens is paramount, and, if online counselors cannot meet their duties in a time of crisis, such services should not be allowed.

At the most basic level, however, all mental health providers have an ethical duty to provide competent care (e.g., ACA, 2005, § C.2). Legal duties can be informed by ethics codes, and a key question in litigation will be, "what entails competence when it comes to online counseling?" Simply being a competent f2f counselor may not suffice. Online counselors are wise to engage in some sort of professional training (continuing education or self-training) so that they may show that they have made reasonable efforts to acquire the level of skill required to be considered competent in the field of online counseling. A number of experienced online mental health professionals have begun to offer such training and certification classes (e.g., http://counsellingresource.com; http://www.onlinetherapyinstitute.com). Other chapters in this book discuss the special skills necessary to be effective in text-based care.

CONSENT

Mental health professionals should be well-acquainted with the concept of informed consent. The current legal standard is that health care providers must

> disclose those facts and opinions that a reasonably prudent health care services provider in the medical community, exercising diligent and reasonable care, would disclose to the patient regarding the risks and probable outcome of the proposed course of medical treatment
> **25 Am. Jur. Proof of Facts 3d. 117 § 8, 2009**

If something goes wrong in the treatment, the professional may be sued for malpractice on the grounds that the client was not properly informed of the risks. Thus, in any mental health treatment, clients should be made aware of the risks of undergoing the treatment (e.g., limitations, the chance they will get worse). Online counselors need to inform their clients of the additional risks due to the online medium that might impact their decision concerning whether or not to engage in online counseling versus f2f counseling (Berger, 2003; Dreezen, 2004). These might include the risk that their confidential information might be inadvertently disclosed (see discussion below), the risk that technical difficulties might cut off the communication in the middle of a session (for synchronous modalities), the risk that misunderstandings might occur due to limitations inherent in text-based communications, or the risk that the counselor might be unable to intervene in the event of an emergency. Health care professionals offering innovative therapies or experimental treatments must disclose that the treatment is new, and "should always disclose the existence of the standard practice alternative" (15 Am. Jur. Proof of Facts 2d 711, 2009). Likewise, online counselors should disclose that their services are still part of a developing field for which there is not yet a comprehensive body of efficacy research as compared with traditional therapeutic modalities. In sum, because

> many jurisdictions recognize a presumption of valid and informed consent in situations where a written consent to treatment is executed by the patient and where the consent meets the criteria established within both the medical community and the legal arena where the [. . .] treatment occurs,

conscientious online counselors must have written informed consent built into the intake procedure and make sure that their clients understand the risks specific to this treatment modality (25 Am. Jur. Proof of Facts 3d 117, 2009).

CONFIDENTIALITY: PRIVACY AND DISCLOSURE

Aside from licensure and competence, potential privacy breaches are probably the most prevalent concern in connection with online counseling. In most states, mental health professionals have a legal duty to protect their clients' confidential information. For example, under Colorado law,

> A [mental health] licensee, school psychologist, registrant, certificate holder, or unlicensed psychotherapist shall not disclose, without the consent of the client, any confidential communications made by the client, or advice given thereon, in the course of professional employment; nor shall a licensee's, school psychologist's, registrant's, certificate holder's, or unlicensed psychotherapist's employee or associate, whether clerical or professional, disclose any knowledge of said communications acquired in such capacity; nor shall any person who has participated in any therapy conducted under the supervision of a licensee, school psychologist, registrant, certificate holder, or unlicensed psychotherapist, including,

but not limited to, group therapy sessions, disclose any knowledge gained during the course of such therapy without the consent of the person to whom the knowledge relates.

Colo. Rev. Stat. Ann. § 12-43-218(1)

Unauthorized disclosure may lead to a private cause of action (*Gracey v. Eaker*, 2002; Spielberg, 1999), depending on the state. Therefore, informed consent includes the potential privacy risks of online counseling (e.g., lost or stolen computers, prying eyes, etc.). Like the question of what constitutes clinical competence online, the standard of care for protecting confidentiality online has yet to be established. A court would try to determine what is reasonable, given the risks to the client, standard industry practice, and technological feasibility.

Health Insurance Portability and Accountability Act (HIPAA)

Under federal regulations promulgated pursuant to the Health Insurance Portability and Accountability Act (HIPAA), effective as of February 17, 2010, a person who knowingly "discloses individually identifiable health information to another person" may be fined up to $50 000, imprisoned for up to a year, or both (42 USC. § 1320d-6). Because the HIPAA applies to any providers who do any electronic billing to third-party sources for services rendered, virtually all mental health professionals must be HIPAA compliant, with exemption only for those few who "have no interface [...] with any insurance carrier, hospital, managed care company, state or federal program, or other third-party payer that currently or in the future may require some form of electronic transaction" (American Psychological Association Insurance Trust, n.d.). Online counselors should be particularly aware of the HIPAA because of the increased volume of electronic transactions and the increased use of electronically stored private health information in the e-therapy modality. The APA Insurance Trust has assembled an informative and comprehensive guide on the HIPAA for mental health professionals (APAIT, 2002). The HHS also has a comprehensive website that is worth reviewing. See "Health Information Privacy for Covered Entities," available at http://www.hhs.gov/ocr/privacy/hipaa/understanding/coveredentities/index.html.

Duty to Warn

As mental health professionals are also aware, the law in many states mandates that professionals have a legal obligation to break confidentiality under certain circumstances, such as when the client is in imminent danger of harming himself or others. In some states it will be sufficient to notify the appropriate authorities, but in other jurisdictions it is necessary to warn an endangered third party. Kentucky, for example, requires that (among other things, and with certain exceptions) mental health professionals make "reasonable efforts [...] to communicate" an "actual threat of physical violence" to a "clearly identified or reasonably identifiable victim" *and* to "notify the police department closest to the patient's and the victim's residence of the threat of violence" (Ky. Rev. Stat. Ann. § 202A.400(1)-(2)).

If the online counselor resides in a state, or is working with a client in a state where such reports or warnings are required, the counselor may be subject to criminal penalties or a civil lawsuit (e.g., wrongful death) should a client harm himself or someone else (assuming that the counselor was in a position to know the danger). In many states, mental health professionals also have a duty to report any knowledge of abuse (to children and/or the elderly). For example, California mandates that mental health professionals report suspected child abuse or neglect "to any police department or sheriff's department, not including a school district police or security department, county probation department, if designated by the county to receive mandated reports, or the county welfare department" (Cal. Penal Code § 11165.9).

In-person therapists take care to inform clients about limits of confidentiality at the outset of their work, and online counselors have a similar obligation. Online counselors are at a significant disadvantage, however, when it comes to their ability to take action when their clients are geographically distant. It is especially difficult for counselors who are willing to work with clients who choose to remain anonymous. Clients may sign agreements acknowledging counselor limitations that might preclude a civil suit, but those agreements may not affect the rights of a third-party victim or family member who decides to bring a claim. Such agreements would also not shield providers from professional civil sanctions by state authorities, not to mention potential criminal liability. Working with anonymous clients might create other risks as well; if there is no way to authenticate the client's identity at the outset of a session or at the beginning of treatment, the therapist runs the risk of disclosing confidential information to the wrong individual (e.g., a malicious spouse posing as the client).

Maintenance of Records

Mental health professionals are ethically (and often legally) obligated to maintain records of their work with clients, documenting observations, actions, and treatment plans (e.g., ACA, 2005, § A.1.b). In one sense, online counselors have an advantage because they have the capacity to store transcripts of every session with their clients via chat logs or emails. The chances are that clients also will be preserving this information. In fact, this is considered one of the benefits of online counseling, since the client has the opportunity to go back and review the interactions with their counselors and reflect on what transpired (Speyer & Zack, 2003). Professionals should be aware, however, that the entirety of their interaction with a client may be used as evidence in a lawsuit brought by the client. In other words, counselors used to having some latitude in the verbatim content of f2f sessions are well-advised to avoid saying (writing) anything that they would not feel comfortable with a judge or jury hearing. Every session should be treated as though it is being recorded. Like many aspects of online counseling, this may be both a benefit and a drawback, given that clients always receive a copy and the therapist has no control over how that copy is used. As mentioned above, online counselors should make special efforts to protect their records, using the many technological solutions available to them today.

Business Issues

Most online counselors will be offering services in exchange for some sort of fee, and a variety of remuneration structures are available to providers. The simplest system involves online counselors charging clients directly for individual sessions or session packages (e.g., four email exchanges for $100). Payments may be received by personal check or through online credit-card processing services (e.g., PayPal). Other online counselors join services such as Breakthrough.com, which offer secure communications technology platforms and ancillary services such as client scheduling, record-keeping, and payment processing. Counselors using both options are also beginning to bill their online therapy services to third-party payers. Aside from the application of the HIPAA, discussed above, there are several legal issues related to the way in which online counselors structure their business.

THANK YOU FOR YOUR PATIENTS: REFERRAL FEES

Online counselors who join practice groups or who use technology service platforms should evaluate their terms carefully before deciding which service to use. Unlike other industries, which allow a variety of incentives to generate business, the health care industry is heavily restricted and certain business practices are illegal (Bodenger & Raphaely, 2002). Online counselors should be aware that, if federal funds are involved, fee-splitting arrangements are potentially violations of the federal anti-kickback statute (42 USC.A. § 1320a-7b(b)). Such arrangements may violate state anti-kickback rules as well. For example, under California law,

> [T]he offer, delivery, receipt, or acceptance by any person licensed under this division or the Chiropractic Initiative Act of any rebate, refund, commission, preference, patronage dividend, discount, or other consideration, whether in the form of money or otherwise, as compensation or inducement for referring patients, clients, or customers to any person, irrespective of any membership, proprietary interest or co-ownership in or with any person to whom these patients, clients, or customers are referred is unlawful.
>
> **Cal. Bus. & Prof. Code § 650(a)**

Because services *other than* the referral of patients may be allowable so long as the fees are commensurate with the value of the services provided, a counseling platform provider might charge a technology-related fee as a safer option. Monthly virtual office fees, not based on number or length of transactions, are even better (avoiding situations where the platform's revenue is associated with the amount of business they generate for the clinician). It is important for online counselors to confer with legal counsel if there are any doubts about the propriety of the platform's fee structure (Bordeau, 1996/2007). In reviewing agreements with platform providers, online counselors should ask

> 1) Is a party in a position to receive patient referrals or to refer patients to another party? 2) Does the referral source receive anything of value? 3) Who is the referral source? 4) What is the purpose of the remuneration? 5) How is remuneration determined?
> **Bodenger & Raphaely, 2002, p. 127**

THIRD-PARTY PAYMENTS

Some advocates of online counseling have long argued that the practice will be fully accepted and flourish once insurance companies pay for it. Indeed, traditional third-party payers appear to be looking more closely at online counseling services. Some EAPs have reported great success in implementing online counseling services for covered employees (Labardee, 2009). Private health insurers may be the next to follow. An encouraging first step was code 0074T for "[o]nline evaluation and management service, per encounter, provided by a physician, using the Internet or similar electronic communications network, in response to a patient's request, established patient" (Online Therapy Institute, 2010). Online counseling advocates quickly asserted that this code could be used to bill insurance companies for Internet therapy sessions (Grohol, 2006; OnlineClinics. com). In 2008, this code was revised to 99444: "Online evaluation and management service provided by a physician [98969 for non-physicians] to an established patient, guardian, or health care provider not originating from a related E/M service provided within the previous 7 days, using the Internet or similar electronic communications network" (Porter, 2008). It should be noted, however, that the code definition refers to "established patients."

Providers submitting claims to third-party payers must ensure that the service for which they are billing conforms to the service that was provided, or they may be liable for insurance fraud or penalties under the federal False Claims Act (1994). Online counselors should check with the client's third-party payer in advance to determine whether their services are reimbursable and how they should be reported, carefully documenting the conversation in case of any future disputes. Unless directed otherwise by the payer, billing online counseling services as standard "individual psychotherapy" sessions may be a risky move leading to mandated remuneration and stiff penalties.

Finally, although it is unclear how many online counseling clients are eligible, federal regulations indicate that Medicare Part B will pay for telehealth services, including individual psychotherapy, under certain conditions, but only if the psychotherapy is "furnished by an interactive telecommunications system," with audio and video, specifically defined to exclude email and text-based modalities (HHS Regulation on Telehealth, 42 C.F.R. § 410.78, 2010).

Website Issues

INTELLECTUAL PROPERTY

Online counselors should take care in their use of copyrighted materials, both in their clinical work and the development of their web presence (McMenamin, 2003). Mental health professionals should be aware that sending an article to a client or reproducing it on a website without permission may violate the author's exclusive rights to reproduction and publication under the Copyright Act (1976). There appears to be no legal problem with hyperlinking to content on other sites, so long as the linked material is not itself known to be infringing and it is made clear that the linked material is not associated with the counselor's website (Dockins, 2005; Pokotilow & Gornish, 2005). There are exceptions for "fair use," but, in the context of a commercial endeavor such as online counseling and where the work is substantially reproduced with little if any transformation, fair use would probably not apply were the use to be challenged by the copyright holder (Nimmer, 2006). It therefore behooves online counselors to ensure that they have permission to use the materials upon which they rely in their practice.

ADVERTISING

Online counselors must be accurate in the representations they make on their websites and group service provider profiles. Many states consider false or misleading statements to be examples of unprofessional conduct. For example, under Arizona law,

> 'Unprofessional conduct' includes the following, whether occurring in this state or elsewhere: [. . .] Any false, fraudulent or deceptive statement connected with the practice of behavioral health, including false or misleading advertising by the licensee or the licensee's staff or a representative compensated by the licensee.
>
> **Ariz. Rev. Stat. Ann. § 32-3251(12)(d)**

Note that the statute prohibits misleading advertisements by Arizona licensees *anywhere*. Mental health professionals should take care to accurately represent the skills they truly possess and the services they offer, and should be clear about where they are licensed or certified to practice.

For example, the pronouncement "Available 24/7!" could be problematic if the provider does not actually monitor incoming contacts 24 hours a day. They must also avoid making any promises or guarantees about the effectiveness of their services.

CONCLUSION

As reviewed above, a variety of state and federal laws apply to the delivery of mental health services via the Internet, and a number of concerns arise that simply are not factors in traditional f2f psychotherapy. Further, numerous issues involving jurisdiction and licensure are as yet unresolved and are likely to remain that way until courts have had an opportunity to rule or legislatures have decided to enact statutes. This in itself is relevant to online counselors because it means that, should they find themselves involved in litigation, there is the potential for it to be particularly time-consuming and expensive. Whether a therapist needs to be licensed in both his or her home state and the client's state is an open question, though it appears that dual licensure may be strictly necessary until telehealth licensure portability is established. Counselors who choose to work with clients in states where they are not licensed may risk criminal charges or board sanctions.

As for protection from client lawsuits, the wisest legal course for clinicians is to act responsibly. Professionals will be most protected if they presume that the laws governing traditional f2f counseling apply, both in their home and their client's jurisdiction. When therapists begin to work with someone in another state, they should become familiar with the legal standards of that state for mental health professionals and err on the side of the laws that are most protective of their clients. If a duty is impossible or particularly burdensome, therapists should make their best efforts to comply – not simply assume that a particular responsibility is inapplicable. Following any guidelines promulgated by state boards and professional organizations is a good place to start, as those may be used as evidence of the standard of care in a negligence suit. For example, recommendations for online practice have been published by the ACA (2005), the Clinical Social Work Federation (2001), the APA (1997),[6] and the ISMHO (2000).

It would be short-sighted to suggest that the best or only course of action is to avoid online mental health service delivery at all costs. "To abandon or ignore e-health because of risk considerations is to throw the baby out with the bath water" (McMenamin, 2003, p. 56). There is a need for such services, as legislatures (state and federal) have begun to realize: they have drafted bills and enacted online service-related laws, if only to fund pilot projects. It has been said that "technology is a sprinter

---

[6] Considered inactive because issued under the APA's 1992 *Ethics Code*, superseded by the 2003 *Ethics Code*.

and the law is a marathon runner" (A.K.T. Rex). If that is the case then tech-savvy counselors will be prepared to have the law plod along behind them, and those who may benefit from their services will appreciate their efforts. The most important thing for trailblazers to remember is that the law has developed in an attempt to balance competing interests in a responsible way. Online counselors need to follow existing f2f laws as guideposts for proper general practice and not fear them as obstacles to providing effective online services.

REFERENCES

Ainsworth, M. (n.d.). ABCs of "Internet Therapy." Retrieved March 20, 2010 from http://www.metanoia.org/imhs

American Counseling Association (ACA). (2005). ACA code of ethics. Retrieved March 20, 2010 from http://www.counseling.org/Resources/CodeOfEthics/TP/Home/CT2.aspx

American Psychological Association (APA). (1997). APA Statement on Services by Telephone, Teleconferencing, & Internet. Retrieved March 20, 2010 from http://www.apa.org/ethics/education/telephone-statement.aspx

American Psychological Association Insurance Trust (APAIT). (n.d.). HIPAA for psychologists — Questions & answers. Retrieved March 20, 2010 from http://apait.org/apait/resources/hipaa/faq.aspx

American Psychological Association Insurance Trust (APAIT). (2002). Getting ready for HIPAA: What you need to know now: A primer for psychologists. Retrieved March 20, 2010 from http://www.apait.org/apait/download.aspx?item=hipaa_booklet

Berger, K. (2003). Informed consent: Information or knowledge. *Medicine & Law, 22,* 743–750.

Blum, J. D. (2003). Internet medicine and the evolving legal status of the physician — patient relationship. *Journal of Legal Medicine, 24,* 413–455.

Bodenger, G. W., & Raphaely, R. C. (2002). Fraud and abuse: Overview of business and legal issues. In B. Bennett (Ed.), *E-health business and transactional law* (pp. 113–142). Washington, DC: American Bar Association.

Bordeau, J.A. (1996/2007). Illegal remuneration under Medicare anti-kickback statute, 132 ALR Fed. 601.

Clinical Social Work Federation. (2001). CSWF position paper on internet text-based therapy. Retrieved March 20, 2010 from http://www.cswf.org/page.php?pageid=3670

Copyright Act, 17 USC § 106 (1976).

Darling v. Charleston Cmty. Hosp, 211 N.E.2d 253 (Ill. 1965).

Dockins, M. (2005). Comment, internet links: The good, the bad, the tortious, and a two-part test. *University of Toledo Law Review, 36,* 367–404.

Dreezen, I. (2004). Telemedicine and informed consent. *Medicine & Law, 23,* 541–549.

False Claims Act, 31 USC § 3729 (1994).

Golob v. Arizona Medical Board, 176 P.3d 703 (Ariz. Ct. App. 2008)

Gracey v. Eaker, 837 So.2d 348 (Fla. 2002).

Grohol, J. M. (1999, October 31). Best practices in etherapy: Legal & licensing issues. *PsychCentral,* Retrieved March 20, 2010 from http://psychcentral.com/best/best4.htm

Grohol, J. M. (2006, January 25). CPT code for online counseling: *World of Psychology,* Retrieved March 20, 2010 from http://psychcentral.com/blog/archives/2006/01/25/cpt-code-for-online-counseling

Hageseth v. Superior Court of San Mateo County, 59 Cal. Rptr. 3d 385 (Ct. App. 2007).

Halkett, K.A. (2003, May). Determining personal jurisdiction in Internet-related litigation, *L.A. Lawyer*, 21−28.

Hazard, G. C., Tait, C. C., & Fletcher, W. A. (2005). *Pleading and procedure: State and federal cases and materials* (9th ed). New York, NY: Foundation Press.

International Shoe Co. v. Washington, 326 US 310 (1945).

International Society for Mental Health Online (ISMHO). (2000). Suggested principles for the online provision of mental health services (v. 3.11). Retrieved March 20, 2010 from https://www.ismho.org/suggestions.asp

Johnson, L. J. (2003). Malpractice consult: Legal risks of telemedicine. *Medical Economics, 80*, 101. Retrieved March 20, 2010 from http://medicaleconomics.modernmedicine.com/memag/article/articleDetail.jsp?id=111223

Jones v. N.D. State Bd. of Med. Exam'rs, 691 N.W.2d 251 (N.D. 2005).

Kaye, R.E. (2000/2007). *Internet web site activities of nonresident person or corporation as conferring personal jurisdiction under long-arm statutes & due process clause.* 81 ALR 5th 41.

Koocher, G. P., & Morray, E. (2000). Regulation of telepsychology: A survey of state attorneys general. *Professional Psychology: Research and Practice, 31*, 503−508.

Labardee, L. (2009). Online therapy crosses the chasm. *EAP Digest* (Summer), 12−20.

Manhal-Baugus, M. (2001). E-therapy: Practical, ethical, and legal issues. *Cyberpsychology and Behavior, 4*, 551−563.

McMenamin, J. (2003). Risks of e-health. In S. Callens (Ed.), *E-health and the law* (pp. 45−56). The Hague, the Netherlands: Kluwer Law International.

Nimmer, D. (Ed.), (2006). The defense of fair use. In *Nimmer on Copyright* (Vol. 4−13, § 13.05). New York: Matthew Bender & Co.

OnlineClinics.com (n.d.). CPT code 0074T allows healthcare consults online. Retrieved March 20, 2010 from http://www.onlineclinics.com/pages/content.asp?iglobalid=44

Online Therapy Institute. (2010, January 15). Insurance and online therapy − What's the scoop? Retrieved August 16, 2010 from http://www.onlinetherapyinstituteblog.com/?p=534

Pokotilow, M. D., & Gornish, D. (2005). Internet linking & framing issues. *American Law Institute − American Bar Association Continuing Education, April 21−22: Internet Law for the Practical Lawyer*, 31−49.

Porter, S. (2008). New, revised CPT codes target online, telephone services, AAFP. Retrieved August 15, 2010 from http://www.aafp.org/online/en/home/publications/news/news-now/practice-management/20080229cptcodes.html

Ragusea, A. S., & Vandecreek, L. (2003). Suggestions for the ethical practice of online psychotherapy. *Psychotherapy: Theory, Research, Practice, Training, 40*, 94−102.

Rannefeld, L. (2004). The doctor will e-mail you now: Physicians' use of telemedicine to treat patients over the internet. *Journal of Law and Health, 19*, 75−105.

Rice, B. (1997). Will telemedicine get you sued? *Medical Economics, 74*, 56.

Sammons, M. T., & DeLeon, P. J. (2003). Foreword, whither online counseling: Conceptualizing the challenges & promises of distance mental health service provision. In R. Kraus, J. Zack, & G. Stricker (Eds.), *Online counseling: A handbook for mental health professionals* (pp. xxi−xxxvi). San Diego, CA: Academic Press.

Speyer, C. M., & Zack, J. S. (2003). Online counseling: Beyond the pros & cons. *Psychologica, 23*, 11−14.

Spielberg, A. R. (1999). Online without a net: Physician − patient communication by electronic mail. *American Journal of Law & Medicine, 25*, 267−295.

Telehealth and Medically Underserved and Advancement Act of 2006. H.R. 6394, 109th Cong. (2006).

Telehealth Improvement Act of 2004. S. 2325, 108th Cong. (2004).

Zippo Mfg. Co. v. Zippo Dot Com, Inc, 952 F. Supp. 1119 (W.D. Pa. 1997).

Zitter, J. M. (2008). Construction and application of electronic signatures in global and national commerce act (e-sign act), 15 USCA §§ 7001 to 7006.

Chapter seven

The Business of Online Counseling

Ron Kraus
Editor, EthicsCode.com

It may be true that there is no business like show business but then, without business, there would be no show. And yes, it is honorable to say that the show must go on, but what if tickets are not sold? How far could a business go without generating profits to support operations? Unfortunately, while some slogans sound true and even rhyme well, real life is a bit more complicated than what Broadway tunes would have us believe.

When it comes to running a business, the rules are simple but tough. Either the business is making a profit or it eventually closes. The same is true when it comes to any business, including online counseling. When clinicians bring their practice online, investing time, resources, and effort, they expect to sell their professional services. How is this done? What is required in order to operate a successful practice online? This

129

Online Counseling. DOI: 10.1016/B978-0-12-378596-1.00007-1

chapter will take clinicians through the steps needed to run a professional business online.

A GROWING MARKET AND THE NEED FOR SERVICES ONLINE

In his 1997 State of the Union address to Congress, President Clinton spoke about the need to connect every hospital to the Internet. By now, most hospitals in the US are indeed online. As Internet use expanded since its introduction in the mid 1990s, many health insurance companies, organizations, and individual providers also began providing health care information, services, and resources online. The potential benefit of immediate and private access to health-related information, resources, and services online is undeniable, and the need for such services will always exist.

The Harris poll from 2002 found that nearly 90 percent of people with Internet access expressed a wish to communicate with their physician, ask questions, set up appointments, refill prescriptions, and get test results online (Foreman, 2003). In a study designed to investigate the use of the Internet and email for health care information, Baker et al. (2003) found that 40 percent of individuals with Internet access use it to obtain health information. Considering the size of the market, this level of interest in health-related services online is quite substantial.

The business potential of health-care-related services online has not escaped the attention of the health care industry. Most health care entities have for some years now had presences online. Interestingly enough, most health care sites do not offer fully interactive services such as online counseling. Horgan et al. (2007) found that health plans frequently used the Internet to provide information but used it less often to provide clinical services directly. Most products offered just online provider directories and educational information. Two-thirds offered behavioral health self-assessment tools, and almost one-half provided online referral. About one-third provided personalized responses to problems. However, only two percent offered online counseling (Horgan et al., 2007).

Compared with the vast array of health care and mental health resources currently available online, and considering the substantial interest shown by the public, it is quite surprising that only a very small percentage of clinicians are offering online counseling. Still, considering the APA's early cautious position and clinicians' hesitant attitude regarding the new service modality (discussed in Chapter 3), the fact that only a small number of clinicians provide interactive services online is perhaps understandable. And yet, as research findings accumulate and technology spreads, more and more clinicians are expected to discover the potential of online counseling. Already, clinicians seem increasingly comfortable online.

According to the 2008 APA Health Service Provider Survey, from 2000 to 2008, the number of clinicians using online communications to provide services such as counseling, consulting, and supervision gradually increased (APA, 2010).

From the information discussed so far, one conclusion can be drawn: although Internet use is clearly growing and significant interest in health care services online exists, the full potential for interactive health and mental health care online has not yet been fully realized. In other words, most clinicians are still not offering interactive counseling services online. Business people consider situations where there are demand and need on one side and available products and services on the other as great opportunities. Clinicians reading this chapter in order to build a successful practice online need to think like business people and consider the opportunities that exist in the field.

SETTING UP AN ONLINE PRACTICE

Getting a Domain Name

To set up an independent online practice, the first step is to register a domain name. A domain name is basically an Internet address. Google. com, for example, is a domain name. A domain name indicates who the legal owner of that domain is. Once a domain is registered, a website can be built at that Internet address. To borrow from real estate terms, registration of a domain name is like getting the legal rights to own a piece of land, while a website is the store that can be built on that property.

When the Internet was first made public, a company called Network Solutions was the only entity that registered domain names. Today, many companies are allowed to offer domain name registration and the market is competitive. A simple search online for the term "domain names" will reveal the array of companies currently offering this service. Competition between the various groups that offer domain names allows consumers to shop around for the best deal. The annual or monthly price for registering a domain name is usually very affordable, and the same entities that offer domain names often also sell do-it-yourself websites and related services, such as email, marketing tools, billing capabilities, professional web design services, and the like. And yet, while there are so many products in the shop, one must stay focused on the task at hand.

At times, people wish to have easy-to-remember, prestigious, or "catchy" domain names for their website. This approach makes some sense, as such names may save on marketing expenses, bring more attention to the business, and help to establish brand-name recognition. People experienced in these matters know that "good" names were grabbed early in the Internet domain name game, and, if some are available today, their price may be significantly higher than that of a less valued one. Both companies and individuals offer regular as well as prized names for sale, but clinicians need to consider their options carefully according to their budget and goals. One can invest much in a catchy, easy-to-remember domain name but then have less of a budget left to promote traffic to the site. Another option to consider would be to promote a less catchy name — such as your own name, for example http://www.DrJoeSchmo.com — gradually on a budget so that it eventually becomes recognized. After all, getting new clients to visit the site and consider the services offered is how new business is generated online. Catchy names are easy to market and remember, but quite often their price may be prohibitive. It is important to remember that traffic to a new site does not always depend on the name of the domain, as catchy as it may sound, but rather on marketing efforts and the benefits or services the site offers.

Clinicians have to remember that domain name registration requires periodical renewal, without which the registration expires and the domain may be resold to other customers. Most companies warn their customers before the registration period expires, but it is still the responsibility of the registrant to renew their domain name registration.

The Value of a Trademark

To ensure that the unique domain name and its associated business are not copied or misused by others, clinicians can consider the value of a trademark. The US Trademark Office (http://www.uspto.gov) allows online search of existing trademarks as well as registration of new trademarks.

The one-time registration of a trademark costs quite a bit, but, if brought to completion, the process ensures ownership. Once a trademark is registered, no other entity will be allowed to use a similar-sounding name for a similar type of business. If, for example, one business were to register the trademark for "DrFill.com" and specialize in giving advice to confused adolescents, no one else in the US would be allowed to operate a competing site for the same type of business carrying the name "DrFill.com." The rightful owner of the trademark in this imaginary case could go to court and force the shameless competitor to close shop or change name so it does not unfairly compete with and steal business from the legal owner of the trademark.

In most cases, clinicians who operate a small-scale business online do not need to register a trademark. Still, it is possible that a successful site online will draw attention from competitors, who in turn may use similar-sounding domain names to offer similar services. In such cases, trademark registration would be the best legal way to defend against unfair business practices and competition.

Building a Website for Online Practice: Creation, Design, Tools

One must remember that registering a domain name is but the first step. After a domain name has been registered, regardless of whether or not a trademark process has also been initiated, the next step is to actually set up a website for that domain, otherwise visitors will see nothing but perhaps a "page under construction" note. Obviously, clinicians could provide consults to clients via email, chat, or videoconferencing, even if they had no website, but most people feel that a website for the practice is good to have. A website is like a store front in the global marketplace. As such, the website is primarily a marketing tool, even though it also allows much more, such as interaction with customers and billing for services. Details about the clinician, the available services, hours of operation, fees, specialties, interactive schedule, email, chat capabilities, videoconferencing tools, etc. can all be placed on the website so that potential clients are informed about the services and invited to use them.

Before clinicians start spending time and money on the creation of an online office, the purpose and objectives of such a project need to be considered. Will the website be used to simply advertise and promote the practice, or to provide information? Will the website be interactive? What interactive options should be used to comfortably and securely communicate with clients — telephone, email, chat, or videoconferencing? Perhaps a combination of the above would be best? Should the site offer billing by credit card or should this service be handled by a third-party provider? Clinicians have to know about these matters in order to decide what works best for them, considering the cost of the various features as well as expected marketing expenses. Obviously, if the website is mostly built to promote the business and refer potential clients to call and use the regular office, the cost is significantly lower than that of a fully interactive office online.

The cost of setting up a website ranges quite significantly as it depends on several factors. The companies that register domain names and ISPs usually offer do-it-yourself website-building tools as well as professional website development solutions. Additional products that are offered often include email or secure email services, various online marketing tools, website traffic statistics tools, credit-card billing capabilities, online shopping carts, and the like. When it comes to getting a website up and running, clinicians need not worry too much about a lack of technological skills. Today's do-it-yourself website products are built for the general public, which means that the ability to read simple instructions, enter details, select between various options, and pay with a credit card is all that is required. People with experience can get a domain name and a new website up and running in a few minutes. Brave first-timers will probably be done in less than an hour. The time-consuming part is usually the search for the perfect domain name (see above). Often, the combination of your name and degree will be available, with a ".com" at the end. This option for naming the practice online may save time, but, if you are looking for something more professional, creativity is your greatest ally. Good domain-name hunting!

Clinicians and health care groups who wish to create elaborate and sophisticated web services usually hire professionals to create their site instead of using the do-it-yourself option. Obviously, such projects range in cost and vary greatly as they depend on budget, complexity of the project, and business goals. At times, people spend a great deal of money on their web developer before they realize that ready-made solutions and site-creation tools are offered for a fraction of the cost.

When it comes to the issue of website design, things can get a bit complicated. Not only do many design options exist, but design, as an art, relates to people's subjective esthetic taste — a totally personal matter. The do-it-yourself solutions usually provide various website templates that can be edited and modified. Images can be uploaded to fit the clinician's preference or style. Colors, font, and other features on the pages can be manipulated and the website can be ready in minutes. It is really not so hard to design a ready-made website template with the editing tools provided to customers, but when people hire a professional designer the task gets more complicated. Rather than flipping through many predesigned website template options and editing them to fit, a professional designer will sometimes make more and more designs for review before the client is happy with the way it looks. Obviously, such a process can be both costly and time consuming.

If the purpose of a website is not just to advertise and promote the business name but also to interact with visitors and to bill for services, creation and setup must include the installation of security measures. Both clinical text communications and monetary transactions online require security measures to ensure privacy. It is not enough for an interactive site to be set up with a nice image, an impressive résumé, a phone number, and an email address. To be fully interactive and charge clients for services, it is necessary to get online secure email and/or chat as well as secure socket layer (SSL) for billing (see also Chapter 4).

While free email encryption software is easy to find and use, the SSL service requires a fee. Various companies offer SSL services for businesses online and so it is wise to shop around for the best deal. The best place to start the search may be with the bank that holds the business account. Often, banks offer SSL solutions for customers who wish to do business online. Another simple solution for secure billing online would be to use the services of a third-party provider to process payments. Some entities online specialize in doing just that. When a third-party solution is selected, clinicians need not worry about their site's billing security, in the same way that customers are protected when their credit card is stolen and misused. When a third party is used to process payments, it is that provider's responsibility to ensure that payments are processed accurately and securely.

Secure chat is not as easy to find online as the free email encryption solutions. Still, if clinicians wish their website to include this feature, options do exist out there. Secure chat software solutions can be bought and integrated into the site. Secure chat platforms for rent by third party are also available. A search online will show the current options for these services. Comparison and careful consideration of the various options are recommended.

Promoting and Marketing an Online Practice

Once a domain name has been registered and the website becomes active online, the next important step is to ensure that it is visited by potential and existing clients. The most elaborate and impressive website could just sit there and produce nothing unless customers are made aware of the offered services. When people ask how to best invest in real estate, they are told that the three most important factors are location, location, and location. When it comes to business online, the three most important factors for a website are traffic, traffic, and traffic.

There are many ways in which to promote traffic on a website. Much like the cost of website creation and design, the price of marketing can vary greatly. In the most budget-restricted scenario, a clinician would register a domain name and get a one-page do-it-yourself type of a website. Using free email encryption software and a third-party provider to process credit cards online, the website is ready to market. Often, companies that offer registration of a domain and setup of a do-it-yourself website also allow free registration of a new site with search engines. Search engines, such as Yahoo.com and Google.com, allow users to search for services and products online. True, your new website may just be one among many, many millions of sites and web pages flickering in cyberspace, but, if all your existing clients and contacts were notified of your new site, traffic may start moving in. Using the search engine's submission option (most do-it-yourself website companies offer this service for free) will also help get your site noticed online.

Word of mouth and email campaigns, possibly with a polite request to spread the word around, are not bad ideas for clinicians who have a new online practice and a limited budget. There probably are many leads in your address book right now for such campaigns. Colleagues, clients, family members, and friends can all be notified about the grand opening of your new website. Don't be shy when it comes to promoting your website. Tell everyone you meet about your business online. Putting your website address on your business card is another way to spread the word. Give cards with your website to as many people as you can. Remember: everyone needs a good therapist every now and then.

When marketing budgets are low, websites can still be promoted as links at other Internet locations. A link is a clickable name or advert on another website that connects to your website. Often, site owners will agree to link your site if it has value or if you do the same with their link on your website. The more places your website appears in, the greater the chances that search engines will find it. Are you participating in online discussion groups? Do you belong to any online professional groups? Do you write a blog? Do you ever lecture, give presentations, or appear as a speaker at events? Don't forget to mention your new website when introducing yourself. Your website is like a permanent business card online. Make sure everybody knows about your site. When it comes to creativity, the sky is the limit. Be creative when thinking about how else to promote your business.

If the business is well funded and a larger marketing budget exists, various promotion strategies can be considered. One may elect to purchase marketing products and promote directly, or pay an Internet marketing company to have promotional work done by professionals.

Large companies such as AOL, Yahoo, and Google, which provide search-engine services online, offer to promote customers' businesses for a fee. Payment can be charged to display a website at the top of the page when certain key words are searched. When keyword searching is the marketing strategy, customers decide depending on their allocated marketing budget how often, or for how long, their website will be shown prominently on the search results page to those who look for related terms. While statistical data on this subject are not an exact science, it takes roughly 75–200 visitors to produce one paying customer. Once the website owner knows the average statistics, such as the ratio between number of visits and service purchases, the real cost-effectiveness of this method can be assessed. The marketing companies sell the keyword tool by number of displays. Often, the exact calculation of how much it costs to bring in clients becomes easier once the operation is in motion. Usually, people new to the business expect better results and are disappointed when they realize that only one or two percent of visitors actually become clients. Still, the numbers vary greatly and, if the website is user-friendly, attractive, and useful, marketing success can improve.

Another strategy for online marketing is known as pay-per-click. Customers pay the company promoting the website an agreed-upon fee every time their link or advert is clicked by a visitor. Customers can pay for as many referral clicks to their site as they wish. In this way, customers have much more control of their marketing expenses. Again, having visitors sent to your site will not guarantee sales unless these visitors are actually looking for the services provided on the site.

Well-funded operations can hire the services of an Internet marketing company to do all of the above-described promotional work for a fee. In these cases, the marketing company explains its marketing strategies and specifies the tools it will use, the cost of various components, and their projected effectiveness. The well-funded website's owner only needs to approve the plan and, of course, cover the cost of the campaign. Still, fine tuning the campaign based on initial and ongoing results is always a good idea. Careful monitoring of the marketing campaign will show which of the strategies is most effective and allow adjustments for best results within the budget.

Clinicians need to carefully examine the various marketing options available. In real life, big decisions and grand plans always depend on cost and budget. Often, the challenge in marketing is stretching a limited budget to maximize the sales effort.

MANAGING AN ONLINE PRACTICE

To put it simply, the management principles of an online practice are similar to those used in a real office. After an initial assessment is completed and an agreement to start the therapy process exists, a therapeutic relationship is legally established. Once this happens, clinicians have certain case-management responsibilities. As in a "real" office, clients' treatment records must be kept safely, and profits from online counseling services need to be reported as income.

In the interests of keeping treatment records, electronic files are acceptable as long as they are kept secured. Passwords can protect against unauthorized entry to the file and computer, and when files are kept on CDs or similar portable storing devices they must be stored safely under lock and key.

Clinicians need to become familiar with the privacy regulations concerning their practice. State boards as well as professional organizations publish their rules online, and compliance with these is very important. A review of the HIPAA regulations can aid better understanding of how to maintain clients' privacy when records are managed online (see http://www.hhs.gov/ocr/privacy). A few basic principles may help with improving record privacy:

- Do not keep sensitive material in unprotected hard drives or files.
- Use email encryption or password-protected webmail programs.
- Before you put sensitive information online, pause and review.

TRAINING AND PREPARATION

No one should try to drive a bus full of passengers on a highway without a license and previous training. Although it may seem exciting and adventurous to some action movie fans who are thrilled by speed and suspense, the potential risk to self and others makes it very unwise in real life. In the same way, ethical regulations require clinicians to be competent in their field. When it comes to online counseling, clinicians need to be familiar with the relevant literature, research, and practice strategies; master the necessary communication tools; and know the limits, potential risks, and relevant ethical regulations prior to starting their practice.

It is a good thing that you are reading this book, as doing so is one way to get instruction about online counseling. However, much like learning to drive a car, theoretical knowledge is not a sufficient prerequisite to providing psychotherapy. Clinicians are not currently mandated to get a separate certificate to practice online, but one day such may be the case. Clinicians can train and practice the running of their online office with colleagues and friends. Mock sessions are a good way to simulate real-life situations and experiment with various features and tools.

In order to train, clinicians can consider giving the public free service for a while. Providing educational services for free will help to define such interaction as an exchange of opinions rather than therapy. If a person provides free advice to another, the obligations of a therapeutic relationship are not there. Still, one must be very careful not to mislead the public in any way and to always practice within the limits of the professional license. If a clinician offers free services that are not psychotherapy, it would be best to have the client sign an informed consent for the arrangement. In fact, the informed consent procedure is important every time services are provided.

Another way to obtain training for the practice of online counseling is to select an experienced supervisor or actually take a course. Several providers of training and education are currently offering such classes online. As always, one would want to carefully check the providers of these programs; compare prices, course content, and quality; and try to get as much information as possible from people with experience of the course. Joining professional forums and mental health organizations online may also be good ways to get advice and information from colleagues.

PROFESSIONAL LIABILITY (MALPRACTICE) INSURANCE FOR ONLINE PRACTICE

To operate a private mental health practice in the US, clinicians must have a state license as well as liability insurance for malpractice. In the office, the professional license needs to be displayed in such a way that clients can see it and also know who issued the license in case a dispute arises. Liability insurance is important for clinicians in the same way that car insurance is crucial for drivers. Even good Samaritans are sometimes sued for damages and in such cases the liability coverage is absolutely essential.

When it comes to liability insurance coverage for services that are provided online, clinicians must be cautious when obtaining or renewing a professional liability insurance policy. Insurance companies are obligated to specify what types of professional service the policy does or does not cover. Typically, allegations of sexual misconduct by a therapist are not covered by their liability insurance. In the same way, some companies specify that online counseling is covered by the policy while others do not mention it. Obviously, clinicians would want to make sure that their professional liability insurance specifically states that such practice is covered. In case the insurance company is unfamiliar with this type of service, it may help to mention CPT code 98969 when calling to inquire. Many professional liability insurance companies already include coverage for clinical services delivered over the phone or Internet and, as long as these are conducted with careful consideration of state license limits, there should be no problem.

CHARGING FOR ONLINE COUNSELING SERVICES

In the real office, clinicians can bill the client's insurance company, if such exists, or accept a check, cash, or a credit card. Online, the same options exist. Clinicians can submit insurance claims through their network or via a third-party provider, such as WebMd. Clinicians can either set up credit-card billing capabilities through their do-it-yourself website-building tools or work with a third-party provider to collect charges online. Thus, collecting payments and submitting invoices online is not as arduous as it sounds.

Another issue that clinicians are usually concerned about relates to the value of their work online. How much should a session online cost the client? After all, web office rent is insignificant compared to the cost of an office in a professional building and there are no utilities to pay or transportation overhead costs when working online, so how much should be charged?

As a rule, clinicians need to think about the value of their time when calculating their fee scale for online work. Some feel that the time a clinician spends on helping a client online should be as valuable as when the encounter is f2f. Others feel, partly for the reasons just mentioned above, that the price charged for online work should be reduced. In any case, clinicians are free to set their own price for their services, unless the company that rents them a web office has a set fee policy. There are really no laws when it comes to setting the fees for online counseling. Often, the price of a therapy session depends on geography – that is, in what state or city people are located and the customary price range in that area – and the clinician's level of education or expertise.

It may be a good idea for new online clinicians to offer some service to customers for free. Such a strategy may appeal to potential customers and is a good way to increase traffic. When fees for professional services online are set, several options for billing exist. Some examples include:

- First email or online chat session for free.
- Set rate for each email reply, with no limit on length.
- Set rate for every email reply, with limit on length such as one page.

- Set rate for a series of email exchanges.
- Set rate for unlimited email exchanges over a period of time.

When it comes to live chat and videoconferencing sessions, clinicians usually charge the same rates as they would in a real office. After all, an hour with a client online is the same as an hour with the client in an office. If clinicians spend the same amount of time online as in the office, they expect to be compensated at the same rate. Still, the bottom line often comes down to what the insurance company is willing to pay for the service and how much more the client pays out of pocket according to their policy terms. If payment for the service is out of pocket, for clients who have no insurance or who elect to pay cash, the clinician and customer can usually negotiate a fee that is acceptable to both. Many clinicians post a set fee scale but at the same time also have a sliding scale policy that makes their service affordable.

ONLINE PROVIDERS AND RENTED WEB OFFICES: BENEFITS AND RISKS

As discussed above, clinicians can work independently with relative ease. They have to register a domain name, create a do-it-yourself website, get education and seek training, market their service, and open a business online. All of the above is quite do-able and not too complicated, especially when done step by step. And yet, some may still find the aforementioned steps to be too much technical work. For those who wish to save the effort of setting up an independent office online, there is a ready-made solution.

Several existing entities rent out online offices to clinicians. A simple search online for terms such as "online counseling," "therapy online," and the like will reveal the entities that offer interactive counseling services to clients, as well as web offices for clinicians to rent. Often, the cost of renting a ready-made web office from one of these networks is less than that of setting up a fully interactive website independently. Still, clinicians need to be familiar with the benefits and possible risks of renting an online office from a third-party company.

The obvious benefits of renting an office are quite clear. There is no need to register a domain name and set up a website, no need to spend effort and money on marketing, and no direct responsibility for general operations, such as billing, servicing the system, security, and the like. If all works well, registration and setup is all it takes. Now, all that remains is to wait for those customers, who will surely visit the new office. Does it work like that in real life? Well, partially it does. Registration and payment of web office rent is usually done very smoothly, but then new clients do not always come.

Some groups check new members' backgrounds carefully and reject those who lack training, credentials, or liability insurance for independent practice. Other groups are in business to rent offices and make a profit, and so their membership requirements are minimal. In any case, while registration is usually the easy part, getting new referrals remains an issue. Some ways to overcome this problem are to invest in marketing of the rented office independently or shop around for other groups, who may perhaps generate more customers.

One problem with network membership is that some of the companies have business practices that may conflict with the clinicians' obligation to follow professional regulations. For example, some groups do not allow members and customers to know who the other is in order to maintain exclusivity, yet such practice may be unethical. Some groups sell access to the mental health service provider's web office by time segments and will disconnect callers, regardless of their emotional state, if their time runs out. Some groups charge a referral fee or take a percentage of the clinician's profit. While these practices are perhaps acceptable in the business community, such conduct would be considered unethical for psychologists in the US. Fee splitting and referral fees are forbidden by ethics regulations because a referral to health care or mental health needs to be motivated by need rather than greed. The principles that guide clinical ethical regulations value the provision of responsible care more than monetary profit.

Clinicians need to be selective and careful when choosing the rental of a web office through a network, company, or group online. As many options exist, it is easy to make comparisons and shop around for a decent service. Otherwise, one can always consider setting up and working independently. Some clinicians actually feel that doing both may produce better exposure and thus create more business opportunities. As mentioned earlier, when it comes to a business online, the name of the game is traffic, traffic, traffic. If clinicians have their services registered and advertised in many places, such as mental health networks, directories, interactive web office companies, and search engines, the chance of being found by potential clients is indeed improved.

SUMMARY

Unlike what many clinicians who are unfamiliar with online practice may think, setting up a web office or renting one is neither overly complicated nor very costly. Clinicians can either pay developers to build them a website or they can rent a do-it-yourself template with website-building tools for design, marketing, communication, and billing, and get fully interactive independently. Another option available to clinicians is to rent a ready-made web office from one of the groups that currently provide online counseling. Each option has its benefits and risks, so careful consideration is recommended.

In order to be in business, one needs to ensure that the website is profitable; that is, that it gets visited and used. The main concern for a business online is to find cost-effective ways to generate enough traffic to the website. Traffic brings potential clients to the business and, without clients, the operation has little financial justification.

Before launching a web office into cyberspace, clinicians would be wise to become familiar with the new field, research the various tools and products, compare prices, and consider their best options. It is imperative to know the relevant regulations of the state boards and professional organizations and to ensure that malpractice insurance is in place. These are crucial to the survival and success of any online therapeutic practice, along with good business management decisions.

KEY TERMS

Chat A communication method online in which back-and-forth text messages are delivered immediately. "Chat room" is the name for the online environment where such instant text communications take place.

Domain name The address on the Internet, usually starting with "www" (standing for Word Wide Web) and ending with ".com," ".net," or ".org," is called a "domain name." Domain names require registration and allow a website to be built on that address.

Email encryption An extra measure used to ensure email privacy. Email encryption software converts text and data to encrypted code so that unauthorized users are not able to read the information when it is delivered online.

Internet A global network of computers that are connected with each other.

Internet Service Provider (ISP) A company that operates and/or provides basic and various other Internet services for customers.

Key words In marketing online, certain words or combinations of words that, when entered in a search engine, result in a specific website being displayed on the results page. Customers can pay the marketing company to have their website displayed to a pre-specified number of potential visitors who are searching these key words.

Online counseling A method of treatment in which clinical consultation services are provided to clients over the Internet via communication tools such as email, chat, and videoconferencing.

Pay-per-click In marketing online, an arrangement whereby every time an advert or link online is used to direct potential clients to a website, the owner of that site is charged a set fee by the marketing company. In this way, the owner can decide how many visitors will be diverted to their site and for what price this will be done.

Search engine A computer program that allows customers to enter a term and find all the places on the Internet where it is mentioned. There are many companies operating search engines, such as Google, Yahoo, and AOL. Similar in concept to telephone directories, paid advertisements can also be placed on search engine result pages. Having a website (and its key words) submitted and registered on search engines allows visitors to find it when searching online.

Secure socket layer (SSL) The extra layer of encryption protection needed for private transactions and communications online, such as monetary transaction and secure data entries. Various companies provide this service to websites that wish to maintain security.

Telepsychology Another term for the theory and practice of addressing mental health issues online.

Trademark To ensure exclusivity in commercial use, registration of a trademark through the United States Patent and Trademark Office (http://www.uspto.gov)

limits the ability of competitors to use the same or very similar marks for their business.

Videoconferencing A method of communication online in which both parties can see and hear each other in real time.

Website Once a domain name has been registered, a website can be placed at that Internet address. A website is what visitors to that domain online actually see. In fact, the website is stored on a computer, but visitors see the projection of that site on their screen.

Website traffic A term that relates to the number of website visitors or users in a given time period. Website statistics are often offered by do-it-yourself website companies for free.

REFERENCES

American Psychological Association (APA). (2010). Telepsychology is on the rise. *Monitor on Psychology, 41*(3), 11.

Baker, L., Wagner, T. H., Singer, S., & Bundorf, M. K. (2003). Use of the Internet and e-mail for health care information. *JAMA, 289,* 2400–2406.

Foreman, J. (2003, February 25). Doctors resist e-mail system for patients. Boston Globe, p. C3.

Horgan, C. M., Merrick, E. L., Reif, S., & Stewart, M. (2007). Internet-based behavioral health services in health plans. *Psychiatric Services, 58,* 307.

CLINICAL SKILLS FOR ONLINE COUNSELING

Chapter eight

Text-based Online Counseling: Email

John Yaphe
Associate Professor, Community Health, School of Health Sciences,
University of Minho, Braga, Portugal
Cedric Speyer
Co-founder, InnerView Guidance International; Clinical Supervisor,
E-Counseling, Shepell·fgi, Toronto, Ontario

CHAPTER OUTLINE

"Writing is a strong easement for perplexity [. . .] That is the reason for this journal. Everything is all connected up [. . .] the unaccustomed putting down of my own thoughts in black and white helped me to clarify them and find out my own aims and beliefs."

Emily Carr (Journals)

INTRODUCTION

Online asynchronous text-based counseling is the exchange of therapeutic communication between a client and a counselor using electronic mail. It does not attempt to simulate an in-person counseling session.

147

Online Counseling. DOI: 10.1016/B978-0-12-378596-1.00008-3

Instead, it features the containment, pacing, and contemplation of time-delayed interchanges, as in traditional letter writing. It is called "text-based" to distinguish it from voice-based services that are similar to traditional telephone or in-person counseling. It is called "asynchronous" to distinguish it from the synchronous chat version characterized by the flow of messages back and forth between client and counselor, who are online at the same time. Both methods require that counselor and client have access to electronic mail services or a password-protected website with designated fields for writing and receiving messages.

Many people communicate their thoughts and feelings more easily when they are unobserved and consequently reveal more of themselves while writing. Without verbal and physical cues, the counseling relationship takes place behind the scenes of self-presentation (Goffman, 1990). For this reason, online relationships can have a remarkable intensity and intimacy, referred to as "text-based bonding."

This chapter will present a description of this form of online counseling, the therapeutic structure of the medium, its uses and limitations, skills required for practitioners, the theoretical framework, and a sample transcript as a clinical example of its application.

ASYNCHRONOUS ONLINE COUNSELING

Therapeutic Benefits

As in many forms of counseling, it is the compassionate relationship that may help the most. The history of letter writing demonstrates that it is possible to form meaningful and helpful relationships through written correspondence. Clients have consistently reported that there is an added impact to the written word that has proved to be remarkably beneficial. Instead of working in the *absence* of nonverbal cues, we are working in the *presence* of text-based cues and the wealth of the written word. For many, it is "better than being there" (Fenichel et al., 2002).

There are many unique practical and therapeutic benefits to asynchronous online counseling for the client, the counselor, and organizations providing online clinical services (Speyer & Zack, 2003).

CONVENIENCE
Access to professional counseling is not restricted by geographical location or scheduling difficulties. Clients are able to send messages at any time of the day or night. In rural areas, online counseling has provided access to counseling services that were once available only in larger urban centers. This has been of great benefit to many in isolated communities. Physical and other limitations to mobility may also be overcome with online services. Clients with agoraphobia who avoid even the use of telephone counseling may feel safe with online services. One

client wrote, "When I went online and found I could seek help without having to leave my house or talk in person I thought it was worth a try." Clients with speech disorders or hearing impairments have also been appreciative of the easy access to a counselor.

TIME TO REFLECT

E-counseling offers clear boundaries and a way to contain the problem while new associations and insights arise. Writing, instead of talking, helps some people to focus feelings and can speed resolutions with the validation of seeing them in print. The very process of composing, rereading, and rewording emails increases self-awareness. The introspective, asynchronous nature of the service allows clients time and space to tell their story without interruption. One client wrote at the end of an initial 5000-word exposition of their situation, "Now that I've got all that down, I feel better already." What might be lost from the immediate give-and-take of natural conversation is gained from slowing the process down so that clients have all the advantages of keeping a journal of their thoughts and feelings while still participating in a healing interchange.

WORDS TO HOLD ON TO

Asynchronous replies also give clients and counselors time to reflect on what has been written. There is no need for an immediate response, as is often felt in face to face and chat situations. Reflection allows time for new insights to emerge. Many clients print out the e-counselor's messages and carry them around, rereading and referring to them later. While both the problems and the solutions are externalized in print, the client is internalizing an empathic listener. The record of correspondence is another way to witness personal progress. Clients report that they often print the letters. They find comfort in words of encouragement that can be referred to at a later time. One client wrote, "I have printed out all of your responses so that I'll still have them if ever I feel the need to reflect on what you have told me, and how you helped me turn around what seemed like an endless downward spiral." Supplemental self-help resources can also accompany and complement the personal exchanges.

PRIVACY

Many clients report that they feel more comfortable discussing sensitive issues with an online counselor and that they would not have accessed counseling any other way. Others find the fact that they are not being judged by their physical appearance to be a unique advantage of this medium. Those who value time to slow down appreciate the "zone of reflection" that they experience behind the computer. It allows them to "compose themselves"; that is, to sort out feelings and thoughts while still in a dialogue with a professional counselor who helps to put their predicament into perspective.

DISINHIBITING EFFECT

There is literally no need to "save face." The increased sense of privacy and initial anonymity can remove the usual reticence to spontaneously self-disclose. Writing about the issue also offers more control over the pace, rhythm, and content of the process for clients who feel "on the spot" while talking. It can reduce the stress of self-consciousness and free the psyche. It offers both parties the opportunity to go beyond the distractions of external appearances. While keeping up socially acceptable appearances may inhibit communication in the face to face encounter, decreased inhibition in the online setting allows a "cut-to-the-chase" effect. The physical distance provided by online counseling allows an emotional closeness that many clients find safe and free from embarrassment. Clients have said, "I could never look you in the eye and tell you this" and "I could never tell my doctor this."

FURTHER BENEFITS

An additional advantage is the witnessing or "externalizing" that clients experience upon seeing their issues put into words. Rather than feeling that their "nose is pressed against the glass" of persistent problems, the medium enables clients to take a step back through the act of writing, thereby fostering healthy emotional disengagement.

The following is typical of client feedback at the conclusion of a short-term case:

> Through e-counseling I was able to see things more objectively, was able to read what I was saying and thinking. It enabled me to reach a healthy state of mind and give me a sense of peace and understanding. The true content of our discussions is the focus, not the other stuff that can often impede effective communication. I had no idea it was possible to form such a strong bond and a trust with someone based solely on the written word. Thoughts and feelings just seemed to flow out of me in a way I never could have imagined. My e-counselor helped me put things in perspective and look at things going on in my life in a whole different light. I was apprehensive about trying e-counseling but found it was the best move I ever made.

On the practitioner's side of the screen, there are also numerous benefits unique to the asynchronous method. Of course, the same advantages related to ease of access apply. Counselors located in isolated areas have access to an international client base. Widely separated time zones and differing work schedules are not barriers to providing care. Issues of physical mobility are also less relevant. The e-therapist has a wealth of online resources to turn to and consult throughout the process, which can then selectively be made available for ongoing client support. Therapeutic specialists are also available for peer consultation or referral without geographical restrictions.

See Chapter 6 for discussion of legal issues pertaining to geographical scope of practice.

The medium offers clear boundaries as well as safety and containment. The absence of the physical presence of the e-therapist takes the pressure off the client to speak, please, perform, and fill in silences. There is no threat of physical breaches of trust. There is much less danger of any intrusion, violation, or harassment on the counselor's part and no physical risk to therapists from aggressive clients.

As for the client, the time-delayed nature of email exchanges allows the e-therapist to pay close attention to thoughts and feelings while still engaging in a dialogue. Both client and therapist have an opportunity to witness strong feelings and gain perspective on reactive emotions before responding; when consciously used, the medium is conducive to mindful awareness on both sides of the screen and can reduce countertransference.

Just as writing can help the client to think through and reframe their situation, the writing process allows the therapist to enter the zone of reflection while assessing and reflecting upon the issues. Both client and therapist are able to print out and refer to exchanges as needed. Online counseling provides a written record of every word expressed in the counseling sessions. Counselor accountability is greatly enhanced by virtue of having complete written records of every case. Every word is documented, highlighting the need for impeccable ethics. Transcripts can be used for case review, to facilitate performance audits and/or self-study, and to serve as a basis for clinical supervision, teaching, and research projects. All this, of course, must be conducted within an acceptable ethical and legal framework with respect for confidentiality and informed consent when it comes to any use of material outside the immediate counseling context.

There is a socially conditioned power in the written word that gives the e-therapist's guidance added impact. On the other hand, though, differences in status are less apparent within the egalitarian nature of exchanges; clinicians tend to be perceived less as authorities and more like consultants. Therapists can mirror the tone, vocabulary, and voice of clients as a way of establishing and maintaining the therapeutic alliance. A conversational writing style as well as the creative use of idioms, metaphors and analogies all enhance the process.

The disadvantages of absent face to face cues range from missing facial expressions and general appearance to the lack of spontaneous clarification. These may lead to misunderstandings or misreading of the real issues. However, both the client and therapist can easily quote the text to clarify any misconceptions about tone, language, and content. Advanced training in text-based communication can also improve clinical acumen.

Another advantage of writing is the window it opens into the client's thought process, revealed to the reader as visible "self-talk." "There is a special type of interpersonal empathy that is unique to text relation-ships. Some claim that text-only talk carries you past the distracting, superficial aspects of a person's existence and connects you more directly to the other's psyche" (Suler, 2004).

Asynchronous exchanges provide an effective way to supervise e-therapists. The raw material of case management is readily available to the supervisor; in other words, quality assurance is *hands-on*. Supervision is more directly accessible. It is not once-removed as it is when viewing or hearing a recording of a session, or in a verbal consultation based on the therapist's perception of the sessions. Supervisors can offer guidance by responding to the client's text before the e-therapist composes a reply and/or review the e-therapist's primary process before or after it is shared with the client.

These remarkable benefits extend to organizations that provide or purchase online services for their members. Employers appreciate the ease of access their employees have to counseling services from the workplace or from home, which can reduce absenteeism caused by time off work for in-person appointments. Within the limits of confidential-ity, the service provider in turn can use online transcripts for quality assurance, supervision, and training (Rochlen et al., 2004).

Scope of Practice

The scope of issues addressed through online counseling has been extended in recent years to resemble that of traditional in-person counseling. Online counseling services have helped clients with symp-toms of anxiety, symptoms of depression, relationship issues, parenting issues, difficulty coping with illness, workplace conflict, and addictions.

While initial concerns regarding the safety of distance counseling have been raised and continue to be voiced, experience over the last 10 years has demonstrated the effectiveness and safety of the asynchronous method. Most online services warn clients during intake that certain issues are best dealt with through telephone or in-person services. Imminent risk of harm to self or others requires immediate referral. Any form of abuse or risk to minors requires reporting to appropriate author-ities. Intoxicated clients or those with a formal thought disorder are best served by other means. Aside from these limitations, the scope of prac-tice for online counseling is extensive.

Supervision Standards

As described earlier, the written transcripts allow for close and accurate supervision of the therapeutic process. One EAP provider has set a mini-mum standard of a Master's level degree in psychology or social work with a focus on counseling, membership of a professional college, and adequate malpractice insurance coverage to qualify as an online counselor. This is followed by a period of training involving the use of simulated clients to test writing and counseling skills. An experienced supervisor then closely follows the first few cases assigned to a new counselor, which includes vetting of responses before they are sent to the client. This hands-on supervision continues until the counselor is ready to independently manage a full caseload. Supervision may include telephone contact, yet is often conducted online in a process closely paralleling online counseling with clients.

In addition to initial training and supervision of new counselors, ongoing supervision takes place with experienced e-therapists as the need arises. Random case review and audits are periodically used for quality assurance. Counselors may also select difficult or high-risk cases for discussion with a supervisor. A number of best practices for online counseling have emerged in response to case-management challenges (Yaphe & Speyer, 2010).

CLINICAL APPROACHES TO ONLINE COUNSELING

Specialized Skills

The online counselor requires special skills beyond those needed by a traditional in-person counselor. The foundational traits of the therapist remain the same: the ability to "join" with the client, hear what matters most, guide, support, encourage, reorient, empower, and part ways at the end of the process. However, the online counselor must acquire expertise unique to the medium. This section will describe some of these skills.

Text-based bonding is a term used to refer to the process of engaging the online client in a therapeutic alliance. One of the initial criticisms against online counseling targeted the supposed lack of personal contact with the client due to the absence of nonverbal cues. It is clear, however, from reviewing counseling transcripts (such as the one included later in this chapter) that skilled counselors can quickly and effectively bond with clients through compassionate and understanding letters.

In one example, a client requested help dealing with feelings of anxiety following the end of an abusive relationship. On the intake forms, she described symptoms typical of panic attacks and reported feeling disoriented when it appeared that her doctor did not fully hear her struggle with those feelings. The counselor responded with words of understanding and encouragement, and concluded the first exchange with this text-based embrace:

> I can appreciate how confusing things may seem now but there are
> actually many good options open to you. Something in your message
> makes me optimistic that you are the kind of person who gets through
> these situations. I look forward to receiving your next letter with your

responses and news of your progress forward. Until then I want to wish
you strength and courage to meet the challenges you face.

The client responded, "I cried when I read what you wrote. I immediately felt you were with me and it would be okay."

Therapeutic Orientations

The therapeutic orientation of asynchronous online counseling is associated with solution-focused, narrative, and cognitive-behavioral approaches.
Counselors are encouraged to incorporate solution-focused (Shazer, 1982)
and narrative (White & Epston, 1990) methods, both of which are conducive to the medium and have been successfully adapted to text-based interventions. While the medical model is preoccupied with what is wrong with
people, short-term online counseling focuses on what is right with them
and on abiding essential value. Counselors may choose to explore the
strengths and resources that clients already have within them in order to
foster emotional self-reliance. Since many counseling services are short-
term, this basic solution-focused orientation is conducive to the goal of
finding a direction forward.

The CARE Model

The CARE model is a general framework for short-term, solution-focused
case management. The acronym stands for Connect and contain ("your
challenge is human and manageable"); Assess and affirm ("you've got
what it takes to get through this"); Reorient and reaffirm ("you are not
defined by your life situation"); and Encourage and empower ("keep
going, one step at a time"). Each letter from the e-counselor ideally
represents a self-sufficient or stand-alone therapeutic intervention. Yet,
as further back-and-forth exchanges take place, the client is implicitly
encouraged to build on the CARE continuum in an adaptive spiral of
healing and personal growth.

As a therapeutic template for the e-counselor, the CARE model
engenders observation without judgment, bringing to light the kind
of feelings, needs, intentions, and choices that support fullness of per-
sonhood. The goal is to help clients to become more conscious of
strengths and essential qualities so that we can leave them after short-term
counseling with the confidence they need to overcome present and future
challenges (Speyer, 2010).

ONLINE CASE MANAGEMENT CHALLENGES

Online Intake and Risk Management

The process of online text-based counseling begins with a request for services from a client. This may range from a few words or lines to several

pages of text on the intake form. The first step of online triage is the assessment of risk and the appropriateness of the online asynchronous text-based method. Many websites have screening and risk-assessment tools built into the intake process. This may take the form of a question-naire with space for free text replies or a structured questionnaire with required fields and multiple-choice-type responses. The clinical assessment includes degree of suicide risk including suicidal ideation, current plans, intent, and history of past attempts. Assessment of potential harm to self or others is ethically and legally required. Involvement in current or past physical, emotional, or sexual abuse is an important part of the online assessment, as are questions about substance abuse and other addictions (e.g., gambling, sex).

The initial screening questionnaire may include questions about previous attempts that the client has made to receive help. It may also include questions eliciting preferred psychological and emotional states by asking how the client's life would be changed if the current issue were suddenly resolved ("miracle" or "magic wand" questions). In order to ensure client safety, the intake also needs to include client contact information such as a telephone number, address, and emergency contact details.

Text-based Alliance

Establishment of a text-based assessment is an ongoing process informed by the CARE model: connecting with the client, affirming their strengths, reorienting in new directions, and empowering them to continue.

A suggested format for a first exchange with a client may include the following:

1. Introduction, welcome, presentation of the counselor, parameters of counseling
2. Reflection on and positing of therapeutic goals
3. Initial impression of what is going on and ways to cope
4. Restatement of the presenting issue in positive terms
5. Understanding and validation of the client's feelings; restatement of goals
6. Exploration of inner and outer resources; impression of client strengths
7. Clarification of current issues, and previous treatment received
8. Exploration of precipitating factors ("why now?"); positive reframing of events
9. Exploration of options for change; specific suggestions and homework
10. Closure with affirmation and hope

Short-term Methods

Short-term text-based counseling is emotionally supportive in the present and does not allow for delving into, psychoanalyzing, or historically situating the presenting issue to any great degree. Yet the impact on clients can be equal to or even more profound than the outcome from traditional psychodynamic approaches (Labardee, 2009). The sense of connection, safety, and containment that the online counselor conveys in order to help the client cope with pressing concerns is paramount. The therapeutic bond with the client is achieved primarily through warm, respectful, caring letter writing. Empathy with the client's situation is expressed by identifying it as something "we" (by virtue of being human) are prone to; for example, "We are all slow learners when it comes to breaking personal patterns"; "Isn't it amazing, the way we give away our power").

Our therapeutic mandate calls for strategic, short-term, solution-focused, problem-solving interventions, yet they are secondary to the text-based bonding or rapport-building that clients deeply appreciate. The main goal of the correspondence is to demonstrate an empathic understanding of the presenting issues and faith in the client's capacity to resolve them.

In containing the issue within the context of the client's strengths, the counselor can ask about a time when the client overcame similar circumstances, did not feel the issue as acutely, or experienced some relief from it. This type of inquiry is designed to illuminate social supports as well as emotional self-reliance. Further, the resolution of the issue from the perspective of the future, a loved one's point of view, or the client's values can have an empowering effect in itself as clients respond to the genuine interest in what is right with them, not wrong with them (Speyer, 2010).

ANNOTATED CASE STUDY

The following case study is based on a story in the case files of one of the authors. Clinical and other details have been modified to create a composite case. Some elements have been transposed from other cases to help capture a typical e-counseling experience. The life situation from the original case has been fictionalized and abridged for brevity.

> Dear E-Counsellor,
>
> I don't even know where to begin right now because I feel so lost, not to mention miserable. I feel I have nowhere to turn at this point because everywhere I look is a source of stress. I have reached a breaking point at work, and I can't even turn to the comforts of home for escape. I just want to run away from it all, from everything, but I can't.
>
> To make matters worse, all of this stress is affecting my health. I'm having trouble sleeping and don't even feel like eating. I've even developed some kind of rash that's painfully itchy and totally embarrassing — as if I didn't have enough to deal with. I feel like I'm falling apart. And all I want to do is sleep all the time. But of course, I can't, because I'm too stressed!

The irony though is that at one point I thought this was all that I wanted, the job, marriage, a new home. I'm an interior designer and my husband and I just went into business together because he's a contractor. We thought it would be perfect, us combining our skills and building something of our own. We'd finally be free of working for other people. We knew it would take a lot of work, but we really thought it would be worth it. But instead, it's turned into a nightmare for so many reasons.

Even worse, we also — don't ask me why — decided to buy a gut reno house and turn it into our dream home. Yes, at the same time as running our own business. I know, you probably think we're crazy. And that's how I feel right now! I go to work and feel like tearing out my hair and then when I come home it's no better. Our house is a complete disaster. I hate coming home. But I also hate being at work. I just want to pack it in.

I haven't admitted this to anyone, but at times I feel like I don't want to keep going. I feel like there's no way out of this. And there's no way I can tell my family about any of this because I know how they'll react and I just can't deal with that right now.

Please help.

Mary

Counselor's comments: I am impressed by the intensity of her emotions. There is something strong brewing here and I am curious to find out what it is. The client has set clear goals and that is a good sign. It sounds initially that she feels her life is out of control, certainly beyond her own control. There are also feelings of depression, frustration, and a sense of being trapped. I'm curious about the relationship with her husband and the dynamic of her family. All this may be explored in our first exchange.

Hello Mary,

Welcome to InnerView. My name is John and I am a family physician. In this forum, we can share a number of exchanges to explore the issues you raise and to look together for a new way forward. Of course I can't practice medicine by email and I can't replace your family doctor, but I do have experience helping people with stress-related symptoms and work and relationship difficulties. I'm confident that you can get through this difficult period and out the other side.

I like to start with the "CARE" model and the "C" of "connecting and containing." Her problem is familiar and manageable.

Mary, the strongest feelings I sense when I read your letter are your desperation and your frustration. You are in a tough situation with your business, and then even at home you're at a loss for what to do. It sounds like it's having an impact on your health and you feel your life is slipping beyond your control. Is that a fair summary of your situation?

This is an attempt to "touch the pain." It sends the message that I know what the client may be feeling.

> If it is, I can understand your reactions and want to reassure you that you are not alone. Many people are dissatisfied with their work, their home life, and their relationships, but some do find a way to mobilize their strengths and resources, overcome the obstacles, and move forward. That can be our objective here if you like. I see myself as a kind of guide at the crossroads who can help you on your path. This route may be new to you but I have been this way many times before with many different people. I can point out some important landmarks and pitfalls along the way. Does that sound reasonable?
>
> In order to do that, I would like to get to know you better as a person. I usually like to start by learning about a person's strengths. For example, it sounds like you are a creative individual, with clear ambitions, who likes to try new experiences.

Although she has not described herself in these words, I have surmised these attributes based on what she has revealed about her goals, career choice, and current situation.

> It means too that you must have intelligence and perseverance to have been able to start up your own business. I'd like to hear more about that from you. I would also like to hear what you like most about yourself and what others like about you. For example, what attracted your husband to you and you to him? I'd like to hear about your accomplishments and the things you have done in your life that you are most proud of. I believe we build on our strengths to get our bearings.
>
> I am also interested in hearing about the supports that are available to you now. For example, how has your husband responded to your current situation, both at work and at home, and how is he helping you?

My circular question implies that he could be helping and, if not, why not?

> Similarly, how have your closest friends responded and how are they helping? I'd like to know if you have something you enjoy doing outside of work like a sport or hobby that helps you to keep the needs of body and soul in balance. Do you have a spiritual or a religious nature?
>
> Mary, we say that when we are faced with an impossible situation we have three basic options: we can run away, we can stay and accept it totally, or we can stay and fight to change it. I wonder what these options mean to you. Let's look at work first. You say you have considered "packing it in," which I assume means that you've considered folding up your business. What exactly would that mean to you, or to others, including your husband? What is the cost and what is the benefit? What would you rather be doing if you had your choice? When I

hear you say that you hate work right now, I am struck by the intensity of that statement. I imagine you like a tigress, full of pent-up power.

It is great to have that kind of energy in you, but I wonder how you could channel it in a way that best serves you?

I also wonder who or what is pushing your buttons at work to trigger such a powerful response. Can you tell me a little about what is going on with your business so that we can do some problem-solving together? That is the nature of the stay and fight option. As to the third option, I just don't see you as a passive acceptance kind of person. Am I right?

In the same way I would also like to hear a little about your home situation and your options there. Is it just the carpentry of the house that is unfinished or is it also the bricks and mortar of your marriage? How solid are the foundations of your relationship?

I am looking for the right image to promote change.

I am curious to hear what you were referring to when you briefly mentioned not wanting to deal with the reaction of your family. What are you expecting?

Mary, as to an immediate option to help with control of your stress symptoms, I wonder if you have gone to see your family doctor recently. Talking to your doctor often helps and it's important to know if there is any physical basis for the symptoms of anxiety and/or depression.

I know that this is a tough time for you and that you feel lost, but I am optimistic that there is a healthy core in you that can find the path ahead. I look forward to receiving your reply with your responses. Until then, I want to wish you strength and courage to meet the challenges you face.

With warm good wishes,
John

Hi John,

Wow, you really seem to have a sense of what's going on for me right now. I do feel trapped and haven't felt that I had any options, which is why I've been feeling so tired and frustrated. And crazy!

I think part of what really bothers me is that I thought this is what I wanted. I couldn't wait to have my own business, and own a home, and then even have a family — which feels like such a stretch right now. Instead though nothing is going the way I imagined. We've invested so much time and energy in our business and now into this house, and all we're faced with are problems. Huge problems. I feel like all the decisions I've made were somehow mistakes. But now if we sold the business or the house we'd lose way too much money. So there's really no way out of all this.

This explains some of the trapped feeling.

You asked about my support system, and right now that's pretty much my husband, but he's totally involved in all the work and house stuff too. So even though he seems to be managing better, I know this is hard for him as well. And as for friends? Who has time for that? I can barely keep my head above water managing everything. I've really let my friendships fall to the side. And the same goes for hobbies or interests. My life is renovation and design 24/7. I have no time for anything else! I used to enjoy cycling once upon a time. But now my bike is locked up in storage just collecting dust.

Here is another area of her life that she feels is out of her control.

So as you can imagine, it's hard for me to tell you what I like about myself right now. Right now, I can't think of one thing.

Okay, the one decision I guess I didn't screw up on was marrying my husband. Even though he's involved in all this stuff right now, I still feel so thankful that he's in my life. While I'm the one to lose my cool, screaming or crying over things, he's the one to remain calm. I know he's frustrated too, but he still manages to put things in perspective, or remind me to take a deep breath — I need a lot of those these days! He also still remembers to tell me that he loves me almost every day. He's probably the reason I keep going right now.

I am reassured to read that description of her marriage. That's something I'll want to highlight for her to hold onto now.

Everyone warned us that starting our own business would be hard, especially together as a couple. I guess I didn't really believe it. But it's such a challenge because our suppliers and contractors are so unreliable. The clients we have right now can't commit to anything and keep changing their minds. We feel like we're living day to day not knowing what kind of income we're making and the bills just keep piling up. I feel like I spend my days just putting out fires, running around everywhere, but never getting anywhere. I'm exhausted and irritable and for what?

But the worst part for sure is our house situation. We're so tired from work that we can't keep up with the plans for our home. Plus we can't manage our budget properly because it depends on our work. So the kitchen is pretty much gutted right now, and work remains to be done in every room, so we have stuff everywhere, half opened boxes, we can't find anything. I'm literally living out of a box. I come home and just want to scream or cry when I walk in the door.

And don't get me started about my family, my parents especially. They were the first ones to warn us that we'd be making a mistake starting our own business. I can just imagine them shaking their heads at me. It makes me feel so small.

Her relationship with her parents is something else we may want to explore.

> Thanks again for listening to me rant on. It even helped just to get some of these things off my chest. And to know that I'm not totally alone.
>
> Mary

It is good to see confirmation of the text-based bond that is forming.

> Hi Mary,
>
> Thank you for your thoughtful and informative reply. You have confirmed my initial impression of you as an intelligent, likeable woman. I am pleased that my words hit home and that I was able to relate to what's going on in that emotional storm in there. That's an important start because, really, I am in your corner and my objective is to march us out of there. Only you have to help me a little with some hints about the direction you want to take.

I define this as a collaborative effort. I will assess her strengths and affirm that they work for her. This is the "A" of the CARE model.

> You deserve to feel proud of what you have accomplished so far, even if it doesn't look exactly the way you thought it would. You pursued your dreams. You are a homeowner, and now own a business, which is based on your talents, vision, and hard-work. You didn't mention that there's anything else you'd like to be doing right now, so I'm going to guess that this design work is still something you love, but it's just the business side of things that has been wearing you down. I wonder, are there any options for you to be less involved in that side of the work? Maybe a different division of responsibilities? Or hiring an intern who is willing to exchange learning for the work? It sounds like you want to go back to enjoying your work, reminding yourself why this is a dream of yours.
>
> The housing situation is a tough one because it sounds like you don't have anywhere to go and relax or unwind at the end of a hard workday, which is probably exactly what you need at the moment. Instead, while it's in the process of becoming your dream home, your house feels like an extension of work. Could there be a way of making this a priority? Even finishing one room so you have a space for yourself to leave all the renovation work behind? I wonder if part of your understandable frustration is that you don't have any small daily "escape" from this world of renovations.
>
> It also sounds like you don't want to feel like you've made the wrong choice. So although you are having problems with the house and business, it still sounds like these are things that you want. Is that right? I'm wondering what happened to that feisty tigress from the first

letter, the one who can go after what she wants no matter what anyone else thinks?

Now I want to challenge her and explore a deeper understanding of the situation.

First I hear about this visionary, someone who is ambitious, creative, and willing to take risks. She works hard and achieves her goals. Despite the rough times, she still manages to maintain a strong, loving marriage to someone whose support is unwavering. She is able to appreciate what she does have. As well, she is able to adapt and persevere as she is faced with the challenges that come with pursuing a dream. Mary, I like and respect this person. That's you, by the way, in case you didn't recognize her.

Then we hear about another person who is afraid of making mistakes, or feeling small. She doubts herself when things become challenging, or when problems arise. She is afraid to admit she needs support because it may be seen as a sign of failure, instead of strength. Do you recognize this person too?

Mary, health and healing are about being or becoming whole. The words come from the same root. How do you join these two facets of your being in order to become a whole person again? We need to be whole in order to grow and develop and achieve our dreams.

To do this I would like to hear more from you about where some of these fears and doubts may come from, the things that tend to hold you back. Were there events or situations in your past that might have contributed to these feelings? You've already mentioned concerns about your family's reaction, how you may feel judged by them. How does their perspective on your choices affect or shape how you feel about them? Thinking about these questions may help you recognize patterns that have formed in your life. This may then lead to the possibility of change and a different way of responding to similar situations in the future.

I'm trying to separate what belongs to the present from what belongs to the past.

Mary, I sense that you are a strong woman who needs to draw upon these qualities in yourself to keep working toward your vision. It has been said that a crisis is both a threat and an opportunity. And while I know how tough this time is for you, it can also be a time to learn to take care of yourself in new ways.

With warm good wishes,
John

Hi again John,

Thanks for your thoughtful response. I really feel that you understand where I'm coming from and what actually seems to be the problem. I didn't see it quite that way until now, but I think you're so right that I am having a hard time reconciling my expectations with reality and the ways things are going right now.

I am pleased that this is going in the right direction.

I have talked to my husband and he agrees that I should focus more on the creative, planning part of the business, and not so much on the administrative/budget side, which is what really overwhelms me. We also thought the idea of an intern might be something worth pursuing. I hadn't even considered that. We knew we couldn't afford to hire someone, but maybe we could find a design student who would be willing to help with some of the admin tasks. You were so right too that I do love the design work and I don't want the business side to detract from that. I want to do what I can to be as successful as possible in this field, without losing my love for the work.

She is able to express her strengths too and remind herself why this was a dream of hers.

We have also made it a priority to build the walk-in closet upstairs first so that at least our bedroom will be finished and we can unpack our clothes. Again, you're right that I am someone who needs "down time" after a long day. Even if there's one room in the house — for now — that I can be in without being reminded of renovations, it will be a big help, I think. I've also been thinking that I need to get back on my bike, just do something that gets me away from everything for a little bit. I think I really just need a break!

And yes, I am afraid of failing. I'm terrified of making mistakes, which is why starting this business was such a huge accomplishment — until all the problems started of course. We talked about this business for years before finally doing it. It was really scary because no one in my family takes risks like that. We're a very conservative, "playing it safe" family. My mother has been a teacher her whole life and my father has worked in the same insurance company for almost 30 years. Playing it safe is considered a positive quality in my family. That way you can't make mistakes. So I guess there's this part of me that dreads having to admit that maybe I made a mistake. But then again, I'm not so sure it was a mistake??

I can't even tell my parents I'm struggling because they won't understand. They will only see it as a sign that I did make a mistake, that I should have kept my safe job at the hotel chain (even though I wasn't doing design work exactly). My husband tells me that they're the ones who have compromised by not taking any risks, or pursuing their dreams (my father is an amazing cook, loves food, and I think he could have become a chef if he wanted instead of staying in a job that he has never really enjoyed). But it's really hard to believe that right now. A big part of me wishes that I could rewind and go back to when life was simpler, even if it means just playing it safe.

Here is something worth exploring.

I guess I'm also worried about the future, especially having children. I feel like I can barely cope right now following these dreams. I can't imagine adding children to the mix. And that upsets me greatly. I've always wanted a big family and so does my husband. But I'm terrified that we'll have children and I'll feel as regretful or resentful about them as I do about our business right now. It's like I'm this person with moments of courage to pursue my dreams and big ambitions, but really inside I'm this little girl who just wants to run back to safety as soon as things get hard.

I am cheering for the brave character and will address that.

Thanks again for being here, just listening to me. It helps more than you know.

Mary

In the third exchange we entered the "R" phase of the CARE model, which is "reorienting and reaffirming" her new perspective. Mary was encouraged to acknowledge her need for space and support, and to see that as a strength, not a weakness. She was also invited to differentiate between failure and the need to persevere through challenging times in order to achieve her goals. As well, to reconnect with the part of her that loves the work she does.

Similarly, she was encouraged to express her fears and feelings directly to her partner about having children, as it seemed that that this was an underlying issue contributing to her intense reaction and difficulty coping.

The client responded positively to these suggestions, as follows:

Hi John,

Again thank you for your kind, supportive, and wise words. It sounds like you are a visionary too in your own field, someone who has put much effort into pursuing his dreams.

I have talked to my husband about my fears of failing at motherhood. I can't believe how emotional I became talking to him about it. I think I surprised myself that I've been carrying this weight around with me without even knowing it. As usual, he was very supportive and told me that there's no rush and we can definitely wait until the house is finished to start thinking about a family. He also agreed with what you said that just because something is hard doesn't mean it's a mistake. When you asked me what else I'd rather be doing, I couldn't think of anything else. This design work is what I love doing. And I do like the idea of having my own business. It's just the reality that's so incredibly hard. But I guess it's not bad enough yet to give up on it. I think it's worth seeing how it goes for a while longer.

I also think that once we finish our house then it will be much less overwhelming. I'm realizing that I do tend to get easily stressed and anxious when there's a lot going on, especially when so much of it feels out of my control. I'm not good at letting go too. And I need to learn how to relax or take a break. I can't keep going like this 24/7. I appreciate you reassuring me that no one can sustain this pace. I can't tell you how relieved I feel that you, a doctor, have told me that I'm not crazy, or going crazy. For a while I really felt like I was losing it, which in itself stressed me out even more!

So my plan is to let go a bit more of my plans and to realize that things aren't going to go exactly as I want them to, even if it is something I have long dreamed about. And that it doesn't mean that I've failed or made a mistake. I'm also going to get back on my bike again to remind myself that there is more to life than just work. As you reminded me, I am someone who does what she wants when I put my mind to it. So that's exactly what I'm going to do.

Thanks so much again John, for helping me step back for a moment from all my problems. I need that kind of break more than I even realized.

Take care,
Mary

In the final exchanges with the client, I focused on the "E" of the CARE model, to empower and encourage. The client was reminded how she moved from feelings of frustration, stress, and desperation in a situation that seemed out of her control to a sense of mastery through a process of reflection and self-discovery. She recognized the importance of work—life balance and the need for self-care. She understood how the culture of her family of origin was still contributing to her emotional belief system. She experienced how taking ownership of her needs can be a path to understanding, acceptance, and change.

DISCUSSION QUESTIONS

1. In your own words, what do you consider to be the main therapeutic benefits and possible drawbacks of asynchronous online counseling?
2. Describe the personal and professional characteristics of a clinician who you think would make a good online counselor.
3. What is "text-based bonding" and how can it be established in an online dialogue?
4. Have you ever kept a journal? What do you find to be healing about the act of writing in itself? What is the value of telling your story in writing rather than in a conversation?

5. What are the advantages of online supervision and how does the process resemble or differ from that of supervision for in-person cases?
6. Keeping in mind the 10 suggestions for creating a therapeutic alliance online, write a first exchange to each of the following clients.

    Client 1:

    I am very worried about a lot of things. I recently got remarried to a man with two teenage children and I have two younger children. We are living in the same house. It is been rough on all of us but my stress level has gone through the roof and I am worried that my relationship is beginning to turn sour with my husband as a result of all of this. What should I do?

    Client 2:

    I am in a terrible bind. I am a senior sales person with a very good company. I have been there for 12 years and have built a great career. Two days ago, I got a wonderful promotion but the new job is in another city and province. I rushed home with the exciting news and my wife and two teenage daughters told me I could go if I wanted to but they are staying. I am so upset. I do not know how to handle this nonsense.

7. What is the difference between an online counselor and an advice columnist?
8. Putting yourself in the position of an e-supervisor with respect to the case study with "Mary," what would be your feedback? What does the counselor do well? Where would you say there is room for improvement?

REFERENCES

Fenichel, M., Suler, J., Barak, A., Zelvin, E., Jones, G., & Munro, K., et al. (2002). Myths and realities of online clinical work. *Cyberpsychology and Behavior, 5,* 481−497.

Goffman, E. (1959/1990). *The presentation of self in everyday life.* London: Penguin Books.

Labardee, L. (2009). Online counseling crosses the chasm. *EAP Digest, Summer,* 12−20.

Rochlen, A. B., Zack, J. S., & Speyer, C. (2004). Online therapy: Review of relevant definitions, debates, and current empirical support. *Journal of Clinical Psychology, 60*(3), 269−283.

Shazer, S. D. (1982). *Patterns of brief family therapy: An ecosystemic approach.* New York, NY: Guilford Press.

Speyer, C., & Zack, J. (2003). Online counselling: Beyond the pros and cons. *Psychologica, 23,* 2.

Speyer, C. (2010). From products to persons: Psychology with a soul. *Psychologica, 32*(1), 20−26.

Suler, J. R. (2004). The psychology of text relationships. In R. Kraus, J. Zack, & G. Stricker (Eds.), *Online counseling: A handbook for mental health professionals* (pp. 19−50). San Diego, CA: Academic Press.

White, M., & Epston, D. (1990). *Narrative means to therapeutic ends.* New York, NY: WW Norton.

Yaphe, J., & Speyer, C. (2010). Using email to enrich counselor training and supervision. In K. Anthony, D. M. Nagel, & S. Goss (Eds.), *The use of technology in mental health: Applications, ethics and practice* (pp. 194–205). Springfield, IL: Charles C. Thomas, Publisher.

Chapter nine

Text-based Online Counseling: Chat

DeeAnna Merz Nagel
President and CEO of MerzConsulting, Inc.
Kate Anthony
CEO of OnlineCounsellors.co.uk

CHAT IN COUNSELING AND PSYCHOTHERAPY

The use of Internet relay chat (IRC) (referred to herein as "chat") for the purpose of delivering counseling and psychotherapy has certainly been established in the literature (Adlington, 2009; Anthony & Nagel, 2010; Derrig-Palumbo & Zeine, 2005; Nagel, 2008; Rochlen et al., 2004; Stofle & Chechele, 2004; Stofle, 2001).

This chapter will illustrate how chat can be employed in a therapeutically effective way using varying modalities and theoretical orientations. The traditional phases of online therapy will be reviewed in the context of synchronous therapeutic chat. The discussion of chat as a viable therapeutic medium concludes with a case study excerpt.

169

Online Counseling. DOI: 10.1016/B978-0-12-378596-1.00009-5

Chat as Counseling

The term "counselor" connotes an "advisor" and the professional designation is often used within several different contexts. For instance, spiritual guidance and financial planning are both considered types of counseling (Schimelpfening, 2007). Within the mental health professions, counseling is often identified as a short-term intervention.

According to Hardy (2008), counseling involves the client and counselor working together to identify a problem and find solutions to it. Sessions address life situations directly and are limited to the presenting issues of the client, with problem solving being the key focus. The counselor offers solution-focused strategies during sessions that can subsequently be applied in the client's life. Counseling is a short-term therapy usually only lasting as long as it takes the client to achieve a new perspective, learn new life skills, or achieve short-term goals set in the earlier sessions.

According to the *Dictionary of Psychology* (Reber & Reber, 2001, p. 162), counseling is defined as "a generic term that is used to cover the several processes of interviewing, testing, guiding, advising, etc. designed to help an individual solve problems, plan for the future [...] var., *counseling.*"

Given the definitions of Hardy, and Reber and Reber, the stand-alone term "counseling" can be applied with a broad brush. With such a general description, it is easy to see how any medium could be adapted to delivering counseling services, with chat just as effective as any other option. Counselors can adapt their conversational tone to the chat room environment during sessions and engage in problem solving and goal attainment.

Chat as Psychotherapy

The term "psychotherapy" is more clinically definitive than "counseling." Consequently, there is much controversy about whether psychotherapy can be achieved through synchronous methods such as chat (Essig, 2010; Howard, 2008). Psychotherapy generally involves longer-term treatment, with the goal of fundamental changes in mental and emotional outlook. The focus is on the client's thought processes rather than specific problems (Schimelpfening, 2007). The focus of psychotherapy is insight into underlying personality dynamics for the purpose of optimal psychological growth and development, so that the person can change to improve life overall (Hardy, 2008).

Reber and Reber (2001, pp. 586–7) offer the following definition of psychotherapy:

> In the most inclusive sense, the use of absolutely any technique or procedure that has palliative or curative effects upon any mental,

emotional, or behavioral disorder. In this general sense, the term is neutral with regard to the theory that may underlie it, the actual procedures and techniques entailed and the form and duration of treatment [. . .] in the technical literature the term is properly used only when the treatment is carried out by someone with recognized training and using accepted techniques [. . .] the term is often shortened to *therapy*

Anthony and Nagel (2010) reviewed the Reber and Reber definitions of counseling and psychotherapy and concluded that, while the method of delivery may be different online, the therapeutic processes remain the same.

When therapy occurs in a chat room, the therapy or consultation room is not an influential part of the therapeutic process in the way that most therapists have come to understand (Nagel, 2008). Influences such as artwork, decorative pillows, a box of tissues (creating an expectation of tears), and framed degrees are absent from the chat room. The chat room may be simply a bordered box that allows each participant a space in which to type. Depending on the chat platform, different fonts and colors as well as emoticons may be utilized if the chat platform includes a rich-text editor feature. While rich-text editors are fairly standard and allow for more descriptive chat as well as hyperlinks, some chat programs still remain relatively simple, relying on the richness of the written word to convey the full meaning of the conversation.

CHAT MODALITIES

It is often assumed that e-therapy, or online counseling, is a new *modality* of therapy. This assumption is incorrect. Online therapy implies that the therapy (regardless of modality) is delivered online. To use chat therapy as an example, the method of service delivery is the online medium and chat is the form of technology being utilized. The actual therapy being delivered may be one of several modalities including individual, group, couples, and family.

Individual Therapy

Individual therapy that occurs in a chat room most resembles traditional f2f therapy. While there are differences in the pacing and layering of the conversation, the conversational flow is akin to an f2f interaction between therapist and client. Typically, the transcript of a chat will match that of a 50-minute "hour" f2f session. Online therapists develop their own structure and rhythm, however, which may vary from client to client. Clients may show a pre-existing comfort level with text-based conventions, including the use of emoticons, acronyms, and emotional bracketing (see Anthony & Nagel, 2010, p. 31). Therapists may wish to match the client's use of text language or remain consistent with their own text style. Variations may also become evident depending on the age of the client.

For instance, adolescents tend to be much more casual in text-based conversation, often using a wider range of truncated text methods.

Group Therapy

Group therapy in a chat room becomes more challenging, being similar to facilitating an in-person group with one's eyes closed but where the voices of each group member can still be heard. With synchronous chat, auditory cues are missing, leaving the therapist to rely on visual cues. In chat rooms, which scroll either from top to bottom or bottom to top, it is often difficult to "see" all of the members in the group at one time. Both facilitator and clients tend to remain attentive to the next entry. While the facilitator attends to one group member by typing a response, other chat entries may be missed, requiring the facilitator scroll back and find them. Holding a chat discussion with more than a few participants can become challenging due to this lack of immediate visibility and related communication cues (Barak & Boniel-Nissim, 2010). Even so, group therapy in a chat room can be a very dynamic way to deliver group therapy services. As Colón (1996) so eloquently stated, "There is no way to quantify what happens in an online group. And yet lives can change" (pp. 215).

Couples Therapy

Couples therapy allows both partners to express their feelings in a safe manner using text language instead of spoken conversation. Often, when couples are having a difficult time communicating, especially listening to each other, the use of text-based interventions can be helpful. During a structured chat session, the therapist may employ ground rules, such as instructing clients to wait until after the other has finished responding before beginning to type again. In this way, clients take the time to read carefully each other's responses and mutual "listening" is enhanced. Ideally, the therapist and the clients learn to read with a "third ear." In describing this process of inner listening, Reik (1948) explained, "The voice that speaks in him, speaks low, but he who listens with a third ear hears also what is expressed almost noiselessly, what is said *pianissimo*" (p. 145, emphasis in original). Further, encouraging text-based dialogue between formal sessions reinforces listening skills and can be a helpful tool to build communication between couples who have not been successful in listening to one another in the past (Derrig-Palumbo & Zeine, 2005).

Family Therapy

Family therapy can be conducted in a chat room as well. The considerations established thus far with regard to individual, group, and couples therapy all pertain to family therapy. Teaching the family to listen and communicate respectfully by pacing its members' chat entries is an important way to ensure that they are not talking over each other. This is sometimes a more structured and deliberate process than facilitating a group therapy session with chat. Family members coexist outside the therapy session and often the fundamental challenge is hearing another family member's perspective. While this is important in group therapy as well, it may be advantageous to instruct family members to take turns during a family chat session. Derrig-Palumbo and Zeine (2005) suggest that family therapy chat sessions can be used when framed as family meetings. Once the therapy has concluded, family members are encouraged to continue with the online weekly meetings. The meetings tend to foster continued communication among family members and younger members tend to respond more openly and feel "heard" when online.

CLINICAL APPROACHES TO THERAPEUTIC CHAT

Humanistic Perspectives

One of the central principles of humanistic work is the therapist's use of the self, and this is central to the online practitioner. When working within a chat-room setting, the therapist's example of a strong, expressive, self-aware persona can be a model for the development of the same in the client. Through *text-based* bonding (and plenty of clarification in case of misunderstandings), and with the perceived presence of the therapist, the client can experience freedom of self-expression and growth in self-awareness by means of the online dialogue. Since any progress depends on the acceptance and respectful understanding of issues clients bring to the therapeutic setting, genuineness in text represents the personal qualities of the therapist otherwise experienced via the tangible attributes of an f2f presence.

The "disinhibition effect" of feeling less reserved or cautious when online (Suler, 2004) means that more distressing or uncomfortable issues are often presented much earlier than they would be in f2f sessions. Most novice online practitioners think that the foundation of unconditional positive regard needs to be in place in order to make self-disclosure safe for clients. They are therefore surprised by the apparent level of trust the client places in them on first contact and need to adjust to these kinds of differences in the nature of the online therapeutic alliance.

Psychodynamic Perspectives

Interpretation of the client's words in chat is a skill that takes practice and specialized skills as well as attention and care, particularly with the conversational nature of the synchronous medium. There is a risk of premature interpretation, which can miss the mark, especially given the disinhibition effect on the therapist's side. However, the stream of spontaneous dialogue can provide the therapist with a window into unconscious processes that may become apparent as the client is typing and revealing states of mind that would not necessarily be voiced f2f.

Suler (1998) asserts that "we recreate in our relationship with the computer some ASPECT of how we related to our family members" (para. 9, capitalization in the original). By this, he means that, in addition to the usual transference process for the practitioner and the client, there are feelings toward the hardware and software that are part of the therapeutic context, whether openly interpreted as such or not.

Without a physical presence or voice, it is likely that a fantasy of the therapist – and usually an idealized one – will develop, which may exaggerate the transference factors. While not necessarily having a significant influence on the therapeutic work, it certainly must be kept in mind by the therapist while engaged in online therapy and addressed directly as the need arises. Good boundary-setting and awareness of any projected images are imperative for the online clinician.

As Anthony and Nagel (2010, pp. 20–1) point out,

> The ability to work with issues of denial, and challenge, in online work is often more dynamic than face-to-face work, simply because once the words are 'spoken', they don't fade away or get ignored – they are there in black and white on the screen [...] Some chat software programs provide a function whereby you can see what the other party is typing as they type it, which means that deleted words can be seen as well. This is not recommended for therapeutic work, firstly as it could arguably be intrusive if clients do want to change their text, and secondly because it is distracting within a therapeutic session if you are watching for changes to the text.

Given the level of clinical skill required to confront clients with challenging patterns of behavior in general (Jacobs, 1988), it should also be noted that this is possibly more important within the chat-room environment simply because of the ease with which the client can disengage. It is easy to hit a disconnect button or "hide" in a synchronous text session. If this does happen, it can raise countertransference anxiety for the online therapist. In f2f therapy, there are often physical clues signaling a client's mounting resistance or wish to leave the room. In chat, however, there is usually just a notification that a client "has left the chatroom," or something similar. If this is not due to a technical glitch, careful review of what was going on in the session before the sudden departure is needed, as a case management learning opportunity on the therapist's side and/or for possible debriefing if and when the client re-engages in another session.

Cognitive-behavioral and Solution-focused Therapy Techniques (CBT)

The premise of CBT is that, by reframing how we perceive life events, we can make them less disturbing or traumatic (Beck, 1979). CBT and similar solution-focused theories are often viewed as ideally suited to online work due to the nature of the medium intrinsically allowing for thought processes and perceptions to be clarified in text.

Homework assignments fall within the purview of online interventions, regardless of the theoretical orientation of the actual assignment, because by their nature they are traditionally text-based. Therefore, psychoeducation and bibliotherapy are therapeutic tools that work well with online clients and can accompany any clinical approach. Treatment plans that rely upon objective and measurable goals often use techniques drawn from CBT, brief solution-focused therapy, and neurolinguistic programming (NLP). Challenging a client's "private logic," "limiting beliefs," and "mistaken convictions" in chat can be very effective because the evidence remains on the screen, allowing clients to pause and consider feedback that they might dismiss or tune out in an f2f conversation.

Similarly, therapies that employ narrative, metaphorical, or journal-keeping methods also translate well to the online environment. Although not without its own issues (Nagel & Anthony, 2009), blogging is an effective way of using technological means to create a story and examine feelings associated with it. Similarly, searching online images to enrich and illustrate feelings and emotions can enhance the therapeutic discourse.

PHASES OF ONLINE CHAT THERAPY

The phases of online chat therapy mirror those of the traditional f2f process. Each phase represented below, while not necessarily occurring in sequential order, is an important part of the therapeutic blueprint. Examination of a therapist's subset of skills within the context of the empathic listening skill (Pickering, 1986) and application of that subset of skills to text-based chat therapy set the stage for understanding how chat therapy is a viable therapeutic process. At the same time, these main therapeutic components can be applied to text-based chat therapy as a viable means of treatment.

Rapport-Building

Rapport is established through the felt presence of both the therapist and the client. While traditional f2f therapy allows for all the reassuring features of physical presence, online therapy extends the experience of presence into cyberspace. Realizing that two people can enter into a relationship without physical presence is the first step in understanding how rapport can be established online. In text-based therapy, whether asynchronous or synchronous, the quality of the written communication compensates for the lack of physical presence. The use of text-based conventions on the Internet, or "netiquette," can help to facilitate rapport in chat therapy sessions. Consider "attending," "acknowledging," and "supporting" as skills that aid in building rapport. For example, during a chat session, moments of silence can be acknowledged as such. The therapist might indicate to a client that time is needed to respond by writing, "Pause for thought, okay?" (often truncated to "PFT, k?") or "Take your time." Showing support can be demonstrated by emotional bracketing. For instance, a therapist can encourage a client's positive statement by responding with "[smiling]." These are selected examples from a variety of rapport-building techniques unique to the context of a chat therapy session (Anthony, 2000).

Assessment

Assessment within the chat therapy session is similar to that in an f2f session. The therapist interprets what a client says in person using various skills including but not limited to "restating," "paraphrasing," "probing," "giving feedback," and "checking perceptions." During a chat session, these skills can be utilized as well, sometimes to greater effect since the client is "seeing it in print." For instance, the client may write, "I had such a hard day today. Work was just awful. Nobody there respects me!" The therapist can paraphrase or restate by reflecting back the following: "I am so sorry you had such a rough day. It sounds like you are not feeling appreciated at work." Probing involves questioning the client in a supportive way to elicit more information or clear up any possible misinterpretations. The therapist may pose a question such as, "Anne, I just want to be sure I understand what you are saying...," or, "Can you tell me more about...?" Questions not only help the therapist further to assist the client but also foster continued development of the therapeutic alliance. Giving feedback is a way of sharing and comparing perceptions with the client for the benefit of increased insight. A therapist might pose a statement to a client that begins with, "I am wondering if you...." This is an open-ended way of giving the client an opportunity for further introspection while following the lead of the therapist in a constructive direction. Again, there are a variety of ways in which traditional assessment skills can be translated to text.

Goal-Setting

Goal-setting can be a formal or informal process that engages the client in positive outcomes. Once the therapist has assessed the client's situation, focused feedback and questioning can result in goal-setting that is client-centered. The e-therapist may take a more directive approach, depending on the circumstances; for instance, "I would like for you to make an appointment to see your psychiatrist next week. Will you agree to do that?" Alternatively, the goal-setting may be more collaborative. With the help of paraphrasing and feedback, the therapist can support client-driven goals: "It sounds like you are not feeling appreciated at work. It might help to find ways for you to be able to leave your job at the end of the shift and not carry that stress with you. Tell me about an activity that helps take your mind off work."

Engagement

Engagement refers to the client's involvement in the therapeutic process. Through the skills mentioned above, the therapist is able to establish a therapeutic alliance. When the therapeutic alliance is present, clients will engage in the process. During a chat session, this is evident by statements that acknowledge the therapist's contribution to the dialogue. The client may reply to encouraging observations with "Thanks!" or "That makes sense." Alternatively, the client may reply with a simple emoticon such as "☺." The therapist can generally sense when the client is taking ownership of their part in the dialogue. Other ways to increase client engagement may take place between sessions. A client may complete reading assignments or other homework, or test out new life skills between chats, with "progress reports" a feature of follow-up sessions.

Closure and Follow-up

Closure and follow-up occur within each chat session as well as at the end of the therapeutic relationship. As in the f2f setting, therapists utilize "summarizing" and "synthesizing" skills to offer the client focus and understanding. The summaries can be strategically positioned within as well as at the end of the chat session. Reinforcing goal-setting and corresponding client progress within the session is one method of summarizing. At the end of each session, the therapist can wrap it up with key points and review ongoing issues needing more attention in the next session. The final session can include a wrap-up statement about the client's successes, with an optional follow-up email summarizing therapeutic achievements, new perspectives, and further recommendations. Online closure includes necessary referrals and appropriate clinical documentation just as it does in f2f treatment.

CASE STUDY EXCERPT

The following chat transcript is excerpted and slightly modified from a case study used for training purposes. ReadyMinds, in partnership with the Center for Credentialing and Education (CCE) and an affiliate of the National Board of Certified Counselors (NBCC), has created a national new credential category in the US. The Distance Credentialed Counselor (DCC™) qualification has been offered since 2004. The "Case of Anne" (Nagel & Anthony, 2010) is utilized as part of the DCC training curriculum. Anne is a composite client and not an actual person. Background information about Anne is as follows.

Anne filled out an intake questionnaire on the therapist's website. That questionnaire was delivered via encrypted channels to the therapist, who reviewed the questionnaire before the first scheduled chat session. In addition, the therapist sent a welcome and introduction email to the client reviewing informed consent, privacy rules, and other "housekeeping" matters.

Anne is a 44-year-old married woman who reports feeling depressed and moody. She reports a history of depression in her twenties "but not with the mood swings like this." She is taking Wellbutrin to stop smoking but she continues to smoke half a pack of cigarettes daily. She takes ibuprofen as needed for "heavy menstrual cramps." She received counseling in her early twenties due to depression and reports a rape at the age of 17, but did not receive counseling after the incident. She and her husband have a good relationship but "we don't have sex anymore because I don't want to." She has a 16-year-old daughter. Anne states that her preference is to receive counseling services through email or chat because she works long hours and is comfortable online.

This case excerpt represents a 30-minute chat session.

Counselor: good morning, Anne… thanks for being right on time for our chat session.

Anne: no problem …I'm anxious to talk to you … I have a lot on my mind.

Counselor: want to tell me about it…?

Anne: well, there's a lot going on …am not sure where to begin …

Counselor: it's really up to you, Anne …you sound like you want to talk.

Anne: am drawing a bit of a blank here …

Counselor: you're feeling overwhelmed? …or are some of these things just hard to talk about?

Long pause while Anne is typing…

Anne: not sure … hard to sort everything out …

Counselor: remember the intake questionnaire you filled out before we began our chat sessions?

Anne: yeah, I've got it here…I read it again this morning …am wondering if what I wrote sounds kind of desperate.

Counselor: what does feeling "desperate" mean to you?

Anne: like I'm not in charge …can't get what I want…not sure what I even want …

Counselor: In your initial email you stated you were "depressed" and in the questionnaire you used the term "moody" to describe yourself …do you feel like you are not quite in control of your feelings?

Anne: yeah, that's it…

Counselor: In my initial email back to you I gave you a link that gave some information about depression. Did you have time to review any of the information on that website?

There is a very long pause here, and depending on the chat program used, the counselor or client may not know whether the other person is typing. To offer assurance that the counselor is "listening," the counselor states the following:

Counselor: Anne I know you are typing your feelings and that is good. Take your time, but if you want to, go ahead and "enter" parts of your passage to me. I can be reading while you are typing more. And when I am giving you a lengthy response, I will do the same.

Anne: I did. And you know, I don't know, I mean, it doesn't feel like depression so much as just not feeling "right" — I am just not myself. I guess that is why I described it in the questionnaire as moody. I can't quite put my finger on it. But that is the main reason I am seeking some sort of help. Which feels weird too — to reach out to a therapist this way but it fits with my schedule right now.

Anne: Ok good.

Counselor: Thank you for sharing. That helps me know where you are at. You mentioned a couple of issues in your intake . . . your mood swings and the effect it is having on your marriage . . .

Counselor: As well as a rape that occurred earlier in your life [imagining that was so difficult for you] . . .you also said that you have a 16 year old daughter.

Anne: yes . . .

Counselor: let's just pick one of these areas to discuss . . . maybe the one that feels easiest to talk about right now. I'm right here to help you.

Anne: I guess that would be my daughter . . .

The following 2 entries come in simultaneously demonstrating the pacing difference with chat as compared to a conversation:

Counselor: tell me about Stacey.

Anne: She is just a wonderful child. She is so thoughtful — she helps me around the house and with her grandmother. She is an excellent student. . . and she is fun to be around!

Counselor: I get the feeling you have a smile on your face right now . . .

Anne: that's for sure . . . She is my bright spot these days.

Counselor: sounds like you enjoy being a mom.

Anne: I do . . . but I worry about how my mood swings are affecting her.

Counselor: how so?

Anne: Well she has commented on me being grumpy and she has asked me if I am upset or sad at times. She asks if there is anything she can do or if it is her fault.

Counselor: That sounds like a normal response from a caring daughter. Chances are, if these mood swings have not been going on long, she is just noticing a difference and is concerned.

Counselor: You are taking a big step with counseling so you will figure this out.

Anne: Yea, I know. . .just wish Peter was as understanding ☺

Counselor: Do you want to tell me about that?

Anne: I will maybe next session. Not quite ready to talk about it but I know I need to. We have not had sex in a long time and it is a problem. I just don't want to.

Counselor: It sounds like you have a lot going on right now. I am going to switch gears. It may seem like I am going off topic, but I think it might be related. Do you mind?

Anne: No, go ahead.

Counselor: You stated on your intake that you are having heavy cramping and sporadic periods. You said yourself you should probably go to the doctor. I am wondering if you shouldn't go and explain to your doctor too about your mood swings and your low sex drive.

Anne: Yea I know.

Counselor: Can you agree to do that? I would like for you to schedule an appointment. We can make that your homework assignment for next week.

Anne: I will try.

Counselor: Anne I really encourage you to do this. We need to rule out anything medical while we are working together. We can certainly continue with counseling but it would help both of us to know if something else is going on.

Another very long pause here.

Counselor: Do you agree?

Anne: You are right. I just hate going.

Counselor: How are you feeling right now?

Anne: fine I guess. A little depressed and anxious. Going to the doc . . . well anyway. I don't want to talk about that just yet either.

Counselor: Ok. I think we have covered some ground today.

Anne: Can we do this time again next week? This is good for me.

Counselor: Yes. We can plan on that. In the meantime Anne, think about a way that you might document your moods — maybe on a calendar so that we can see if a pattern emerges.

Anne: Hey I never thought of doing that! Thanks!

Counselor: No problem. Take care. "see" you next week!

The chat transcript demonstrates the therapist's ability to implement solution-focused techniques while adhering to his or her own psychodynamic theoretical orientation. The therapist encourages the client to seek a medical consult to rule out any biophysical reasons for her heavy cramping and low sex drive. The therapist's orientation, while not explicit in this excerpt, influences the direction the therapist will take with the client. Assuming that the medical consult does not reveal new information, the therapist might speculate that one reason for her mood swings and low sex drive, along with her initial hesitancy to see a medical doctor, could be unresolved emotional repercussions of the rape she experienced when she was 17. Her 16-year-old daughter may be a trigger point for that, since her daughter is near the age when the client's own traumatic event occurred.

In future sessions, the therapist will work carefully with the client on maintaining rapport, continuing with further assessment, setting goals, and promoting ongoing client engagement through homework exercises and bibliotherapy recommendations. The therapist will be diligent in assisting the client in pacing the self-disclosure, particularly related to the traumatic event, offering therapeutic boundaries within the chat session and containment techniques the client can use between sessions. If difficult material emerges during the chat sessions, the therapist may choose to send between-session communication in the form of positive affirmations or additional readings through email.

CONCLUSION

The discussion in this chapter has underscored how counseling and psychotherapy within an online chat environment can include benefits common to f2f therapy yet also unique to the medium and that do not try to replicate the in-person experience. Of course, every therapist or counselor will have his or her own preferred methods, theoretical orientation, and training; therefore, each session with an individual, couple, family, or group will have its own nuances and pathways of therapeutic progress. It should also be stated that the use of technological innovations for therapeutic services is not something that should be imposed upon the practitioner – indeed, this is often unsuccessful online because the therapist's resistance will affect the sense of authentic presence and congruence of communication crucial to rapport-building. However, when approached with an open outlook, postgraduate training, and an ethical awareness of the issues involved, chat-room therapy is a dynamic, convenient, and effective way of delivering therapeutic services.

REFERENCES

Adlington, J. (2009). *Online therapy – Reading between the lines: A practical NLP based guide to online counselling and therapy skills.* London: MX Publishing.

Anthony, K., & Nagel, D. M. (2010). *Therapy online [a practical guide].* London: SAGE. p. 16.

Anthony, K. (2000). The nature of the therapeutic relationship within online counselling. Retrieved April 4, 2009 from http://www.kateanthony.co.uk/thesis2000.pdf

Barak, A., & Boniel-Nissim, M. (2010). Using forums for online support groups. In K. Anthony, D. M. Nagel, & S. Goss (Eds.), *The use of technology in mental health: Applications, ethics and practice.* Springfield, IL: Charles C. Thomas, Publisher, pp. 47–55.

Beck, A. T. (1979). *Cognitive therapy and the emotional disorders.* New York, NY: Meridian Books.

Colón, Y. (1996). Chatt(er)ing through the fingertips: Doing group therapy online. *Women & Performance: A Journal of Feminist Theory, 9*(1), 205–215.

Derrig-Palumbo, K., & Zeine, F. (2005). *Online therapy: A therapist's guide to expanding your practice.* New York, NY: Norton & Co.

Essig, T. (2010). WARNING: 'Online therapy' is not therapy, not really. Retrieved March 22, 2010 from http://trueslant.com/toddessig/2010/03/15/warning-online-therapy-is-not-therapy-not-really

Hardy, M. (2008). The difference between counseling and psychotherapy. Retrieved March 22, 2010 from http://www.altmedweb.com/experts/psychotherapy/difference-between-counseling-and-psychotherapy

Howard, S. (2008). Commentary: Filling the void in the virtual consulting room. *Voices, 44*(3), 101–102.

Jacobs, M. (1988). *Psychodynamic counselling in action.* London: Sage.

Nagel, D. M., & Anthony, K. (2009). Writing therapy using new technologies: The art of blogging. *Journal of Poetry Therapy, 22*(1), 41–45.

Nagel, D. M., & Anthony, K. (2010). *Distance Credentialed Counselor (DCC™) training: Mental health concentration training handbook.* Internal Proprietary Training Document. Lyndhurst, NJ: ReadyMinds.

Nagel, D. M. (2008). Filling the void in the virtual consulting room. *Voices, 44*(3), 98–101.

Pickering, M. (1986). Communication. *EXPLORATIONS, a Journal of Research of the University of Maine, 3*(1), 16–19.

Reber, A. S., & Reber, E. S. (2001). *Dictionary of Psychology.* London: Penguin Books.

Reik, T. (1948). *Listening with the third ear: The inner experience of a psychoanalyst.* New York, NY: Pyramid Books. p. 145.

Rochlen, A. B., Zack, J. S., & Speyer, C. (2004). Online therapy: Review of relevant definitions, debates, and current empirical support. *Journal of Clinical Psychology, 60*(3), 269–283.

Schimelpfening, N. (2007). Psychotherapy 101: What is the difference between counseling and psychotherapy? Retrieved March 22, 2010 from http://depression.about.com/od/psychotherapy/a/counseling.htm

Stofle, G. S., & Chechele, P. J. (2004). Online counseling skills, Part 2: In-session skills. In R. Kraus, J. Zack, & G. Stricker (Eds.), *Online counseling: A handbook for mental health professionals* (pp. 181–196). San Diego, CA: Academic Press.

Stofle, G. S. (2001). *Choosing an online therapist.* Harrisburg, PA: White Hat Communications.

Suler, J. (1998). Mom, dad, computer (transference reactions to computers). *The psychology of Cyberspace.* Retrieved April 4, 2009 from http://www-usr.rider.edu/~suler/psycyber/comptransf.html

Suler, J. (2004). The online disinhibition effect. *Cyberpsychology and Behavior, 7*(3), 321–326.

Chapter ten

Counseling Groups Online: Theory and Framework

Yvette Colón, PhD, ACSW, BCD
American Pain Foundation
Stephanie Stern, MSW, LCSW-C
Compassionate Counseling Services, LLC

CHAPTER OUTLINE

INTRODUCTION

When the first edition of this book was published, the rapid development of Internet technologies had opened new and unexplored means of interpersonal communication and brought dramatic challenges and opportunities to the mental health community. The potential of online group counseling on the Internet, as a novel therapeutic medium, was just beginning to be explored. Group counseling venues varied from open-membership bulletin boards to small counseling groups using multimedia

Online Counseling. DOI: 10.1016/B978-0-12-378596-1.00010-1

and voice communication to enrich the therapeutic environment. This chapter will review several different types of online setting for therapeutic groups and provide guidelines for therapists interested in expanding their work.

Although the Internet has been in existence for more than 40 years (Hafner & Lyon, 1996), the World Wide Web — its graphic and hyperlink interface — has only been available for 20 years. The web was created in 1989 and made available to the public in 1991, but did not become popular until 1995 (Kehoe, 1995, p. 78). Even then, the web was driven by text-based menus in what was known as GopherSpace (Kehoe, 1995, p. 102). In those years, the Internet grew from a small academic and military network to an enormous international communications network.

The number of Internet users continues to grow every year and the time they have been online has increased as well. In 1999, approximately 33 percent of Internet users had three or more years of online experience (Horrigan & Rainie, 2002). Three years later, the number of Americans with Internet access had nearly doubled to 60 percent and 38 percent of those had been online for more than six years (Horrigan & Rainie, 2002). In 1988, there were only 60 000 computers online in the world; in 2007 there were approximately 650 million (Markoff, 2007). Twenty-eight percent of all Internet users reported that they have looked online for information about depression, anxiety, stress, or mental health issues and more than half of patients living with chronic disease have consumed user-generated health information (Fox & Purcell, 2010). The Internet has changed greatly in the decades since it came into being and it will continue to do so at a rapid pace, ever-evolving in the direction of new, socially relevant, and culturally creative services.

The last five years have brought unprecedented innovations in web, email, social networking, and other online technologies. It has become commonplace for individuals to use the Internet to find information, education, and support. The wild popularity and near ubiquity of social networking sites and the building of online communities have increased the numbers of people who turn to the Internet, not only for information and recreation but also for mental health support and social connection (Horrigan & Rainie, 2005).

There was a time not so long ago when organizations, businesses, and individual mental health providers were true pioneers if they providing a website, an informational email address, and some kind of online service for the clients they served. Now it is virtually impossible for an organization or business to exist without any of those features. Organizations and mental health practitioners broadcast to clients, receive donations or process payments, respond to emails seeking assistance, provide information and support, and much more.

THERAPEUTIC AND SUPPORT GROUPS

The earliest forums were Internet discussion groups called "Usenet newsgroups" (Hafner & Lyon, 1996). Each newsgroup was a collection of messages, similar to bulletin boards or message centers, organized around a central topic; those with the prefix "alt.support" were open support forums. The newsgroups facilitated an exchange of information among interested people and were global and local at the same time (Usenet has been archived by Google at http://groups.google.com/groups/dir?lnk=od&). Groups of people who used the Internet for social interaction could cluster in Usenet discussion groups, computer conferencing systems, or web-based bulletin boards. People with a shared history, shared values, and a variety of interests could connect and carry on a conversation with anyone around the world, all without leaving their own communities. Online groups themselves offer a number of advantages: smaller costs, less infrastructure and setup resources, better scheduling options, better formats (synchronous versus asynchronous), and numerous methods of service delivery (chat, bulletin board, email) (Colón & Friedman, 2003).

Many of the early studies considered clinical aspects of online group therapy. Finn and Lavitt (1994) analyzed computer-based self-help groups for sexual abuse survivors. Weinberg et al. (1995) reviewed "computer-mediated groups" as an extension of social work services and Meier (1997) proposed new models of online groups by and for social workers. Childress (1998) asserted that the Internet was becoming an important means to conduct psychological research and psychotherapeutic interventions, but stressed the importance of conducting research for online interventions and the need to develop appropriate standards of practice.

King and Moreggi (1998) reviewed then-current efforts of mental health workers who provided fee-based services via email and chat rooms. An overview of online self-help and mutual aid groups was included and the authors described the nature of interpersonal relationships that formed among group participants. Ethical, legal, and moral implications as well as pros and cons of this medium were outlined.

Barak and Wander-Schwartz (1999) compared online unstructured process group therapy using synchronous (real-time) text chat with an f2f traditional process group. Their early findings, although based on a sample too small to establish significance, suggested that synchronous online text-based process groups appeared to have similar psychodynamics to traditional groups. They demonstrated the unique quality of online therapy and the power and impact of anonymity on psychological behavior in groups; people tend to be more disinhibited and self-disclosing on short acquaintance, and interpersonal closeness therefore develops more rapidly. Suler (1999) theorized about psychotherapy in cyberspace, noting the text, sensory, and interpersonal experiences and presence of those in online groups while proposing ways to create group bonding experiences online, promoting a cybertherapy theory and discussing the role of the professional.

Humphreys et al. (2000) considered the ethical responsibilities of psychologists facilitating Internet-based groups. They provided a definition of online groups that deliberately excluded group psychotherapy, believing that it could not be conducted over the Internet for the following reasons: online group members may come from a wide geographical catchment area, hampering the ability to follow ethical guidelines in the event of an emergency; individuals cannot be identified accurately and reliably; and, because all discussions are written, all activity can be copied and distributed, and therefore group members' privacy and confidentiality cannot be guaranteed. Additionally, Humphreys et al. stressed the importance of the facilitator (in this case, the psychologist); whether facilitating in a professional capacity or as a peer member, it was imperative that the facilitator role be defined as clearly as possible.

Childress (2000) outlined guiding ethical principles on providing online psychotherapy (focusing on the use of email to provide online psychotherapeutic interventions), including the responsibility to provide ethical service, the mandate to "do no harm," the issue of informed consent, the provision of effective online interventions, the scope of competent practice, professional accountability, and the redress of grievances. In an extensive article, Rochlen et al. (2004) reviewed recent literature addressing the definitions, ethical and research considerations, and potential strengths and limitations of online therapy; they noted that the integration of technology with the practice of psychotherapy had been one of the most vigorously debated topics among mental health professionals within the previous 15 years. Eysenbach et al. (2004) and Griffiths et al. (2009) conducted systematic reviews of the effects of online peer-to-peer interactions in health-related virtual communities and electronic support groups and did not find convincing evidence of their benefits. Only a portion of the studies they reviewed were randomized trials with control groups. Many had small samples and less-than-optimal research designs. Most of the studies were exploratory and the outcomes measured most often were depression and social support; most did not show any remedial effects. The researchers noted that the absence of measurable objectives was a disadvantage.

Much of the early literature regarding online therapy was anecdotal or impressionistic. Increasingly, researchers are conducting systematic evaluations of outcomes and more studies are available that indicate online group counseling's efficacy. It is vitally important to continue to develop research studies that will help to quantify the effectiveness of online psychotherapeutic support and assess the efficacy of a broad range of online interventions.

PROFESSIONAL PROGRAMS

As a result of this large amount of activity, writing, and theorizing about online groups, it was not long before professional programs took hold and began to be offered by health and mental health social service organizations.

In 1993 and 1994, Yvette Colón facilitated experimental therapy groups for ECHO (East Coast Hangout; http://ww.echonyc.com), a private virtual community based in New York City. The group conference was conducted in text-only bulletin board format. Criteria for entry were simple; in the spirit of adventure, people could join the group simply by being interested in an online psychotherapy experiment, making a three-month commitment to participate and signing a liability waiver. The groups were limited to eight participants each and lasted twelve weeks. The screening process consisted of potential participants supplying the therapist with their real names, addresses, phone numbers, previous groups and/or individual psychotherapy experiences, and any topics they wished to explore. Once participants had been screened and accepted, they were given a password for access to the bulletin board; they had access 24/7 and were free to post whatever and whenever they wished. The group therapist provided group guidelines and helped to maintain structural parameters for each of the created topics, logging in every day to read posts and respond or comment as needed. While one-hour synchronous chat sessions were included at the beginning of the project, they proved to be unpopular and were discontinued. Feedback from all participants indicated that they believed that their online experience had been a positive one and that the groups had provided support, insight, and a safe place to work through issues they had wanted to explore.

Beginning with a small grant, Colón then created an online services program at Cancer*Care*, a national nonprofit organization that provides free, professional support services for anyone affected by cancer. Cancer*Care* has long found innovative ways to extend their services through technology, beginning with telephone support groups in 1993 (Colón, 1996) and online groups in 1997. Both programs became a part of the core services offered by the agency to its clients and remain in operation today. Stephanie Stern, an oncology social work clinician and consultant, facilitated online groups in the program for 13 years.

Initially, the groups were held in bulletin board format and provided online support to people with cancer and cancer caregivers. All online groups were facilitated by staff social workers. The focus of these online cancer support groups was to enable participants to cope more effectively with illness by discussing concerns, gaining emotional support, and finding appropriate emotional and practical resources.

Information about the groups was posted on the agency's website. Applicants completed and sent email registration forms in order to be considered for an appropriate online group. Bulletin board groups were limited to 12 members. Participants completed an online questionnaire, which included demographics; information on their cancer experience, treatment, support system, and reasons for joining the group; and a Brief Symptom Inventory (BSI) (Derogatis & Melisaratos, 1983) that assessed psychosocial distress. Participants were required to commit to participating for three months and to participate/post at least three times a week. Although the groups were designed to be 12 weeks in duration to emulate time-limited f2f groups, one of the online groups continued for one and a half years. After several years the groups were also offered in listserv format and participation was increased to 25 members per group.

As an initial screening tool, the BSI was used pre- and postgroup to assess the effectiveness of the groups. At that time, informal data analyses of the inventory indicated that participants' psychosocial distress, especially anxiety and depression, lessened over the span of the group. The members enjoyed the ease of participation (via both bulletin board and listserv), but felt limited by the early technology, which prevented topics from being well-organized or archived. Overall, participants in those early groups found the online group experience to be a positive one.

Over the last 13 years, there have been many changes made to CancerCare's online program to best serve clients who prefer to receive support group services online. In 1997, three staff social workers each facilitated a group available to people living with cancer, their caregivers, and other family members and friends. There were not as many people online then, so it was more difficult to gather group members. In 2000 and 2001, open forums were offered.

In addition to time-limited groups, CancerCare offered informal, drop-in forums that were designed to provide an immediate response to clients' informational and support needs. Three groups were initially provided: patients, caregivers, and the bereaved. Clients registered for CancerCare's virtual community and then quickly entered the group that best met their needs. Groups were moderated by a staff social worker but did not require intensive screening or commitment. The size of the group was not limited. These support groups were more difficult to facilitate because members could come and go as needed, which resulted in lack of stable membership and commitment, making it difficult for members to connect with one another. There were no beginning, middle, and end phases to each group. In 2006, open forums were discontinued (an archive of some of the groups remains at http://supportgroups.cancercare.org/index.php/board,82.0.html as read-only forums to introduce potential group members to the format and content of CancerCare's online groups).

The organization has more clients using its online services and now offers approximately 30 different online groups to patients, family members/friends, and the bereaved. The groups are available to many different kinds of clients: people with any kind of cancer; people who are lesbian, gay, bisexual, or transgender; caregivers and the bereaved; people with specific cancers (lung, gynecologic, colorectal, blood, and other cancers); age groups (young adults 20−40); relationships (partners' bereavement group, teen caregivers); and cancer survivors who are post-treatment. Many groups have approximately 30 members.

The organization currently offers its online groups on a trimester basis. After many years of running online support groups, the social workers have found that time-limited groups are the most effective and that there are clinical benefits to having beginning, middle, and end phases. Time-limited groups enable members to participate in all phases of the group process and provide an opportunity for reflection. An important aspect of a planned break in the group schedule is that the organization is then able to streamline the administration of the online groups to provide the most effective service to its clients.

The American Pain Foundation (APF) also saw the value of providing support services online early in its development. The APF was founded in 1997 to serve people with pain through information, advocacy, and support, and since its inception in 1997 has used technology as an effective means to reach its consumers. It provides a consumer-focused website, online pain resource locator service and pain clinical trials center, email information service, toll-free telephone number for information services, monthly electronic communications, and, with Colón's help, an online support community called PainAid (http://painaid.painfoundation.org/). The APF has combined the technological strengths of its website with the interpersonal value of group support and created a comprehensive, moderated, online group program for people affected by pain.

PainAid was launched in 2002; its mission is to provide those who live with chronic pain with a "home base" where they can reduce isolation and connect with others; gain support from others in similar situations; share information and experiences; learn about the wide variety of available pain treatments; get questions answered; learn how to deal with related physical, emotional, and financial problems; and dispel myths and fears − all in a quality-controlled environment moderated by trained staff. Anyone is eligible to participate in PainAid: people with pain, caregivers/loved ones, and health care professionals. Visitors who want to join PainAid must first complete a simple registration form requiring a user name and password of their choice and agree to adhere to a set of common-sense guidelines (e.g., conversation and ideas are to be maintained in an atmosphere of mutual respect and appreciation of differences; advertisements, personal solicitations, "shouting," obscene language, and X-rated content are expressly prohibited). PainAid members are not required to provide unique identifying or demographic information. They can explore, learn, and interact with others in the PainAid community through text-based discussion boards and live chats.

PainAid offers over 100 moderated discussion boards on an array of pain-related topics and up to 10 scheduled chat sessions per week, all open to any PainAid user. Twenty volunteers, all chronic pain patients and health care professionals, manage and monitor all of the discussions and chats.

PainAid's chat rooms provide real-time opportunities to interact and learn about the issues that affect many people with chronic pain. Each week, scheduled chats focus on a specific topic or subject relevant to a broad range of patients, including coping skills, effective communication with a doctor or health care team, depression, anxiety, medications, pain-related legal issues, and complementary treatments. On occasion, there is a special-topic chat with a guest speaker.

PainAid's discussion boards typically focus on a single well-defined topic and provide a simple place where a user can go to ask a question, post an item of useful information, or simply engage in an informative and supportive conversation with others interested in the same topic. The Ask-the-Expert section is moderated by six licensed health and mental health professionals, all with strong backgrounds in pain management, who have volunteered to answer individual consumers' questions. The experts provide only general information, offering self-advocacy skills and identifying additional resources a consumer may use for specific advice or assistance.

ONLINE VERSUS FACE-TO-FACE (F2F) THERAPY

Online therapy and support groups have similar "curative factors" to those noted by Yalom (2005) in f2f groups, including a sense of belonging and acceptance, a willingness and need to disclose personal information, honesty about feelings toward oneself and other members, interest in and acceptance of others, good will and support of the group, personal importance, a sense of stability, and hope for its members. The basic tenets put forth by Yalom for f2f groups also appear to factor into online groups:

- Instillation of hope
- Universality
- Altruism
- The corrective recapitulation of the primary family group
- Development of socializing technique – imitative behavior
- Interpersonal learning
- Group cohesiveness
- Catharsis
- Existential factors

Online group therapy is best viewed as a part of a continuum of therapeutic services. It may serve as an adjunct to f2f therapy. A therapist may, for example, have a client visit a group online to explore issues dealt with in traditional therapy. The use of such groups as an adjunct to traditional therapy is set forth, and examples often are given of the ability to connect peers with rare disorders, for which no in-person self-help exists. Members of online groups seek to get the most out of their experiences. They also support other members of the group, feeling that, as part of the whole, they are tied to the outcome of the entire group.

Online therapy groups also may provide an entrée into more traditional f2f therapy. A client who is not ready to visit a therapist may begin with an online experience and then proceed to office-based therapy, after he or she has become comfortable with the process. Online group therapy may also be primary. While therapy groups are usually held in person at a designated place and time, there are people who could benefit from a traditional group but are unable to attend. They may be people who live in rural areas with few support services, medically ill patients who are homebound or debilitated by treatment, or caregivers who have significant demands on their time. The Internet has had the eternal advantage of bringing people together while allowing them to remain in their homes or other comfortable locations. Online group therapy offers a practical, cost-effective option for psychological support. It maintains privacy and serves to diminish social isolation, anxiety, and depression. Many online groups provide an environment in which strong alliances and helpful relationships are formed.

Although technology and program delivery have grown tremendously, the issues and feelings that are discussed in online groups seem to remain the same over time. Online groups provide a safe place in which to talk about thoughts, feelings, fears, and concerns as they relate to group members' experiences and concerns. Group members are very open to talking about their experiences and feelings, and feel fortunate to have the opportunity to be with others (without having to leave their homes) who are going through similar situations.

Group members often disclose that they feel like they cannot openly talk about how they are feeling with their family members and friends. Many feel that they do not want to burden their loved ones and/or feel that their family members and friends just do not understand what they may be going through. For example, issues that are brought up in support or therapy groups focus on support for those with a chronic illness and may include profound explorations of mortality, pain, sadness, independence versus autonomy, financial stress, exhaustion, vulnerability, crying, expression or suppression of anger and other difficult feelings, communicating with one's children, finding information on the illness or clinical trials, and waiting for test/scan results.

Relative anonymity is pervasive in online group interactions as well as one-on-one encounters. This effect dramatically alters the interpersonal environment by making it feel safe to disclose deep personal feelings without fear of being judged or held accountable. Social distance, the disconnection between specific behaviors such as offline and online interactions, may encourage people to be more self-revealing when they are in online groups. The protection of anonymity and social distance may also trigger disinhibited behavior as a result of the perception that behavior that is normally controlled or edited has no consequences in the online environment. The hallmark of the disinhibition effect is the willingness of people to say and do things in cyberspace they would never say or do in the f2f world.

Sitting at a computer in a protected, private world, one is able to focus more closely on inner feelings without being overpowered by the ego's need to look good to its peers. This allows personal feelings to be perceived more intensely and, accompanied by online disinhibition, enhances the expression of content that might not ordinarily be shared. The perception of safety is something people are keenly aware of and is often stated as a reason people are willing to be more open in online groups.

Projective mechanisms seen in traditional online groups, where visual and auditory cues are lacking, may be more powerful than in f2f groups. In the online group, one participant creates an image of another participant tailored to fulfill his or her unconscious emotional needs or to manage unacceptable feelings by attributing them to another. Projections can dramatically increase the positive or negative perception of others in the online group setting. Positive perceptions may result in clients displaying overly positive behavior, deferential attitudes, and showing excessive generosity. Clients may form deep relationships very quickly. This may be dangerous for the more vulnerable client who has problems setting personal boundaries. Negative projections may be reduced in highly structured groups but must be managed by the therapist in order to maintain cohesiveness in the group.

A wider range of emotional interactions are observed in online process groups than in the more structured, subject-focused groups. The impact on psychological behavior appears to be the most positive in groups where issues are mediated by the presence of a therapist and where group norms discourage negative responses.

The presence or absence of a group member in an f2f setting is obvious, even when those present are not actively participating in the conversation. Members in online groups must be cognizant that, while they may enter and exit a group unnoticed, they have a responsibility to tell other group participants that they are present. The group dynamic is affected by all members, whether they are taking an active or passive role. Even in groups where the presence of members is noted on the screen, acknowledging one's presence, and even one's reason for leave-taking, is important to other group members.

Similarly, when a member decides to leave an online group perma-nently, letting others know not only when they plan to leave but also why they are leaving is important to the overall progress of the group. Groups where members just disappear may have a feeling of unfinished business or even a feeling of uneasiness about the sudden departure of a group member, who may have become emotionally important to the group. Paradoxically, for both therapist and client, involvement in an online group surmounts geographical and other physical barriers; as long as there is an Internet connection, they may participate from any-where at any time.

Conflict

Conflict can occur in any type of group therapy, but it is not inevitable. Conflicts in text-based online therapy may occur for many reasons, but can be due to miscommunication due to lack of verbal tone and visual clues. Conflicts arise when members are not feeling safe. Having a pro-fessional moderated group helps to alleviate group conflict. When there is a conflict, it is critical for the therapist to be more visibly present in the group, not only when the conflict is occurring but also in other con-current discussions. Conflicts require that the therapist maintain neutral-ity, clarify what has been said, elicit more information about the conflict, and mediate between the participants. In some cases, the con-flict can be moved to a private area (e.g., a designated discussion board or chat room) in order for the original discussion to continue. This strat-egy is especially useful in online groups, where members can easily absent themselves from the conversation when uncomfortable feelings are stirred. Groups also can quickly lose their focus when disruptive behavior becomes contagious. Disinhibition may be a factor when mem-bers react with intense hostility to perceived affronts. Clear guidelines are necessary in order to help group members to understand how to appropriately work through conflict. Once the conflict has been resolved, there is an opportunity for the therapist to open a discussion about handling anger and conflict in daily lives. Ultimately, it is the responsibility of the therapist to deal effectively with conflict, providing a level of comfort and safety to group members that will ensure their continuing participation.

Group Dynamics

Over the past several years, group members have seemed to be much more comfortable sharing their personal information. They often share their first names (not just their user names) and sometimes their last names. They also share the cities and towns in which they live. This is most likely due to the fact that online use and services are a part of most people's day-to-day lives and increasing numbers of individuals are involved in less-formal social networking communities in which the sharing of information is encouraged and even expected. Group members may set up or share a photo-sharing site for the group if one is not included. Members of some of the CancerCare online groups were able to post their pictures as well as view photos of other members through a password-protected site. This was optional and most group members participated. Sharing photographs seemed to create additional bonding between group members.

Client Responses to Online Therapy

Client reactions to online group therapy have been similar to those of f2f groups with regard to pacing, self-disclosure, bonding, conflict, and transitions. However, participating in online therapy requires that clients have a minimal level of computer literacy. Therapists must have an optimal level of skill in order to provide safe and confidential services online and handle any technological contingency. Online therapists and clients must write reasonably well and express themselves effectively (Rochlen et al., 2004). However, our experience has been that the level of sophistication in our groups has remained high over the years. Group members write very well and are able to express themselves without any difficulty. Members are also very computer-savvy and there are very few instances when a group member needs help with accessing/using the group. In fact, the most frequent help requested by PainAid members is to be reminded of their user names and passwords; those with pain often have difficulty with concentration and memory due to their pain conditions, medications, or associated anxiety. Advances in technology have helped PainAid's groups to run better with little to no technical interruptions.

PainAid groups have no beginning or end; members are able to join through "rolling admissions" and may participate as much or as little as they wish in both chats and discussion boards. An email address is publically posted so that members can ask for individual help with any technical issues at any time, but otherwise they use the groups to get support or discuss their concerns. There is no screening process by PainAid moderators; the community regulates itself and moderators review all posts, deleting any that are grossly inappropriate and otherwise facilitating discussions so that accurate information and helpful support are shared. CancerCare does have a screening process for its time-limited groups, which the staff facilitators have found helpful. There are structured breaks in the groups and group members are encouraged to share email addresses with each other before each group ends. Group members are provided with a contact at the organization along with a toll-free telephone number should they need support while the group is on break. Over the years, more and more group members have shared their disappointments and frustrations with their online support group taking a break. Many do not remember reading about the group's end date in the Welcome folder when they first joined.

Members have raised their difficulties in dealing with large groups featuring active ongoing posting strings; it can be difficult to read so much and keep track of everyone's names and situations. When this occurs, the facilitators invite group members to talk about this further and have validated members' feelings, which they have found to be helpful.

The Role of the Online Therapist

As in an f2f group, the online facilitator shapes the group and sets the tone for the discussion. As mentioned above, the facilitator must also make decisions on the communication pathways to be used as well as the technologies employed. Good writing skills are necessary to communicate not only content but also tone and mood, which will set the standard for the group. An atmosphere of trust and comfort must also be conveyed in writing. Most group members do not often seek out the therapist's thoughts or opinions. Establishing and maintaining a leadership style and providing guidelines are important in keeping the group on track. These include validating members' feelings, asking clarifying questions, providing interpretations of behaviors, and mediating any conflicts.

Understanding when to intervene during conflict and how to diffuse anger is also essential. The facilitator must be comfortable enough with conflict to deal with it and not to take attacks personally. Those experienced in running f2f groups will find the transition to online groups relatively easy, although conversion of verbal communication into the written word may take practice and patience.

In text-based online groups, the therapist and group members do not have the visual or verbal cues that are present in f2f groups. The therapist must "listen" in a different way, by paying close attention to language, the ways in which group members write, and the ways in which they express themselves when they are feeling well versus when they are feeling ill or upset. The therapist must be more active and sometimes more directive in the group to make up for the lack of eye contact and body language. If the therapist does not send messages to the group on a regular basis, he or she is considered to be "absent" from the group. The biggest challenge faced by an online group therapist is the text-based nature of the group environment. The written word, in or out of the context of group communication, can be stark and direct. Humor and sarcasm can be misinterpreted easily and feelings can be hurt. In these situations, the therapist must be a strong presence, with the text-based skills to mediate and guide the group through conflict.

Therapists who have worked in an online setting can be surprised at how much and how quickly they can learn about clients through the written word. Emotions and feelings become easily recognizable. The therapist can often discern when a client is ill, intoxicated, or depressed, and may even uncover untruths by "reading between the lines." Therapists have discovered that levels of intimacy and trust may be greater because participants feel more comfortable disclosing and discussing their most intimate concerns. In asynchronous communications, clients are able to give time and thought to their writings, which leads to richer and more meaningful responses.

Facilitators of online groups must decide how much time they will devote to the group. The posts in large groups operating on a 24/7 schedule may prove too numerous to read and evaluate.

After a decade of experience, many therapists believe that it is important to consider the size of the group before a venue is chosen. Chat groups ideally should be small because of the potential to have multiple conversations occurring at once. Having too many chat participants may prevent the group from achieving any depth of focus. A discussion board group can accommodate larger numbers of participants if organized logically and well; a high number of posts can leave many feeling overwhelmed. An email group appears to accommodate higher numbers of participants without losing intimacy and connection.

Online facilitators also have the role of consultant and gatekeeper. It is the facilitator who decides which of the online technologies will be employed and in what context and combination. It is also the facilitator who can approve or deny admittance to new members, remove disruptive or dangerous members, and keep track of active members and conversations. As technology continues to evolve, the facilitator will need to take an active part in making sure that the group evolves with it. Therapists considering opening an online group must have the level of expertise and competency necessary for these tasks.

Program Design

As with f2f groups, the design of the group must be carefully considered (this process is reviewed in greater detail in Chapter 11). The purpose of the group must be elucidated and the appropriateness of the group for each client must be addressed. Potential clients need to be carefully screened in order to identify fragile or at-risk individuals. Group members must be assessed for mood disorders, suicidal ideation, and previous suicide attempts in order to determine whether a particular online group would be of benefit to them; they can be referred to other resources as needed. For text-based programs, reading, writing, and comprehension skills must be assessed. The following questions must be answered in order to create an online group:

- Will this be a heterogeneous or homogeneous group?
- Will it be a support group, discussion group, or therapy group?
- Will the group be an open-membership or closed group?
- What technology/delivery systems will be used?
- How many members will participate in a given group?
- Will members be screened for admission to the group?
- What is expected of the therapist/facilitator?
- What schedule will be used for synchronous groups?
- Will this be a time-limited or open-ended group?
- What commitment is expected of group members?
- Will group members be asked to sign membership forms and disclaimers?
- What is the fee schedule? How will the group be funded?

Additionally, policies and procedures must be addressed and published, including those pertaining to group norms and guidelines, confidentiality and safety, conflict management, group member and therapist accountability, and parameters of participation. Assumptions about cultural differences and any language barriers must be considered.

Program Delivery

There is enormous diversity in the range of online group therapy options available, and the format depends on selection criteria, degree of structure, leader expertise, and communication pathway chosen. While synchronous and asynchronous text-based groups are the most common online therapeutic venues, videoconferencing and other multimedia experiences are becoming popular, especially as the cost of broadband decreases. As technology progresses and the technical expertise of therapists and clients increases, novel approaches are inevitable. Group forums can easily include video, sound, and graphics along with text. They promote active participation by members and allow for individualized experiences and a self-paced process. Members' choices and preferences can also affect the process.

Some of the delivery modes available to the online group counselor today include:

- Group chat rooms
- Message/bulletin boards
- Email
- Listservs
- Webcam/videoconferencing

Therapists have the option of using one of the above options or combining them to deliver a richer, more beneficial program to clients. There are also online assessment tools available, which can be used to match clients to the mode of program delivery and to assess the viability of the therapy as it progresses. Therapists will also have to develop new assessment tools to clarify which online environments work best for specific client needs.

Technology

Professionals interested in conducting therapy in cyberspace must be familiar with the various formats available to them. They must have the technical knowledge to install and operate hardware and software. They must also understand how clients may be using technology to address their health and mental health needs. Therapists must also educate themselves on the computer basics necessary for facilitating online groups, including troubleshooting certain technical problems; editing, saving, and deleting messages; and ensuring privacy and confidentiality. Consultation with Internet experts who can explain current and emerging technologies is also important for therapists interested in maintaining a viable online clientele.

An example of one of the newer technologies being employed is videoconferencing. Previously, cost and technical difficulties prohibited its use as a medium for therapy. Now, however, webcams may be built into computer systems or available as a peripheral device for minimal cost. Video software is likewise easily available and inexpensive. Videoconferencing allows the group leader to be visible to all members of the group, allows members to speak directly to one another, and also allows the use of concurrent text-based communications. As broadband connections become more and more affordable, counselors and clients are able to easily connect through a variety of simultaneous applications. Multimedia presentations, such as video clips and slide presentations, also serve to dramatically enrich the experience of therapeutic groups on the Internet.

Videoconferencing allows the presentation of a format for group treatment that closely emulates traditional groups. Verbal interactions, even the ability to have more than one person talk at a time, resemble f2f groups. A striking feature of this approach is the impact of having the counselor's face visible throughout the group process, which seems to significantly enhance group cohesiveness and individual commitment to the group. Clients often report that they have a sense of the direct presence of the counselor, as if the counselor is in the room with them. This personalizes the online group experience and clients feel emotionally connected with the counselor. Even at low bandwidths, the appearance of the counselor's image is powerful.

Counselors choosing this mode of therapy delivery will have to develop a professional on-screen persona, learn to talk directly to the camera, and remain aware of the level of participation of each group member while simultaneously reviewing private messages and other activities by group members. They must also remain aware of staying with the group's agenda while facilitating spontaneous discussion.

Confidentiality

While confidentiality of the group members must be scrupulously maintained, it is necessary for the group leader to have the information needed to ensure that there is a proper "fit" between each participant and the group. While most groups use "handles" or screen names during group sessions, it is necessary for the therapist to maintain an accurate list of the real identities of the participants. In many cases, identification will include names, addresses, phone numbers, and as any clinical diagnoses or other information pertinent to participation in the group. In some cases, information such as credit card numbers and social security numbers may also be required. If any personal information will be shared (e.g., with other therapists, a webmaster, or credit card company), this must be authorized by the client. The therapist should also be familiar with the confidentiality policies of those with whom client information will be shared. Mental health and other licensed professionals are legally and ethically required to report clients who may harm themselves or others. To help clients understand in advance how reportable issues will be handled, they should be asked to read and accept a description of behaviors that will be reported. It must be explained that confidentiality will be broken if a client is determined to be a danger to himself or to others.

Security

In all groups, secure communication is a concern. Two important aspects of security are the privacy of the group environment (is it password-protected and do members have handles, user names, or screen names?) and the level of security regarding what is being shared by group members (are group interactions encrypted?). Consultation with an expert in Internet security may aid in deciding how much security is available, necessary, and affordable, as high levels of security may no longer be cost-prohibitive for therapists in private practice.

Due to the perceived anonymity of text-based communication, group members may need to be reminded that they are interacting with real people and that they are accountable for their actions, not only toward the group but also toward the therapist. Group rules and norms must be explicitly spelled out and remedies for disruptive behavior explained. For severe infractions, a removal policy should also be in place and employed when necessary. The leader must have an adequate tracking system and be aware of each member's real name, password, and screen name. This is especially important when it is possible for participants to leave the group, only to return using a different screen name.

CONCLUSION

Over the past 20 years, computer-mediated interpersonal communication has evolved significantly. The Internet has increasingly become more user-friendly and a more powerful tool for information exchange, communication, and connection. Although the Internet can now be seen as an integral part of everyday life, providing many opportunities for communication, education, connection, and support, those opportunities are not without risk. Technology has provided psychotherapists with the ability to reach people who, not so long ago, would have had no opportunity for psychotherapy. For example, even in rural areas, people with Internet access have the ability to join online groups dealing with very specific and focused issues. As new technologies emerge and people become more comfortable with online activities, it is clear that the delivery of health care in general, and mental health care in particular, will be shaped by this technology.

Therapists willing to take the time to become familiar with the technology currently available, and willing to keep abreast of future developments, will be at the forefront of a very satisfying and valuable means of providing group therapy.

DISCUSSION QUESTIONS

1. What are the differences between an online group and an f2f group?
2. What are the important factors in designing an online group?
3. What contributes to group members being willing to be more self-disclosing online?
4. What are the main factors that contribute to the "disinhibiting effect"?
5. What is the role of the psychotherapist in facilitating an online group?
6. What kinds of online behavior are ameliorated by the presence of the therapist?

KEY TERMS

Asynchronous groups Online groups in which participants post responses at any time.

Broadband Telecommunication in which a wide band of frequencies is available to transmit information; the higher the broadband, the faster the Internet connection.

Bulletin board/discussion board A website in which participants can read and write messages at any time, which then can be read by any other participant. The messages remain for the duration of the group, posted sequentially and usually organized by topic.

Chat group/chat room A real-time exchange in which everyone is at his or her computer at the same time, using a program or system that allows what is typed by one participant to be viewed by all the others.

Listserv/mailing list A private email group in which each subscriber receives a separate email of each message that is posted. Through these messages members can maintain ongoing communication with other list members, who share a common interest or concern.

Process groups Groups in which spontaneous interactions occur; these may become the focus of groups without a fixed educational agenda and where the leader takes an observational role.

Projective mechanisms Unconscious perceptions that color how others are perceived.

Social networking A web-based process that focuses on building social relationships among people who share interests or activities. A social network site usually consists of a profile or representation of each user, his or her social links, and a variety of additional features, and provides ways for users to interact over the Internet, such as email and instant messaging.

Synchronous groups Groups that meet during a specified time period.

Text-based groups Online groups based on written text messages; the groups can be synchronous or asynchronous.

Videoconferencing Programs that allow the counselor and others to be streamed onto part of the computer monitor screen so clients can see them when they talk, much like a remote television news reporter.

REFERENCES

Barak, A. & Wander-Schwartz, M. (1999). Empirical evaluation of brief group therapy through an Internet chat room. Retrieved April 2, 2010 from http://construct.haifa.ac.il/~azy/cherapy.htm

Childress, C. (1998). Potential risks and benefits of online psychotherapeutic interventions. Retrieved March 20, 2010 from http://www.ismho.org/potential_risks_and_benefits.asp

Childress, C. A. (2000). Ethical issues in providing online psychotherapeutic interventions. *Journal of Medical Internet Research, 2*(1), e5.

Colón, Y., & Friedman, B. (2003). E-therapy in group practice. In S. Goss, & K. Anthony (Eds.), *Technology in counselling and psychotherapy: A practitioners' guide* (pp. 59–74). Basingstoke, UK: Palgrave Macmillan.

Colón, Y. (1996). Telephone support groups: A nontraditional approach to reaching underserved cancer patients. *Cancer Practice: A Multidisciplinary Journal of Cancer Care, 4*(3), 156–159.

Derogatis, L. R., & Melisaratos, N. (1983). The brief symptom inventory: An introductory report. *Psychological Medicine, 13,* 595–605.

Eysenbach, G., Powell, J., Englesakis, M., Rizo, C., & Stern, A. (2004). Health related virtual communities and electronic support groups: A systematic review of the effects of online peer to peer interactions. *British Journal of Medicine, 328*(7449), 1166–1172.

Finn, J., & Lavitt, M. (1994). Computer-based self-help groups for sexual abuse survivors. *Social Work with Groups, 17,* 21–46.

Fox, S. & Purcell, K. (2010). Chronic disease and the Internet. Retrieved March 20, 2010 from http://pewinternet.org/Reports/2010/Chronic-Disease.aspx

Griffiths, K. M., Calear, A. L., & Banfield, M. (2009). Systematic review on Internet support groups (ISGs) and depression (1): Do ISGs reduce depressive symptoms? *Journal of Medical Internet Research, 11*(3), e40.

Hafner, K., & Lyon, M. (1996). *Where wizards stay up late: The origins of the Internet.* New York, NY: Touchstone Books.

Horrigan, J. B. & Rainie, L. (2002). Counting on the Internet. Retrieved February 16, 2003 from http://www.pewinternet.org/reports/pdfs/PIP_Expectations.pdf

Horrigan, J. B. & Rainie, L. (2005). A decade of adoption: How the Internet has woven itself into American life. Retrieved April 3, 2010 from http://www.pewinternet.org/Reports/2005/How-the-internet–has-woven-itself-into-American-life.aspx

Humphreys, K., Winzelberg, A., & Klaw, E. (2000). Psychologists' ethical responsibilities in Internet-based groups: Issues, strategies, and a call for dialogue. *Professional Psychology: Research and Practice, 31*(5), 493–496.

Kehoe, B. (1995). *Zen and the art of the Internet* (4th ed.). Upper Saddle River, NJ: Prentice Hall.

King, S. A., & Moreggi, D. (1998). Internet therapy and self help groups – The pros and cons. In J. Gackenbach (Ed.), *Psychology and the Internet: Intrapersonal, interpersonal and transpersonal implications* (pp. 77–109). San Diego, CA: Academic Press.

Markoff, J. (2007, January 7). Attack of the zombie computers is growing threat. *New York Times.* Retrieved April 20, 2010 from http://www.nytimes.com/2007/01/07/technology/07net.html

Meier, A. (1997). Inventing new models of social support groups: A feasibility study of an online stress management support group for social workers. *Social Work With Groups, 20*(4), 35–53.

Rochlen, A. B., Zack, J. S., & Speyer, C. (2004). Online therapy: Review of relevant definitions, debates, and current empirical support. *Journal of Clinical Psychology, 60,* 269–283.

Suler, J. (1999). Psychotherapy in cyberspace. Retrieved March 19, 2010 from http://www.rider.edu/users/suler/psycyber/therapy.html

Weinberg, N., Schmale, J., Ukan, J., & Wessel, K. (1995). Computer-mediated support groups. *Social Work with Groups, 17*(4), 43–54.

Yalom, I. D. (2005). *The theory and practice of group psychotherapy* (5th ed). New York, NY: Basic Books.

Chapter eleven

Clinical Work with Support Groups Online: Practical Aspects

Elizabeth A Pector, MD
Spectrum Family Medicine, SC, Naperville, IL
Robert C Hsiung, MD
Founder, dr-bob.org and psychiatrist in private practice, Chicago, IL, USA

CHAPTER OUTLINE

Online Counseling. DOI: 10.1016/B978-0-12-378596-1.00011-3

In Chapter 10, Colón and Stern clearly explain many aspects of work with online groups. Peer support groups share many similarities with online therapy groups, with some important differences. The present chapter narrows the focus to online self-help groups. Following a review of demographic, therapeutic, and interpersonal factors of online peer groups, we discuss the benefits and risks of online self-help communities. Next is a survey of the practical aspects of establishing, promoting, and ending groups. Attention then turns to the moderator's role in developing guidelines, facilitating discussion, and addressing dysfunctional group dynamics. Observations about the future of peer support online conclude the chapter. Some resources for the location of groups and for coping with conflict in online forums are provided.

THE DEMOGRAPHICS OF PEER SUPPORT

A significant minority of Internet users participate in online support groups. By 2003, 70 to 90 percent of Internet had users searched for health information, with 9 to 54 percent of health-searchers in different nations visiting online support or advocacy sites (Fox & Fallows, 2003; Lieberman & Russo, 1999–2000; Taylor & Leitman, 2002). A 2006 survey indicated that 12 percent of all Internet users in the US have participated in – rather than just searched for – online support groups for a personal or health problem (Fox, 2007). With recent US Census Bureau data showing over a threefold rise in the number of Americans online – from 18 percent in 1997 to 64 percent in 2007 (Edwards, 2009) – and a 2009 estimate of 1.7 billion world Internet users (World Internet Use and Population Statistics, 2009), one may infer that an increasing number of people in many countries are using online peer support. The authors have observed more lower-literacy and non-English speakers using online forums in the last decade.

A vast array of forums welcomes these online support seekers. Usenet has hosted discussion groups for health and psychological concerns since the 1980s (Holmes, 2010). As of February 2010, there were more than 98 000 Yahoo! groups listed for health and wellness issues. Topica and Google Groups list hundreds of additional groups in mental health, substance use, and disease categories. The American Self-Help Group Clearinghouse maintains a database of over a thousand support groups, many of them online. Many nonprofit organizations have online support forums, some accessible by the general public and others available only to members.

Online groups have been the most abundant for stressful, stigmatizing, disfiguring, debilitating, rare, and poorly understood conditions (Davison et al., 2000; White & Dorman, 2001). For example, groups for people with breast cancer, a frequently disfiguring illness, far outnumber groups that deal with coronary heart disease, despite the higher mortality rate of heart disease (Davison et al., 2000). People who are more depressed than average may be more likely to seek online support (Fox,

2007; Houston et al., 2002; Klemm & Hardie, 2002). Patients with stigmatizing conditions such as acquired immune deficiency syndrome (AIDS), alcoholism, anorexia nervosa, cancer, depression, and diabetes find abundant group support, while there are fewer groups for other lethal or painful disorders such as emphysema, arthritis, or migraine (Davison et al., 2000). For some conditions, such as alcoholism, individuals may prefer f2f support. Online alcoholism groups are less prevalent than f2f equivalents (Davison et al., 2000).

THEORETICAL AND THERAPEUTIC CONSIDERATIONS

Familiarity with f2f group process will help online group moderators promote benefits and anticipate problems (Yalom & Leszcz, 2005). Empirical theories such as Yalom's therapeutic factors and Tuckman's stages of group development are relevant in the online milieu.

As detailed in Chapter 10, online group process incorporates many therapeutic factors described by Yalom (Fox, 2007; Gary & Remolino, 2002; Lieberman et al., 2003; Yalom & Leszcz, 2005), thus fostering a sense of personal empowerment and control (Barak et al., 2008). The discovery that "there are others like me" on the Internet may be described as incredible and life-changing, providing a sense of community for people who struggle with misunderstood conditions such as zoophilia (Miletski, 2002). Some groups are more factual than emotional in tone. The tone and style of a group is influenced by the group topic and format, posts of moderators, participant reasons for involvement, and single-sex versus mixed-gender composition of the group (Klemm et al., 1999; Mo et al., 2009; Preece & Ghozati, 1998).

Tuckman's stages of group progression — "forming," "storming," "norming," and "performing" — apply to both therapeutic and work groups in f2f settings (Tuckman, 2001). These stages also occur in online groups. Newly convened, closed groups typically go through a "forming" period for members to get acquainted. This is followed by debate ("storming") about the group's purpose and work process, establishment of rules ("norming") to govern the group, and finally work ("performing") to achieve the group's goals. Group leaders need to be fairly directive early in a new group's existence. Gradually, as the group becomes more cohesive through conflict, compromise, and consensus, the leader can adopt a more passive, advisory role. Groups may regress as well as progress, and not all reach the "performing" stage. "Transforming" — or, in Tuckman's original model, "adjourning" — involves redefining the group's purpose and/or bringing the group to a close.

The invisible coming and going of group members and the presence of lurkers may lead to a less cohesive experience in open-ended groups online (Barak et al., 2008). "Lurking," or reading without posting, is reported by 75–95 percent of members in some groups (Finfgeld, 2000; White & Dorman, 2000). Lurking permits members to learn about group culture and norms before writing (White & Dorman, 2001). Lurkers report learning and experience a sense of community despite not actively participating (Preece, 1999; van Uden-Kraan et al., 2008). However, some evidence suggests that greater benefits accrue to more active participants (Cummings et al., 2002; van Uden-Kraan et al., 2008).

One important difference between self-help communities and professional group therapy is that self-help members voluntarily seek support and may not screen themselves for depression, suicidality, or other mental health problems. There is little to no prescreening of members to determine the suitability of group support for them (Barak et al., 2008). Anyone who forms or moderates a peer group will thus need to be vigilant for signs of problems. Fortunately, Pector's survey (2009) of online group moderators indicated that disturbing posts from people with substance abuse or mental health disorders were less worrisome than episodes of purposeful deception or disruption. Deceptive and disruptive behaviors may, of course, be associated with mental health disorders.

Another important difference is that there may be limited or absent leadership in peer groups. Many leaders do not have training in mental health or group facilitation (Gary & Remolino, 2002), although unofficial leaders often emerge, with skills similar to those of trained moderators (Lieberman & Russo, 1999–2000). Most importantly, peer groups generally focus on supporting existing coping mechanisms and psychological defenses, whereas therapy groups aim to effect change in emotion, thought, or action. This is a major difference between peer groups and therapy groups, and neither is a substitute for the other (Barak et al., 2008).

Online and f2f support may complement each other. Some groups combine f2f meetings with online support (Cummings et al., 2002). Online groups may help those needing more support between f2f meetings (White & Dorman, 2001) or when illness or caregiving responsibilities prevent attendance at f2f meetings. An online group may be a step toward a f2f group or professional treatment. One study indicated that people with hearing disorders experienced greater benefits when their real-world significant others joined their hearing-impaired online support group (Cummings et al., 2002).

INTERPERSONAL FACTORS IN ONLINE PEER GROUPS

The disinhibiting effect of anonymity is a two-edged sword. On the positive side, anonymity accelerates trust and intimacy (Barak et al., 2008). Hidden identity also facilitates discussion of sensitive topics such as sexuality (Miletski, 2002; Wolfradt & Doll, 2001), ethical controversies (Casey & Hardy, 1998), and suicide (Baume et al., 1997; King, 1995; Miller & Gergen, 1998). Anonymity expands support to socially ostracized individuals by concealing their atypical appearance, behavior, demographics, and communication style (White & Dorman, 2001). On the other side of the sword, anonymity can facilitate deception, anger, and fictitious personae (Feldman, 2004; Fox, 2007; Suler, 2007; White & Dorman, 2001). Individuals who falsely claim to have a condition may cause substantial distress to honest members in a support forum (Feldman, 2004; Finn & Banach, 2000).

About one in five group members drops out of professional therapy, and equal or greater discontinuation rates are seen in online support groups, although membership fluctuation may be invisible to users (Gary & Remolino, 2002; Lieberman et al., 2003; Miller & Gergen, 1998; Yalom & Leszcz, 2005). People who have difficulty controlling anxiety or who tend to suppress feelings about illness may be more likely to drop out (Lieberman et al., 2003).

BENEFITS AND EFFECTIVENESS OF PEER SUPPORT ONLINE

Despite the popularity of online groups, few well-designed trials have sought to quantify the medical or mental health benefits of peer support communities (Barak et al., 2008; Eysenbach et al., 2004; Griffiths et al., 2009a; Klemm et al., 2003). Many published studies are merely descriptive, or they incorporate a complex combination of peer and professional interventions. Most trials assess depression or social support instead of learning, behavior change, or quantitative health measures (Barak et al., 2008; Eysenbach et al., 2004; Griffiths et al. 2009a). Randomized or controlled trials, of variable quality, document modest but statistically significant benefits for patients with depression (Griffiths et al., 2009b), back pain (Lorig et al., 2002), breast cancer (Lieberman et al., 2003), and diabetes (Glasgow et al., 2003), among other conditions. Perceived social support and functionality may increase (Brennan, 1998; Barak et al., 2008; Glasgow et al., 2003), while depression, pain, health care utilization, isolation, and stress may decrease (Barak et al., 2008; Barrera et al., 2002; Brennan, 1998; Griffiths et al., 2009a; Lieberman et al., 2003). The major benefits of online groups are thus enhancement of a participant's sense of wellbeing, confidence, control, and social and emotional support (Barak et al., 2008).

Another advantage is the low financial cost of online support. The only significant financial outlays are for Internet access and for a computer or other device that permits Internet access. These may be free at a location such as a public library. An online group member might also incur fees to join an organization, such as a nonprofit entity dedicated to his or her health condition, that provides access to private discussion forums as a membership benefit. Thus, substantial psychosocial support can be obtained for little financial investment.

RISKS OF ONLINE GROUP SUPPORT

Empirical experience triggers concern about psychosocial harm to group participants as a result of deception, disruption, the influences of mental health disorders on self-expression, and suicide (Barak et al., 2008; Feldman, 2004; Herring et al., 2002; Hsiung, 2000; Hsiung, 2007; Pector, 2009; White & Dorman, 2001). There are reports of hurtful interactions, unhealthy advice, faking, and suicide in emerging Web 2.0 formats, especially blogs and social networking sites (Associated Press, 2007; Janssen, 2009; Peng, 2008; Schwartz, 2008).

Arguments, insults, misinterpretations, and hurt feelings may result from the tendency to "objectify" others online (Miller & Gergen, 1998; Suler, 2007). In any group setting, members may develop unwarranted optimism or fear when encountering others with more benign or more severe forms of a situation (Lieberman et al., 2003; Winzelberg et al., 2003; Yalom & Leszcz, 2005). Misinterpretations may become more common as more people of low literacy or with a non-English background become active in cyberspace. Improving online translation tools may, however, ease that transition for non-native speakers. Expressions of hostility can have especially negative consequences for vulnerable individuals (Casey & Hardy, 1998; Hollander, 2001; Hsiung, 2000).

Risks are not limited to psychosocial concerns. Since traditional medical and psychological treatments are often criticized in self-help groups, patients may delay seeking needed health care (Barak et al., 2008; Davison et al., 2000; Finfgeld, 2000). Inaccurate medical information may not be corrected by other group members (Davison et al., 2000; White & Dorman, 2001). Groups may, however, empower members to become strong readers (Heffernan, 2010). Even accurate information may cause information overload. Some groups validate and normalize practices that clinicians may consider to be disorders (Miletski, 2002; Peng, 2008). Potential breaches of anonymity and confidentiality must also be considered. Such privacy breaches may arise in the workplace and at home, and are often unrecognized or underestimated by participants (Gary & Remolino, 2002). Less commonly, identity theft, harassment, cyber stalking, and victimization may occur (Finn & Banach, 2000; Gary & Remolino, 2002).

PLANNING, STARTING, PROMOTING, AND ENDING AN ONLINE PEER GROUP

In addition to Colón and Stern's excellent advice, two classic articles explain technical and practical aspects of establishing or finding an online peer group. After useful overviews, Madara (2010) explains the creation of a Yahoo! group, while Grohol (2002) explains the institution of Usenet newsgroups and other formats. Message boards, or forums, are very popular (Barak et al., 2008). Dozens of message board systems and hosting services, both fee-based and free, are listed at http://thinko-fit.com/webconf/hostsites.htm. Facebook, other social networking sites, and blogs may function as public support forums, but they are not discussed in detail here.

As Madara and Grohol point out, there is no sense in reinventing the wheel. If a group already exists for a counselor's topic of interest, the therapist might join the existing community. However, a counselor with an innovative approach or special expertise may wish to create a new forum. When establishing a group, it is important for the founder to clearly define inclusion and exclusion criteria. Perinatal loss support is a useful example. One could offer support to mothers, fathers, siblings, grandparents, or all of the above. A group could include, or exclude, people who experience early pregnancy loss; late pregnancy loss; infant death; termination for medical or for non-medical reasons; loss following fertility treatment; death of twins; or pregnancy or parenting after a prior loss. Similar distinctions can be identified for many conditions. Some groups serve a diverse population, while others address a specific subgroup.

It is optimal for a group moderator to identify alternatives for people who do not qualify for group membership, especially in a group with narrowly defined criteria. Such individuals may benefit from peer support in another setting or from individual therapy. Some type of assistance can often be found even for rare circumstances through a careful Internet search or professional networking.

To promote a group, the founder may request a listing in a self-help group database such as the American Self-Help Group Database, Google Groups, or the National Organization for Rare Disorders. It is also worthwhile to seek reciprocal links with organizations dedicated to the situation of interest. F2f promotion at conferences related to the condition may be useful. One might also contact leaders of related groups to alert them to a new support option. Professional networking sites, therapist discussion forums, and social media offer additional opportunities to spread the news about a new group.

As members join, they should be informed of group guidelines and encouraged to post a brief introductory announcement to the group. Similarly, a farewell message is customary when a member plans to depart. Groups often go through cycles of activity and inactivity. A therapist-moderator might post a reflection or thought-provoking question to spark activity during dormant periods. If it becomes necessary or prudent for an administrator to terminate a group, it is best for the administrator to allow members to post final messages, to post a list of similar groups and non-group resources, and/or to encourage a suitable member to start a new group elsewhere. The moderator can end by summarizing positive changes that have occurred in the group.

DEFINING QUALITY IN ONLINE GROUPS

People will not remain long in a group that is inactive, abusive, or irrelevant. A healthy group has a stable core membership with some participants departing and others joining (Fox, 2007). Past studies have indicated that the tone of interaction in online groups is influenced by the quality of professional or peer moderation (Lieberman et al., 2003).

Madara (2010) describes good online groups. In brief, a potential member should seek a nonjudgmental, active, caring group whose discussions offer a sense of community and helpful support from multiple participants. The group should not have a hidden sales agenda or promotional pitch. Clear rules of participation help to minimize conflict and abuse.

A good moderator will set and enforce guidelines that ensure the online community is comfortable for as many participants as possible. Common controversies include faith and religion, end-of-life choices, health care choices, disturbing thoughts or news, and politics. Will discussions of faith, deity, or afterlife be welcomed? In a pregnancy loss group, can expectant parents mention a subsequent pregnancy? In a cancer support group, should notice of a member's relapse be flagged? In a depression support group, are mentions of suicidal thinking or suicide methods allowed, banned, or restricted?

Reintegration into society is a goal of a quality group. Speaking of grief support, but with relevance to other conditions, Hollander observed, "There is a danger in becoming too centered on grief and forgetting the remainder of life and the living. To the extent that we, as a society, isolate the grieving into pockets of exclusion we create precarious, alienated and angry subcultures" (Hollander, 2001). As noted, when compared to professional therapy groups, interpersonal learning may be limited in a cohesive forum where members do not challenge each other's opinions or stories. Indeed, some groups serve as a "pity party," endorsing rather than confronting dysfunctional attitudes and behaviors (Hollander, 2001; Madara 2010; Worotynec, 2000). For example, there are pro-anorexia groups that promote eating-disordered behavior (Peng, 2008), and support has been described for decisions to commit suicide (Baume et al., 1997; Miller & Gergen, 1998) or to leave a distressed infant crying for hours in a day care home (Worotynec, 2000). To foster an environment for improved coping, eating disorder groups may need to explicitly discourage unhealthy comparisons of self to others by forbidding mention of members' weights (Walstrom, 2000).

MODERATOR TRAINING: SUPPORT FOR SUPPORT-GROUP LEADERS

Online peer support moderators can benefit from training, since many have no professional mental health experience (Gary & Remolino,

2002). Nonprofit organizations may offer structured training for peer facilitators. Seminars are available for some types of group; for example, grief support. Many books about group facilitation are available, and an Australian pamphlet for cancer peer support facilitators has excellent guidance that could equally apply to other types of group (Commonwealth of Australia, 2009). Yalom's classic text on group psychotherapy provides an excellent background on f2f group theory and practice for the prospective moderator who lacks professional mental health training (Yalom & Leszcz, 2005).

The Australian cancer group facilitator booklet lists several qualities and skills of a competent moderator (Commonwealth of Australia, 2009). Among these are balance (between self and group); empathy (listening skills, positive attitude toward participants); flexibility and creativity (openness to new ideas, theories, and methods); impartiality (facilitator supports group agenda, not the reverse); focus on process; intuition (trust of self, group, and process); inclusivity (everyone has valuable input and can learn from others); and humor (laugh with others and at self, but not at others). A solid grounding in the basic aspects of a condition and common complicating factors is also essential.

A prospective peer moderator should assess his or her readiness to lead, preferably with the input of an objective colleague. After a health crisis or personal crisis such as bereavement, it is recommended that a prospective leader wait one to two years before assuming a moderator role. A diverse array of strong emotions, distress, and conflicts are expressed in online forums, and a moderator must have adequate self-esteem to withstand such assaults and intervene promptly and fairly. Moderator knowledge of technical aspects of group administration (approving, rejecting, disciplining, and dismissing members) is essential, unless a separate group administrator exists. In many forums, two or more co-moderators share responsibility for guiding discussion and making difficult decisions. Peer support from other moderators is invaluable. Both authors have participated in forums where moderators can discuss best practices with other group leaders.

Group welfare generally has priority over an individual's welfare (Yalom & Leszcz, 2005). Individuals with certain problems may not benefit from group support, and they may be detrimental to therapeutic process in professional therapy groups. These include people that have borderline, psychotic, or schizoid personality disorders; factitious disorder (Munchausen's syndrome); obsessive-compulsive disorder; suicidality; and refusal to get better (Feldman, 2004; Finn & Banach, 2000; Hsiung, 2000; Miller & Gergen, 1998; Sansone, 2001; Yalom & Leszcz, 2005). A respondent to Pector's 2009 survey commented that groups function better after "toxic people" depart. Prompt, progressive discipline should focus on the rule violation and not on the person.

Inflammatory labels such as "psychopath," "borderline personality," and "troll" are best avoided. Alternative care and support options should be presented to any member dismissed from a group, as well as to members who seem to warrant assistance outside the group; for example, individual counseling, professional therapy group, or f2f intervention. It should be recognized that it may be difficult to prevent dismissed members from regaining at least temporary access to the group.

An alternative to permanent dismissal is progressively longer temporary dismissals. Conflicts and negative feelings in the group are not eliminated by "shooting the messenger." Inclusiveness is an important value when stigma is an issue for group members.

GUIDE TO GROUNDRULES

Every group and its guiding principles or terms of service will be unique. The following template can be adapted for a variety of situations.

1. **Group mission statement.** Explains group purpose and philosophy, population served, and group goals. Members can share personal stories, practical and psychological coping tips, referrals to specialists, information, health research, and suggestions to help family, friends, and others understand the condition.

2. **Disclaimer.** The self-help group does not provide medical or mental health group therapy. Advice should be considered to be general and not an individually prescribed treatment plan. Readers should consult their own health professionals before acting on suggestions from group members.

3. **Resources.** Frequently asked questions (FAQs) for newbies, background information, and links to authoritative information or ongoing research trials.

4. **Anonymity, confidentiality, and access**
   a. **Anonymity.** Avatars or nicknames may/may not be used. Provision of contact information to the administrator is/is not required.
   b. **Confidentiality.** What is said in the group does/does not stay in the group.
   c. **Access restrictions.** The group is/is not limited to registered and approved members. The group can/cannot be accessed by the general Internet population.
   d. **Research, surveys, and journalists.** Administrators do/do not allow requests from researchers or journalists to study or quote the group. (Generally, research should only be approved after a moderator or administrator has reviewed the research protocol, the researcher's credentials, and evidence of institutional review board approval. Covert study is controversial and administrators

should weigh the risks and benefits of the study.) Members are aware that administrators may not be aware of covert studies.

5. **General netiquette**
   a. **Respect** guides all interactions among members.
      i. **Differences are respected** in situations, opinions, culture, lifestyle, age, race, gender, sexual orientation, partnered status, religion, politics, education, health care philosophy, and parenting style. At the same time, lines may need to be drawn. The tenets of one religion may put down the followers of another; parenting styles may be abusive; etc.
      ii. **Language or technical difficulties.** Members are patient, keeping in mind that English may not be a member's primary language and that some people may be new to the Internet.
      iii. **There are different ways to cope** with a problem. The group recognizes that most people cope the best they can, based on personal experience and resources. The forum does not advocate only one solution.
   b. **Universality.** Everyone's experiences and opinions are important. Members avoid dominating discussions and use "I" statements, not "You are" or "You should..."
   c. **Community.** Members are encouraged to post introductory and farewell messages as they join or leave the group.
   d. **Text-based communication** eliminates tone of voice, expression, and body language. A member may read a meaning the writer did not intend. Members are encouraged to clarify possible misunderstandings.
   e. **Authorship rights.** Posters own their posts. Members do not quote outside the group without permission and do not post material that violates copyright.
   f. **Alerts about sensitive topics** should be posted in subject line (examples: "religion or God mentioned"; "pregnancy mentioned" in a loss discussion group; "relapse mentioned" in a cancer group).
   g. **Negativity.** Members avoid flames, rants, spam, urban legends, and repeated "me-too" posts. The forum does not allow discrimination, personal attacks, profanity, obscenity, slander, and defamation.
6. **Members should be honest and careful**
   a. **Safety and anonymity**
      i. Members are aware that, despite authorship rights, what they write in an online forum may be forwarded or remain on the Internet indefinitely.
      ii. Members are encouraged to consider keeping their real identity, location, occupation, age, etc., private. Their privacy is more protected if they refrain from including in their

signature, or otherwise sharing, identifying information, including email addresses and links to personal web pages (Facebook profiles, blogs, etc.). Members do/do not have access to the email addresses of other members.

    iii. Honesty about feelings and health experiences is expected, even if identity is concealed.

    iv. F2f meetings, though potentially valuable, should proceed only with caution. A meeting should occur in a public place, with a trusted friend or family member accompanying the member or knowing their location.

  b. **Members provide information to confirm statements** about themselves when requested by moderators, to keep the community honest and safe. This may include personal identifying details; the moderator keeps such information as confidential as possible. Refusal to provide information that authenticates statements may result in dismissal from the group.

  c. **If members suspect dishonesty or guideline violations**, they inform a moderator off-list.

  d. **Members provide references** where possible to back up medical or mental health facts that they state.

  e. **Members correct each others' errors gently**, and again with references where possible.

7. **Members take personal disagreements off-list**

  a. Repeated unsolicited messages to a member off-list about the same topic may be considered harassment and can be reported to the moderator.

  b. The moderator is/is not available to mediate in off-list disputes.

8. **Consequences of violating these terms of use**. Violators may be subject to progressive discipline including a warning, moderator pre-approval of posts, and temporary or permanent dismissal. Dismissal may occur for serious violations without warning. Decisions made by the moderator/administrator are final.

TROLLS, FAKERS, AND TROUBLEMAKERS

In Pector's survey, support leaders and participants in online peer groups ranked trolls, fakers, and threats of harm to oneself or others as more distressing than negative expressions of members who had mental health or addiction problems (Pector, 2009). The disruptive potential of troll and faker phenomena may be unfamiliar to online counselors.

Trolls incite conflict and negativity via abusive comments or controversial statements. They may appear less interested in logical debate than in spreading disharmony. They may be motivated by boredom, anger, or a desire for attention, power, or control (Gil, 2010; Herring et al., 2002; SnowyHOST, 2006; "Troll (Internet)," 2010). The advice of most writers is, "Don't feed the troll." A troll's posts can be ignored by members or reported to moderators (SnowyHOST, 2006). Group leaders can decide to moderate (preview before approving) the posts of suspected trolls or may implement progressive discipline: temporary or permanent dismissal. The best strategy is to establish strong group guidelines, educate members about trolls, confront and discipline offenders off-list, and minimize attention to the troll's activity on-list (Herring et al., 2002; SnowyHOST, 2006).

Moderators who delete threads need to strike a balance between two extremes: prematurely deleting a disruptive thread before the members can resolve the issue themselves and keeping a hurtful thread for too long and alienating members who are seeking support but may feel hurt or at risk of retribution if they complain (M. Boyle, personal communication, March 8, 2010). Deleting threads also may cover up conflict and/or may confuse members who see threads one day and do not see them the next.

Fakers present false personae in online groups, sometimes for months or years. They may deceive several online communities at the same time. Feldman characterizes the assumption of a false identity as a disease sufferer as "Munchausen by Internet" (Feldman, 2004). Legitimate members have been known to create an additional fictitious persona in the same group. A faker may introduce a second false identity or "sockpuppet" (often presented as a family member or friend) to legitimize their first false persona (Feldman, 2004; "Troll (Internet)," 2010). Imposters' dramatic stories draw empathy, attention, and energy away from legitimate members. As with trolls, a faker's motivation may be to attract attention, act out anger, or control others. The discovery of deceit can seriously disrupt a group. Members may raise valid concerns about the group's stability and future, and they may be angry if the moderator supported a faker or troll's version of events. In the aftermath, members may leave the group, form a new group, and/or persist in denying that deception occurred. Remaining members may express amusement, anger, embarrassment, sadness, betrayal, violation, or shame (M. Boyle, personal communication, March 8, 2010; Feldman, 2004; Suler, 2007).

To limit faking, a moderator might consider verifying the identity and eligibility of a prospective member prior to allowing them to join, including submission of a street address that can be confirmed via reverse-lookup functions online. This may reassure approved members of safety but at the expense of turning away people that need support but do not want to reveal personal information. To investigate potential faking, a group leader may likewise request validating information from the suspect member such as personal data, photos, medical records, news clippings, or birth or death certificates. These data need to be reviewed skeptically. For instance, a faker might join under someone else's name and supply that person's real street address. Imposters may also creatively edit digital photos and documents to support their claims. For example, fakers have built websites with photos appropriated from the sites of families who have triplets or quadruplets, then claimed the babies as their own. If a person suspected of faking provides inconclusive information, a moderator might compare the member's IP address location with their purported location, or search the Internet for the member's name, ID, email address, career information, or news items. If a suspicious photograph is on a member's website, a moderator using a Windows operating system can right-click to check the "properties" tag for evidence that the photo did not originate with the member. For a purportedly hospitalized member, one could call the hospital and ask for the member's room, although the hospital may not disclose that information. To uncover sockpuppets, a leader may compare members' IP addresses or locations to detect duplication (although different individuals may use the same IP address or be in the same location).

Truth may be stranger than fiction, so it is important in any contact with a suspect member to be nonjudgmental and to emphasize the goal of a safe, honest, supportive community. Maureen Doolan Boyle, founder of Mothers of Supertwins, feels that, if a member's assertions cannot be promptly proven true, it is better to provide unneeded support to a faker than to risk banning a person who genuinely needs help (M. Boyle, personal communication, March 8, 2010). It is helpful to educate members about simple steps they can take to guard against faking; for example, watermark or (in the Windows operating system) right-click-disable photos.

Some group leaders believe that it is too disruptive to expose a faker or troll on-list. Quiet off-list confrontation, discipline, and/or dismissal followed by a brief announcement on-list and time-limited processing of member feelings may be optimal.

Troublemakers may include people whose personality, substance abuse habits, or mental health disorder(s) prompt alarming, negative, inconsistent, or disruptive expressions online. The best approach is to remind such individuals of group guidelines and apply the specified discipline for repeated violations. Psychiatric diagnoses cannot excuse behavior that creates a hurtful instead of helpful group environment.

Pector's survey elicited valuable advice. One respondent related,

> Early in our 'life' we had a moderately serious problem with trolls, fakers and trouble makers [. . .] Over time, a change in management strategy and finely tuned troll radar made this a minor issue. In the last 2 or 3 years, the most disruption we've had were [sic] a few members [whose] mental health issues caused them to be openly hostile [. . .] and [1–2] members with substance abuse issues, swiftly dealt with, negligible wake.

CRISIS AND SUICIDALITY IN ONLINE GROUPS

Crisis management for a group member's sudden illness, suicide attempt, or imminent death may be particularly challenging (Gary & Remolino, 2002; Hsiung et al., 2003). Referral to emergency services may be hampered by lack of knowledge of the member's geographical location or local health care resources (Baume et al., 1997; Gary & Remolino, 2002; King, 1995). It may be hard to confirm that a reported death actually occurred (Baume et al., 1997; Feldman, 2004; Hsiung, 2007; Hsiung et al., 2003). Group members may have difficulty in coping after another participant's death, expressing denial, concern, sorrow, or anger (Hollander, 2001; Hsiung, 2000; Hsiung, 2007; Hsiung et al., 2003; King, 1995). Virtual memorials after the death of a member and the processing of emotional reactions within the group have been shown to be useful for group recovery (Hsiung, 2007; Hsiung et al., 2003; King, 1995).

Mark Stevens, MD, a psychiatry professor, wrote in 1995, "Cyberspace is an anarchy which for the most part works extremely well, but which contains the seeds of disaster as well" (King, 1995). Some forums such as alt.suicide.holiday encourage suicide, discussing the efficacy of different methods and explicitly forbidding referrals to counseling or hotlines (Baume et al., 1997; King, 1995). People in suicide forums or groups for conditions such as depression or addiction recovery may leave suicide notes that trigger deep concern, fear, and anger in those who read them (Baume et al., 1997; Hsiung, 2007; Hsiung et al., 2003; King, 1995). Some people move from group to group leaving false suicide notes, but it can be hard to tell a real threat from a hoax (King, 1995).

Based on real-world experience with teen suicide clusters, there are legitimate reasons to fear suicide contagion online (Baume et al., 1997), but in at least one professionally moderated mental health support network no contagion was evident after a suicide (Hsiung, 2007). The ethical and legal obligations of clinicians and researchers who encounter online suicide threats are not clear (Baume et al., 1997; King, 1995). Anonymity and distance make it difficult, but not impossible, to intervene (Baume et al., 1997; Hsiung et al., 2003; King, 1995).

The authors queried members of the ISMHO about how to proceed when anonymous members express suicidal ideation. Useful suggestions included education on the group home page about common conditions that may trigger suicidal ideation; for example, PTSD or postpartum depression. Contact information for local, national, and international crisis resources, and emergency services and hotlines can be provided, with suggestions for private counseling. Some US crisis resources are posted at http://www.onlineclinics.com/Pages/Content.asp?iGlobalId=3. http://www.suicide.org provides links to hotlines in the US and other countries;

http://www.hopeline.com links to the US 1-800-SUICIDE hotline. The Samaritans, at http://www.samaritans.org, formed in Europe, offer confidential email counseling to suicidal individuals. They have steadily grown and have assimilated the former Befrienders group, http://www.befrienders.org, which offered voluntary support in 40 countries (Baume et al., 1997; King, 1995). In addition, SAHAR, an Israeli Hebrew-language online suicide prevention network, has been successful, and led in one instance to the rescue of a youth in the US after a suicide attempt (Hsiung et al., 2003). Resources cited in older literature include the American Association of Suicidology, the Australian Institute for Suicide Research and Prevention, Suicide Prevention Australia, and Kids Helpline in Australia (Baume et al., 1997). The Suicide Information Centre in Canada, now renamed the Centre for Suicide Prevention, has claimed to be the largest such center in the world (Baume et al., 1997).

Expression of suicidal ideation requires an assessment of suicidal risk, including seriousness of intent, existence of detailed suicide plan, availability of means to harm oneself, and availability of urgent assistance from a social network, mental health provider, hotline, or emergency services. When the member's name and location are known, the local police force can be contacted and emergency intervention can be requested. If the member's name and address are not known but their IP address is, the member's ISP can be contacted, the urgency of the situation can be explained, and the ISP can be urged to notify the local police. In less emergent scenarios, a moderator may discreetly seek the identity and location of the member in crisis from other participants close to him/her by contacting them off-list and stating, "I need to contact X urgently. Do you know his or her real name, phone number, or location?" During this process, confidentiality should be preserved regarding the nature of the crisis and the identity of the informant(s).

A member's expression of a threat to harm others or confession of a crime raises another ethical and legal quandary (Humphreys et al., 2000). Non-therapist peer moderators, or even psychotherapists, may or may not be held to the standards of the California Tarasoff law, which established a therapist's duty to warn a potential victim about serious threats (Ewing, 2005). As with suicidal ideation, it is prudent to assess seriousness of intent to harm and availability of means to carry out the threat. Further, one might refer a threatening group member to appropriate resources, warn the potential victim if known, and notify local law enforcement services.

THE FUTURE

Online forums may be considered to be among the first examples of Web 2.0. Research will be needed to assess the effects of newer "Web 2.1" social networking (Twitter, Facebook, professional networking sites, blogs, etc.) and the extent to which they create de-facto support groups and emulate – or replace – Web 2.0 groups and forums. Social networking may, in Boyle's words, represent the current "Wild West" of support, "unstructured, untrained, with immediate 24/7 connection and feedback" (M. Boyle, personal communication, March 8, 2010; Peng, 2008). The influence of an increasingly international presence in online forums and the availability of online translation tools needs to be further explored. Finally, further clarification of a psychotherapist's role and liability in peer support and social media settings (Hsiung, 2002), and creation of a secure but prompt means to approach ISPs and law enforcement for crisis intervention is needed. Finally, legislation would be welcome if it allowed meaningful action against slander, libel, cyber stalking, and identity theft in group support settings.

Research on the suitability of online group members and improved standards and training for online group moderation is needed, as empirical studies have revealed variable quality of experience for participants. Finally, dedicated discussion groups for support leaders may improve preparedness for difficult situations and may limit the readiness with which trolls and fakers move from group to group.

DISCUSSION QUESTIONS

1. What are some major differences between self-help and professional psychotherapy groups?
2. What are the major benefits and risks of online self-help communities?
3. Why is anonymity both a help and a hindrance in online peer groups?
4. How can a prospective leader set up a new support group?
5. Where can peer group moderators obtain training to prepare them for their role?
6. What are some important elements of effective group guidelines?
7. How do group members react to discovery of faking in their midst?
8. How should a moderator handle a disruptive group member?
9. What strategies can be used to investigate legitimacy of member claims?
10. How should a moderator proceed if a member's assertions cannot be proven?
11. When a group member expresses suicidal ideation, what steps can be taken?
12. How can a moderator help a group to process a disturbing event such as dismissal or suicide of a group member?

KEY TERMS

Administrator Oversees the technical details of message board or email group operation. Sets the rules, structure, appearance, and function of the forum; appoints moderators; may approve, modify, or delete membership terms, or post forum-wide messages. Sometimes also serves as a moderator.

Blog (weblog) A website where an individual posts text, photo, audio, video content, and/or links; on some blogs, readers can respond in a manner similar to a forum post.

Board See Forum. Messaging system for group discussion. Began as Usenet and later evolved to message board formats.

Faker A person who presents a false identity in an online group.

Forum software A type of computer program used to host a Forum or Board. Some are free, some require a fee, and some are provided at dedicated sites for third-party use.

Forum An online discussion network with topics and replies sorted into threads.

Guidelines/Terms of Service (TOS) Rules that govern discussions in/on a Board or online group. Users are expected to agree to these conditions of membership and may need to indicate agreement by clicking on a button.

IP (internet protocol) address A unique numeric identifier for a device participating in a computer network. These may be assigned to localities and can sometimes identify the location of an individual computer.

Internet Service Provider (ISP) The entity that provides Internet access to a computer user.

Moderated post A message in a listserv, email group, or Board that must be approved by a moderator or administrator before it is published or distributed.

Moderator An individual with monitoring responsibility and access to forum posts and membership rolls in a message board or email list. The moderator may either passively observe or actively guide discussion. He or she answers questions; ensures that members adhere to guidelines; and has the authority to delete, censor, or preapprove threads or posts and to warn, suspend, and temporarily or permanently ban members.

Munchausen by Internet Posing falsely in an online group as a disease sufferer or as the parent of a child affected by a disease.

Persona An online identity, including screen name, self-description, and virtual personality. This may or may not correspond to reality; people can develop fantasy or fake personas. An avatar (two-dimensional or three-dimensional; stationary or moving graphic) may be used to represent a persona.

Self-help group A mutual support group composed of individuals who share a common concern. They may involve professionals or reject professional facilitation.

Social media Interactive formats in Web 2.0 that facilitate contact and message exchange. For example, texting, blogs, MySpace, Facebook, Twitter, and professional networking sites.

Sockpuppet A false identity introduced into a group to either support or divert attention from another persona. This may be done by a faker or a legitimate group member.

Troll A person who purposely and habitually incites disturbance or conflict in online groups.

Yalom's factors Therapeutic factors defined by Dr Irving Yalom that operate in a psychotherapy or self-help group. These include instillation of hope, universality, imparting of information, altruism, corrective recapitulation of the primary family group, development of socializing techniques, imitative behavior, catharsis, existential factors, direct advice, and interpersonal learning.

REFERENCES

Associated Press. (2007, November 16). Mom: Myspace hoax led to daughter's suicide. Retrieved March 5, 2010 from http://www.foxnews.com/story/0,2933,312018,00.html

Barak, A., Boniel-Nissim, M., & Suler, J. (2008). Fostering empowerment in online support groups. *Computers in Human Behavior, 24*, 1867–1883.

Barrera, M., Glasgow, R., McKay, H. G., Boles, S. M., & Feil, E. G. (2002). Do internet-based support interventions change perceptions of social support? An experimental trial of approaches for supporting diabetes self-management. *American Journal of Community Psychology, 30*, 637–654.

Baume, P., Cantor, C. H., & Rolfe, A. (1997). Cybersuicide: The role of interactive suicide notes on the Internet. *Crisis, 18*, 73–79.

Brennan, P. F. (1998). Computer network home care demonstration: A randomized trial in persons living with AIDS. *Computers in Biology and Medicine, 28*, 489–508.

Casey, A., & Hardy, G. (1998, February). *Online communities for information exchange and peer support: A case study.* Presented to the Communities Networking/ Networking Communities Conference. Retrieved March 5, 2010 from http:// www.preemie-l.org/netconf98.html

Commonwealth of Australia. (2009). Cancer support groups: A guide for facilitators. Retrieved April 17, 2010 from http://www.canceraustralia.gov.au/media/files/ca/ publications/peer_facilitators.pdf

Cummings, J. N., Butler, B., & Kraut, R. (2002). The quality of online social relationships. *Communications of the ACM, 45*(7), 103–108.

Davison, K. P., Pennebaker, J. W., & Dickerson, S. S. (2000). Who talks? The social psychology of illness support groups. *American Psychologist, 55*, 205–217.

Edwards, T. (2009). Internet use triples in past decade, census bureau reports. Retrieved March 5, 2010 from census.gov/PressRelease/www/releases/archives/ communication_industries/013849.html

Ewing, C. P. (2005). Tarasoff reconsidered. *APA Monitor, 36*(7), 112.

Eysenbach, G., Powell, J., Englesakis, M., Rizo, C., & Stern, A. (2004). Health related virtual communities and electronic support groups: Systematic review of the effects of online peer to peer interactions. *British Medical Journal, 328*(7449), 1166.

Feldman, M. D. (2004). *Playing sick?* New York, NY: Brunner-Routledge.

Finfgeld, D. (2000). Therapeutic groups online: The good, the bad, and the unknown. *Issues in Mental Health Nursing, 21*, 241–255.

Finn, J., & Banach, M. (2000). Victimization online: The downside of seeking human services for women on the Internet. *Cyberpsychology and Behavior, 3*, 276–285.

Fox, S., & Fallows, D. (2003). Internet health resources. *Pew Internet & American Life Project*, Retrieved March 5, 2010 from http://www.pewinternet.org/Reports/2003/ Internet-Health-Resources.aspx?r=1

Fox, S. (2007). Online patient groups. Retrieved March 5, 2010 from pewinternet. org/Commentary/2007/June/Online-Patient-Groups.aspx

Gary, J. M., & Remolino, L. (2001/2002). Self-help + computer = online emotional support. *New Jersey Journal of Professional Counseling, 56*, 2–12.

Gil, P. (2010) What is an Internet troll? Retrieved March 5, 2010 from http:// netforbeginners.about.com/od/t/f/what_is_a_troll.htm

Glasgow, R. E., Boles, S. M., McKay, H. G., Feil, E. G., & Barrera, M. (2003). The D-Net diabetes self-management program: Long-term implementation, outcomes, and generalization results. *Preventive Medicine, 36*, 410–419.

Griffiths, K. M., Calear, A. L., Banfield, M., & Tam, A. (2009a). Systematic review on internet support groups (ISGs) and depression (2): What is known about depression ISGs. *Journal of Medical Internet Research, 11*(3), e41.

Griffiths, K. M., Calear, A. L., & Banfield, M. (2009b). Systematic review on internet support groups (ISGs) and depression (1): Do ISGs reduce depressive symptoms? *Journal of Medical Internet Research, 11*(3), e40.

Grohol, J. (2002). Starting a new online support group. Retrieved March 5, 2010 from http://psychcentral.com/howto.htm

Heffernan, V. (2010, April 18). PharmVille: Dr. Bob's forum for people on psychoactive drugs. *The New York Times Magazine, 26*, 28.

Herring, S., Job-Sluder, K., Scheckler, R., & Barab, S. (2002). Searching for safety online: Managing "trolling" in a feminist forum. *Center for Social Informatics – Indiana University*. Retrieved March 5, 2010 from http://rkcsi.indiana.edu/archive/CSI/WP/WP02-03B.html

Hollander, E. M. (2001). Cyber community in the valley of the shadow of death. *Journal of Loss and Trauma, 6*, 135–146.

Holmes, L. (2010) Usenet newsgroups offer support online. Retrieved March 5, 2010 from http://mentalhealth.about.com/library/weekly/aa061697.htm

Houston, T. K., Cooper, L. A., & Ford, D. E. (2002). Internet support groups for depression: A 1-year prospective cohort study. *The American Journal of Psychiatry, 159*, 2062–2068.

Hsiung, R. C. (2000). The best of both worlds: An online self-help group hosted by a mental health professional. *Cyberpsychology and Behavior, 3*, 935–950.

Hsiung, R. C. (2002). Does a doctor–patient relationship arise from online moderating? *American Medical News, 45*(29), 18.

Hsiung, R. C. (2007). A suicide in an online mental health support group: Reactions of the group members, administrative responses, and recommendations. *Cyberpsychology and Behavior, 10*, 495–500.

Hsiung, R. C., Barak, A., & Silber, D. (2003). Suicide and the Internet. *Technology and Health Care, 11*, 323–324.

Humphreys, K., Winzelberg, A., & Klaw, E. (2000). Psychologists' ethical responsibilities in Internet-based groups: Issues, strategies and a call for dialogue. *Professional Psychology, Research and Practice, 31*, 493–496.

Janssen, K. (2009). Blogger's baby was a hoax. *Chicago Tribune*, Retrieved March 5, 2010 from http://archives.chicagotribune.com/2009/jun/12/local/chi-baby-hoax-12jun12

King, S. A. (1995). Suicidal ideation in virtual support groups. Retrieved March 5, 2010 from http://webpages.charter.net/stormking/suicide.html

Klemm, P., Bunnell, D., Cullen, M., Soneji, R., Gibbons, P., & Holecek, A. (2003). Online cancer support groups: A review of the research literature. *Computers, Informatics, Nursing, 21*, 136–142.

Klemm, P., & Hardie, T. (2002). Depression in Internet and face-to-face cancer support groups: A pilot study. *Oncology Nursing Forum, 29*(4), E45–E51.

Klemm, P., Hurst, M., Dearholt, S. L., & Trone, S. R. (1999). Gender differences on Internet cancer support groups. *Computers in Nursing, 17*, 65–72.

Lieberman, M. A., Golant, M., Giese-Davis, J., Winzelberg, A., Benjamin, H., Humphreys, K., et al. (2003). Electronic support groups for breast carcinoma: A clinical trial of effectiveness. *Cancer, 97*, 920–925.

Lieberman, M. A., & Russo, S. (1999–2000). Self Help Groups and the Internet; Breast Cancer Newsgroups. *International Journal of Self Help & Self Care, 1*, 279–300.

Lorig, K. R., Laurent, D. D., Deyo, R. A., Marnell, M. E., Minor, M. A., & Ritter, P. L. (2002). Can a back pain e-mail discussion group improve health status and lower health care costs? A randomized study. *Archives of Internal Medicine, 162*, 792–796.

Madara, E. (2010). How to develop an online support group or web site. Retrieved March 5, 2010 from http://www.mentalhelp.net/selfhelp/selfhelp.php?id=863

Miletski, H. (2002). Understanding bestiality and zoophilia. Bethesda, MD: East-West Publishing LLC.

Miller, J. K., & Gergen, K. J. (1998). Life on the line: The therapeutic potentials of computer-mediated conversation. *Journal of Marital and Family Therapy, 24*, 189–202.

Mo, P. K., Malik, S. H., & Coulson, N. S. (2009). Gender differences in computer-mediated communication: A systematic literature review of online health-related support groups. *Patient Education and Counseling, 75*, 16–24.

Pector, E. A. (2009). Defense against the dark side: Confronting deception and disruption in online groups. Retrieved March 5, 2010 from http://www .ementalhealthsummit.com/en/symposium-details#Pector

Peng, T. (2008). Out of the shadows. *Newsweek*, Retrieved March 13, 2010 from http://www.newsweek.com/id/170528

Preece, J., & Ghozati, K. (1998). In search of empathy online: A review of 100 online communities. *Proceedings of the Association for Information Systems Americas Conference*. (pp. 92–94).

Preece, J. (1999). Shaping communities: Empathy, hostility, lurking, participation. *Workshop on research issues in the design of online communities*, Retrieved March 5, 2010 from http://www.cc.gatech.edu/ ~ asb/workshops/chi/99/participants/preece. html

Sansone, R. A. (2001). Patient-to-patient e-mail: Support for clinical practices. *Eating Disorders, 9,* 373–375.

Schwartz, M. (2008, August 3). The trolls among us. *The New York Times*, Retrieved March 5, 2010 from http://www.nytimes.com/2008/08/03/magazine/03trolls-t.html

SnowyHOST. (2006). Trolls: Who, what, why and how to deal with them. Retrieved March 5, 2010 from http://bipolar.about.com/od/ourcommunity/a/snowy_trolls. htm

Suler, J. (2007). Online therapy and support groups. Retrieved March 5, 2010 from http://www.rider.edu/ ~ suler//psycyber/psycyber.html

Taylor, H., & Leitman, R. (2002). Four-nation survey shows widespread but different levels of Internet use for health purposes. *Harris Interactive Health Care News, 2*(11), 1–4.

Troll (Internet). (2010). In: *Wikipedia*. Retrieved March 5, 2010 from http://en.wikipedia.org/wiki/Internet_troll

Tuckman, B. W. (2001). Classics for group facilitation: Developmental sequence in small groups. *Group Facilitation: A Research and Applications Journal, 3,* 66–81.

van Uden-Kraan, C. F., Drossaert, C. H., Tall, E., Seydel, E. R., & van de Laar, M. A. (2008). Self-reported differences in empowerment between lurkers and posters in online patient support groups. *Journal of Medical Internet Research, 10*(2), e18.

Walstrom, M. K. (2000). 'You know, who's the thinnest?': Combating surveillance and creating safety in coping with eating disorders online. *Cyberpsychology and Behavior, 3,* 761–783.

White, M., & Dorman, S. M. (2001). Receiving social support online: Implications for health education. *Health Education Research, 16,* 693–707.

White, M. H., & Dorman, S. M. (2000). Online support for caregivers: Analysis of an Internet Alzheimer mailgroup. *Computers in Nursing, 18,* 168–176.

Winzelberg, A. J., Classen, C., Alpers, G. W., Roberts, H., Koopman, C., Adams, R. E., et al. (2003). Evaluation of an internet support group for women with primary breast cancer. *Cancer, 97,* 1164–1173.

Wolfradt, U., & Doll, J. (2001). Health behavior changes after colon cancer: A comparison of findings from face-to-face and online focus groups. *Journal of Educational Computing Research, 24,* 13–27.

World Internet Usage and Population Statistics. (2009). Retrieved March 5, 2010 from http://www.internetworldstats.com/stats.htm

Worotynec, Z. S. (2000). The good, the bad and the ugly: Listserv as support. *Cyberpsychology and Behavior, 3,* 797–810.

Yalom, I. D., & Leszcz, M. (2005). *The theory and practice of group psychotherapy*. New York, NY: Basic Books.

ONLINE RESOURCES

Sample Guidelines

MOST (Mothers of Supertwins). http://www.mostonline.org/agreement.htm

Preemie-L. http://www.preemie-l.org/forumrules.html

Psycho-Babble. http://www.dr-bob.org/babble/faq.html#civil

Listings of Support Organizations and Forums

The Association of Cancer Online Resources. http://www.acor.org

http://www.mentalhelp.net/selfhelp

http://psychcentral.com

http://www.rarediseases.org

http://www.our-kids.org (a resource for families with special-needs children)

Conflict Resolution

http://www.kalimunro.com/article_conflict_online.html

http://www-usr.rider.edu/ ~ suler/psycyber/therapygroup.html

Chapter twelve

Internet-based Psychological Testing and Assessment

Azy Barak
University of Haifa, Haifa, Israel

CHAPTER OUTLINE

Benjamin had been unhappy for a while. He had had trouble sleeping, had generally felt unhappy and unmotivated. Everything seemed to keep going wrong for him and there was nobody he felt he could turn to for help. He was troubled by what he was experiencing, and wondered if there was something wrong with him, but it had not occurred to him to seek professional help. One evening, while surfing the web, he accidentally came across a link to a self-help site (http://depression.about.com) that looked interesting. At the site, he filled in a short questionnaire, called a "Depression Screening Quiz" and was informed that

Online Counseling. DOI: 10.1016/B978-0-12-378596-1.00012-5

he might be suffering from clinical depression and he should consult a mental health professional about it.

Sangeeta was stressed and desperate. She had no idea what was wrong with her — she couldn't get any work done, felt uptight and aggressive, couldn't concentrate well, couldn't sleep, and spent most of the night playing computer games instead of writing the report she should have finished last week. On impulse, she typed "am I depressed?" into http://www.ask.com and followed a sponsored link labeled "Are You Stressed? You could have a chemical imbalance take the self-test and see." This led to a page (http://www.iwr.com/becalmd/stress.html) that mainly seemed to be advertising proprietary remedies. She followed a link to a simple self-test, which presented a list of feelings and instructed her to follow another link if more than a certain number applied to her. She thought they did, so followed the link to a page that told her she would benefit from buying certain dietary supplements. Now, where was her credit card?

Lars was reading one of his favorite online discussion forums when he came across a message posted by a psychologist halfway across the world, looking for people to take part in a study on online counseling. This involved anonymously filling out some online questionnaires before participating in a course of email exchanges and then filling out the questionnaires again afterwards to see whether there had been any changes. He thought it sounded interesting, so emailed the psychologist to let her know he would like to take part.

Dr Jones, an experienced psychologist with a busy caseload, had just met a new client for a brief initial consultation. As part of her normal assessment procedure, she liked to administer a comprehensive battery of psychological tests (personality, ability, and clinical screening measures). However, this was very time-consuming, so she had adopted a new technique. She gave the client a web address and asked him to visit it and complete the questionnaires there in his own time. The website Dr Jones referred the client to was maintained by a test publisher, who offered this service to subscribed clinicians. Later that evening, the client visited the site at his own convenience. When Dr Jones arrived at work the next morning, she found that a full psychological assessment report on the client had been automatically generated and emailed to her. She used it to plan her next session with the client and the issues she wanted to follow up in her assessment of his situation.

These (fictional) scenarios are based on materials found on the Internet at the time of writing this chapter, and represent a few of the ways in which people might come into contact with Internet-based psychological assessment procedures. They illustrate some of the potential uses of such assessments, as well as some of the problems that may be associated with their use. The purpose of this chapter is to describe the principles and different techniques of online assessment, reasons why one might want to do it, and important issues that anyone involved in online psychological assessment need to be aware of.

There are numerous contexts in which online assessments may take place, and several different types of assessment procedure. In their simplest forms, Internet-based psychological assessments may take the shape of a web page on which the items of a traditional paper-and-pencil questionnaire are represented in computerized form. Respondents may view and complete this form using browser software such as Microsoft's Internet Explorer, Mozilla's Firefox, or Google's Chrome. Having answered all of the questions, respondents then typically click on a button that transmits their data to a psychologist, or are scored automatically and presented with some form of feedback.

Such Internet-based questionnaires may be used for a range of purposes by a variety of people. Different types of questionnaire are used (in addition to simple tick-the-appropriate-box-style instruments), and some assessment procedures have been developed that do not rely on questionnaires at all. In the sections that follow, we outline some of the potential uses of online assessments, the types of assessment procedures available, the advantages and disadvantages of their use, and ethical and legal issues that must be considered.

THE PURPOSES OF ONLINE ASSESSMENT

Internet-supported assessment is used for various needs and purposes. It can be classified into three major categories: psychological evaluation, psychotherapeutic diagnostics, and self-exploration and awareness. The term "Internet-supported" has intentionally been selected over "Internet-based" as a title for this area since online testing and assessment may be used as an alternative to the equivalent offline pursuit, but also as a complement to the professional evaluation of a person.

Psychological Evaluation

Psychologists are often asked to evaluate — or assist in the evaluation procedures — of a person's psychological characteristics, usually in relation to classification or selection processes (Groth-Marnat, 2009). The assessment usually includes factors relating to personality traits, abilities and special aptitudes, attitudes and values, and sometimes special dimensions. The Internet has become a very efficient professional source of assistance to psychologists who wish to engage in evaluation, as it provides continuously updated, rich information about assessment procedures (e.g., tests, assessment centers, interview techniques), as well as online devices that can be used — for free or for a fee — by professionals. Although both information and tools are available offline, the Internet makes them available in an easily accessible way to any interested professional whenever needed. In addition, online portals, as well as organizations (e.g., companies, publishers, universities, research institutes), provide ongoing updated information about assessment tools, so that professionals have a quick, convenient way in which to find what is suited to their professional needs. This channel is much more efficient than traditional resources such as the Mental Measurements Yearbook.

Further, the Internet makes it possible to assess people very efficiently using various computerized procedures, unlike the manual, cumbersome activities of traditional assessments. Research studies have consistently reported that online testing produces very similar psychological findings to traditional paper-and-pencil testing (see reviews by Barak & English, 2002; Barak & Hen, 2008; Buchanan, 2007; Lievens & Harris, 2003; Naglieri et al., 2004; Sampson, 2000; Wall, 2000). Online psychological evaluation has been found to be successful in a variety of assessment areas, including various measures of personality (e.g., Aluja et al., 2007; Buchanan, 2001; Buchanan et al., 2005; Chuah et al., 2006; Cronk & West, 2002; Fouladi et al., 2002; Johnson, 2005; Kelly & Jugovic, 2001; Pettit, 2002; Robie & Brown, 2007), psychopathology (Baer & Minichiello, 2006; Bhatara et al., 2006; Brodey et al., 2004; Carlbring et al., 2007; Chinman et al., 2004; Coles et al., 2007; Fortson et al., 2006; Hyler et al., 2005; Le et al., 2009; McCue et al., 2006; Read et al., 2009; Rosen et al., 2008; Spek et al., 2008; Steenhuis et al., 2009; Zlomke, 2009), integrity (Jones et al., 2002), career- and work-related measures (Barak, 2006; Barak & Cohen, 2002; Betz & Borgen, 2009; Gati & Saka, 2001; Gore & Leuwerke, 2000; Kleiman & Gati, 2004; Lumsden et al., 2004; Miller et al., 2008; Oliver & Chartrand, 2000; Oliver & Zack, 1999), online behavior (Riva et al., 2003), offline behaviors (Knapp & Kirk, 2003; Sinadinovic et al., 2010), intelligence and abilities (Ihme et al., 2009; Mooney, 2002; Williams & McCord, 2006), health-related issues (Mangunkusumo et al., 2006; van de Looij-Jansen & de Wilde, 2008), and neuropsychological assessment (Erlanger et al., 2003; Hoffmann et al., 2008; Medalia et al., 2005; Schatz & Browndyke, 2002; Younes et al., 2007).

Of special importance is the use of online testing for job-related assessment of candidates. This procedure enables the use of test batteries in evaluating job applicants from a distance, under some proctored conditions, saving time and expenses while retaining a high level of reliability and validity of measurement (Bartram, 2006; Konradt et al., 2003; Potosky & Bobko, 2004).

It should not, however, be assumed that all psychometric questionnaires will "work" on the web, or that the psychometric properties of online questionnaires will remain the same as offline versions. While most of the research to date has indicated that online questionnaires can be valid, there are reports of instances where factor structures and mean scores have been found to differ (see, e.g., Buchanan, 2001;

Buchanan, 2002; Buchanan, 2003; Buchanan et al., 2002a; and other work cited later in this chapter). The most appropriate interpretation of the body of work that currently exists may be that online questionnaires can be (and usually are) psychometrically acceptable, but this must be empirically demonstrated rather than assumed. One should never just place a test online and expect that it will be the same test as it was in paper-and-pencil format.

Psychotherapeutic Diagnostics

Counselors who wish to take advantage of the Internet might find it very useful to obtain assistance from online procedures when assessment is desired (Jones, 2004). Clients may be guided to engage in online testing — provided by computer stations at a clinic or at a client's home — at their convenience, without the necessity of paper forms, scoring keys, or test administrators. Clients may take various types of test — personality inventories, career-interest questionnaires, or intellectual ability tests — through the web and receive immediate, accurate results. Moreover, the results can be provided simultaneously to the client's counselor, too. Test results may be linked directly to relevant online information resources, making the results much more meaningful and applicable for test-takers.

Counselors may benefit from having their clients engage in online assessment procedures in several ways: first, quite a few counselors may free themselves from the need to administer tests (themselves or through the help of assistants). Second, counselors receive the accurate results as soon as they are available, directly from their personal computers. Third, automated interpretation, of a single test or of a whole (online) assessment battery, can be provided in many cases, saving time and obviating subjective biases on the counselor's part. Fourth, all scores (or even item responses) can conveniently be saved and archived for any future use. Fifth, test upgrades and adaptations, as well as test norms, are centrally administered by test owners, without monitoring on the counselor's part.

Online tests may also be used efficiently as mental-health-screening devices to identify psychological problems prior to or as an adjunct to medical procedures, which require initial and immediate diagnosis (Hill et al., 2002; Wolford et al., 2008). Further, online assessment may be used to evaluate prospective clients' readiness for online counseling (Rochlen et al., 2004). Another example of the practical diagnostic use of online assessment is the successful use of an online measure intended to assess a youth's independent living potential (Bressani & Downs, 2002). A special case in exploiting the Internet for effective diagnosis has to do with sex-function problems (Ochs et al., 2002), for which openness and candor are necessary but might be jeopardized in an f2f interaction. Also, Internet communication channels can be used for the delivery of test interpretation. Jones et al. (2002) showed that interest inventory interpretation can effectively be conducted with test-takers over text chat accompanied by video.

Self-Exploration and Self-Awareness

The Internet is loaded with psychological and pseudo-psychological tests and questionnaires that anyone may take for free or for a fee: intelligence tests, personality measures, vocational interest inventories, and other psychological scales. People may take such tests for their own self-exploration and self-awareness, to know themselves better, to obtain answers to personal questions, to help themselves in making choices, or just for the sake of curiosity. People may thus obtain psychologically relevant information on themselves in almost any area and, in principle, make good use of this information. These experiences, which are becoming convenient and normative due to the Internet, should be considered a matter of human advancement, as they foster career development, personal development and maturity, and decision-making in various areas. Thus, the tests (online or offline) are usually considered an inseparable part of psychological self-help (Tucker-Ladd, 2000). The ease of using the Internet, its prevalence, and indeed its excessive use — related to the "Penta-A Engine" (Barak & Fisher, 2002): availability, accessibility, affordability, acceptability, and aloneness — has brought about a significant increase in the usage of psychological tests for personal purposes, thereby supposedly contributing directly to valuable personal growth. This assertion, however, depends upon the validity of the tests as well as the test-takers' effective assimilation of the meaning and implications of the results. A good example of the use of online testing for self-awareness has been provided by Cunningham et al. (2000), who developed a brief Internet-based self-assessment procedure that provided normative feedback (by gender and age group) to respondents in regard to their drinking habits. Also in drinking assessment, Miller et al. (2002) found that web-based measures of drinking habits were as reliable and valid as were paper-and-pencil measures. Test repositories, such as at http://www.queendom.com (Baker, 2007), include hundreds of tests, many of them professionally constructed and validated, for the use (for free or for a fee) of Internet surfers.

However, we should keep in mind that self-assessment by unmonitored online tests might have drawbacks, too. For instance, most Internet users cannot identify reliable and valid tests among all the available tests on the Internet. Also, interpretations could be erroneous and lead to non-adaptive attitudes and decisions. There are ethical concerns, too, regarding the lack of informed consent as well as the abuse of online tests for criminal purposes (Buchanan, 2002; Kier & Molinari, 2004; LoBello & Zachar, 2007).

TYPES AND METHODS OF ONLINE PSYCHOLOGICAL TESTING

Like traditional psychological testing, online testing is characterized by multiple methods. Naturally, objective testing techniques (cf. Groth-Marnat, 2009), such as multiple-choice tests, are the most commonly published type on the Internet as they can mechanically and automatically be scored without direct human intervention. However, despite this clear preference, other testing methods, including projective techniques and the open-ended format, are possible and available on the Internet.

The first multiple-choice tests to be published on the Internet were those that measured intellectual abilities and they became very common, apparently because of the right—wrong nature of the test items. Several factors should be considered, however, when referring to these tests. First, these tests should be professionally developed, following clear scientific and ethical guidelines and based on common, empirically based psychometric considerations. Many online tests, however, may be amateur efforts and as such, developed and published without an established professional basis by anyone who knows how to create a web page (Barak, 2003; Buchanan, 2007; Naglieri et al., 2004). Second, online tests may be highly technology-enhanced in a way that takes advantage of advanced computer applications, including the rich use of pictures and sound; they may be highly interactive, allow time keeping, and employ complicated scoring techniques; at the other extreme, such online tests might be very simple, using only text, and be scored manually.

Another type of assessment that is common on the Internet is that of personality and attitudes. Here too, use of a response format of rating scales (Yes/No, numerical, or text-based) makes computer-software automatic scoring easy and fast. There are also various levels of sophistication and exploitation of Internet capabilities with these questionnaires. In this case also, there are quite a few well-established, professional psychological tests published and used online, as well as amateur ones. It sometimes takes an expert to differentiate between the two; the problems for lay people are therefore obvious. In this regard, Naglieri and associates (2004) suggested that "Producers of pop-psychology tests should be made to issue more detailed disclaimers, or warnings, describing their tests as entertainment and not as true tests, just as tobacco manufacturers must issue store warnings on cigarette packages" (p. 160). Obviously this suggestion may prove useful for professionals, but — given the fact that online publication is easy and free — it cannot regulate amateurs who launch pop-psychology tests. It seems it would be more effective if web users were trained — perhaps in the context of more general education programs and information dissemination — to differentiate between professional and nonprofessional online tests, as they ought to be knowledgeable in relation to the quality of online information in general (Gerjets & Hellenthal-Schorr, 2008; Trettin et al., 2008).

Online testing can exploit specific characteristics of computers and the Internet to advance assessment. For instance, the use of colorful and animated pictures in test items, as well as short movies, may enhance the test stimuli. This procedure has been successfully implemented in online testing of agoraphobia (Nordin et al., 2007). In a different, computer-unique technique, response time to test items can be measured to assess a person's attitudes or values as used by the Implicit Association Test (see https://implicit.harvard.edu/implicit; Kraut et al., 2004; Nosek et al., 2007).

More complicated assessment techniques, such as those that require human interaction for interpretation and scoring, can also be found on the Internet. For instance, the pictures of the Rorschach inkblot test may be presented at a certain website, and patients may record or write down their responses, which will later be handed to a therapist. It is also possible, and might be feasible, to conduct such assessments using real-time videoconferencing systems, electronically replicating the interactive situation that might occur in a traditional setting. A still more advanced method is possible (and yet rarely used): Stories told following exposure to Thematic Apperception Test (TAT) pictures may simply be typed under each picture into a predesigned form; when test-takers have finished writing their stories, they can submit the form with the click of a mouse. A clinician thus receives a patient's forms through email to facilitate efficient assessment. Volcani (2000) reported a sophisticated online projective test, based on principles similar to the TAT, that proved to be a useful measure of personality. A similar procedure can be used with a sentence-completion test. Drawing software, though widely available, seems unfit for this medium to be used with drawing tests (e.g., draw a person, draw a family, draw a tree) as a user's behavior is not as spontaneous and free as it is in offline testing. Obviously, these types of test must be private and secure because of clear privacy issues, in addition to copyright considerations. Using a secure, password-protected website seems to meet these conditions to a large extent.

Just as open-ended questions are included in paper-and-pencil tests and questionnaires, they may also be included in online tests and questionnaires. Although their evaluation may be conducted as if they had been submitted on paper, digitized materials have the great advantage of the potential to be assessed through computer-based procedures (Shermis & Burstein, 2003). Answers to open-ended questions in questionnaires, as well as essays, may be quickly, efficiently, and more objectively scored following predesigned procedures. This method, however, lacks the *qualitative* component of human impression, just as it is still impossible for a computer to rate the quality of artwork. Attempts have been made in recent years, however, to enable professional computerized analysis of text. One of the more successful developments in this area is the Linguistic Inquiry and Word Count (LIWC) program, developed by Pennebaker and his associates (e.g., Chung & Pennebaker, 2008; Tausczik & Pennebaker, 2010). The LIWC is able to calculate the degree to which people use different categories of words across a wide array of texts and determine the rate at which authors use positive or negative emotive words, self-references, or words that refer to specific contents. Extensive research has revealed that such analyses differentiate among distinct groups and individuals and provide important insights into their personal qualities based on their writings.

NON-TESTING ONLINE ASSESSMENT PROCEDURES

Although testing online is widespread and appears to be the most efficacious Internet-supported assessment procedure, it is certainly not the only available procedure. Efficient, variegated online communication channels, on the one hand, and the characteristics of the online environment itself, on the other, enable other online assessment procedures. These procedures add a unique value to the use of the Internet as an aid in evaluating people and provide a breakthrough in developing distance appraisal.

The Internet may be exploited to conduct assessment interviews through text only, by using the computer's sound capability (i.e., a conversation involving the computer's microphone and speakers, such as through Skype) or through video (by using webcams). Internet-based interviews are particularly useful when interviewee and interviewer are at a great distance from each other, as they save travel time and expenses. Telephone interviews for assessment purposes are possible and actually used, too (e.g., Blackman, 2002; Paulsen et al., 1988), though limited in validity (Cacciola et al., 1999; Silvester et al., 2000). Interviewing through the Internet (especially using text interviews) has, moreover, two special advantages: a conversation may easily be saved for further evaluation and the cost is very low. These special advantages may justify online interviews, at least for initial screening or preliminary diagnostics. Emerging video technologies and recently enhanced communication speed make online interviews not only possible but also quite efficient. However, as with online therapy (e.g., Anthony & Merz-Nagel, 2010; Suler, 2008; see also other relevant chapters in this volume), special professional training, adherence to ethical guidelines, and advanced equipment are necessary in order to make online assessment interviews efficient and valid.

Diagnostic interviewing through the Internet is an exciting method for gathering psychological information about a person. As mentioned above, although phone interviews have the critical disadvantages of lack of eye contact and lack of observable nonverbal cues, online synchronous video technology might lessen this shortcoming. Research in applying this method in actual assessment procedures (Elford et al., 2000; Yoshino et al., 2001) has shown that high-speed Internet communication technology can produce highly efficient, reliable interviews. Still, a text-based interview using chat or instant messaging software is also possible, particularly in cases in which hand-written text may be sufficient to evaluate a person – both by analyzing its content and detecting characteristic online behavior (Cronin et al., 2006; Davis et al., 2004; Hamilton & Bowers, 2006; Hattrup et al., 2006; Leung, 2002; Matthews & Cramer, 2008; McCoyd & Schwaber Kerson, 2006; Peris et al., 2002; Russell, 2007). This verbal-only method might at times even be preferred to the use of video communication, as the lack of eye contact contributes to increasing personal exposure (e.g., Duggan & Parrott, 2000; Hunt & McHale, 2007).

Another method of exploiting the Internet for assessment and evaluation purposes has to do with evaluating resumes and biographical information. Because documents can easily be transferred online, it seems obvious that psychologists could receive material in this way rather than in the traditional, printed manner. Indeed, such attempts have proved useful (e.g., Coffee et al., 1999). An electronic résumé might be appraised differently than a paper résumé in terms of a job applicant's personality and in the context of different jobs (Elgin & Clapham, 2004). However, other sources of personal information can be included in this category: personal websites, which often contain a great amount of private details and expressions (Döring, 2002); weblogs (blogs) – online personal diaries that record even more intimate experiences; poems, stories, and artwork published on the Internet in dedicated sites (e.g., Flickr); and personal profiles in social networks. The latter usually contain extensive personal information shared openly with others, which could easily be exploited to evaluate people for various purposes (Kluemper & Rosen, 2009). All these sources of highly significant psychological input may be analyzed and evaluated by clinicians for the benefit of a client or for improved professional appraisal.

In addition, the Internet allows assessment of another aspect of people's behavior: observations of interpersonal interactions in both synchronous and asynchronous environments, based on the premise that people's behavior online reflects their real personality perhaps more accurately because of the online disinhibition effect (Joinson, 1998; Joinson; 1999; Joinson, 2001; Joinson & Paine, 2007; Suler, 2004). Close observation of people's (text-based) behavior in chat rooms, forums, dating sites, online gaming, social networks, and blogs, as well as in instant messaging and email (and even from email addresses; Back et al., 2008), can provide important psychological information (e.g., Amichai-Hamburger, 2007). Although this information is somewhat limited in scope and context, it may contribute to better understanding one's personal and interpersonal pattern in various social situations (Buffardi & Campbell, 2008; Correa et al., 2010; Gill et al., 2006; Guadagno et al., 2008; Landers & Lounsbury, 2006; Marcus et al., 2006; Ross et al., 2009; Teng, 2008).

In the context of personnel selection, simulative environments can be created online in parallel with observing people's group behavior in a situational test (e.g., Barak & Hen, 2008; McDaniel & Nguyen, 2001; Weekley & Jones, 1999), in order to evaluate social interactions in a challenging circumstance. Observation of behavior on the Internet may lead to special information because of the unique characteristics of cyberspace, which prompt disinhibition. Thus, online observations in a chat room or a forum may serve as a significant source of psychologically relevant information (Anolli et al., 2005; Barak & Miron, 2005), perhaps even more valid than interpersonal behavior in f2f situations. Similarly, group dynamics in online situations (Lee, 2005; McKenna & Green, 2002; McKenna, 2008; McKenna & Seidman, 2005; Michinov et al., 2004; Sassenberg, 2002; Zurlo & Riva, 2009) can disclose significant information about people's various personality characteristics that might be important for therapy. A clinician can benefit from observing patients' behavior in online environments, either in a chat room or a forum, and identifying their typical responses. Taking into account the online disinhibition effect, one can strongly argue that this information contributes significantly to the diagnosis of patients.

One caveat here is the idea that the personae people present online might be constructed or contrived to some degree. There have been speculations and consistent observations (e.g., Davies, 2006; Subrahmanyam & Smahel, 2006; Suler, 2002; Turkle, 2004) that the Internet can be used as a laboratory for identity exploration, and that people may construct or express different selves online. Clearly, this needs to be considered when using the actions of an online persona as a source of data about the person "behind the screen." However, given evidence that people's online personae are likely to be influenced by their "real" personalities (for instance, Buchanan and Smith (1999) found evidence suggesting that the personality trait of self-monitoring was associated with whether or not people chose to use a "handle" or screen name when posting to Usenet newsgroups), observation of online behavior is likely to be a useful source of information as long as one remembers that the context of the behavior may affect its nature.

ADVANTAGES OF ONLINE PROCEDURES FOR PSYCHOLOGICAL ASSESSMENT

Relative to traditional personal assessment in the context of counseling and psychotherapy (e.g., paper-and-pencil testing), online assessment offers quite a few strengths and advanced features that make it attractive.

These advantages — both professional and administrative — are enabled by the special characteristics of online communication and by technological developments. Nevertheless, they are flexible enough to be amalgamated into traditional counseling (and, naturally, into online counseling). Listed below are several of the principal advantages, both those pertaining to testing and those that are related to other assessment procedures.

One main advantage of using the Internet in general, and for testing in particular, is its elasticity (i.e., flexibility); namely, the absence of confinement related to time and place (Barak & English, 2002; Barak & Hen, 2008; Buchanan, 2007; Jones, 2004; Sampson, 2000). In a traditional testing session, tests have to be taken in a particular place and at a particular time. This strict condition has now been overcome, as tests may be taken at any time and in any place where a computer is connected to the Internet (equipped, usually, with basic software). Not only are conditions made more convenient for test-takers, but they may also initiate taking a test when they feel comfortable with this tiring and usually anxiety-provoking activity (e.g., Tseng et al., 1997). Thus, positive personal feelings and sufficient measurement validity are both enhanced. Practically, clinicians may assign eligible tests to patients by providing them only with URLs. Results can be electronically sent to clinicians' as well as to patients' email addresses, as required. Obviously, if necessary, tests might be taken in the clinic, at designated computers, thus saving the clinician's or test administrator's precious time. For example, a client may take an online instrument assessing the constructs of the Myers-Briggs Type Indicator (MBTI) (the Keirsey Temperament Sorter II; see Kelly & Jugovic, 2001) for immediate scoring, results, inferences, and referrals to related information.

Another important advantage relates to the accuracy of raw scoring and standardization conversion. As these two operations are performed by software, human errors are avoided; hence, the scores obtained are accurate and better reflect test-takers' true scores. This is a clear contribution to the reliability of measurement. For instance, it has been found that scoring a simple career-related inventory, such as the Self-directed Search (SDS) (Holland et al., 1994), which simply involves the counting and totaling of "yes" responses, is affected by numerous human errors (Elliott & Byrd, 1985). A computerized version of the SDS has been developed that eliminates these errors (McKee & Levinson, 1990). However, using an *Internet-based* version of the SDS (at http://www.self-directed-search.com), which liberates the user from obtaining the SDS software, can also easily avoid such errors and consequent erroneous interpretations (Barak & Cohen, 2002; Lumsden et al., 2004; Miller et al., 2008).

Another advantage of machine-based scoring of online tests is the speed both of scoring and of obtaining results. With computer-based tests, this stage usually takes a few seconds, with results fed back to test-takers and/or to counselors immediately, saving tension and frustration (Mooney, 2002; Naus et al., 2009; Potosky & Bobko, 2004).

A special advantage relates to saving test-takers' scores, whether for storage, for further professional use, or for any kind of research. The use of digital technology enables data to be saved in pre-existing and preset software (e.g., Excel) or merely in test-takers' personal files. A therapist thus can retrieve test-takers' test results for any professional use — including item responses, raw scores, or normative data — quickly and easily. Moreover, statistical analyses can be done relatively simply and data entry saved.

Still another important advantage relates to the test version being up-to-date. In using an online test, especially if it is at a website provided by the test publisher, we can make sure that the most recent, updated version of any given test is in use, not an obsolete one (as often happens in using paper-and-pencil tests). Related to this, changes in instructions, scoring, and norms are automatically applied to online tests through the testing software located on a server and do not have to be distributed, learned, and supervised with individual users (Barak, 1999; Barak, 2006; Barak & English, 2002; Barak & Hen, 2008). This last consideration is an important matter that is commonly overlooked when using traditional testing at a given agency, as the used version is the version at hand.

One last significant advantage refers to assessment methods other than testing. In online interviewing, through commonly used voice- and picture-enabled systems, there are advantages in addition to the fact that interviewee and interviewer may be at a distance from each other and each at a convenient location (consequently saving time and expenses) and that the interview may easily be saved for later inspection and appraisal. Another important positive aspect is that the interviewee's behavior might better reflect his or her truer personality characteristics, as mentioned earlier, because of reduced inhibitions. This factor may significantly contribute to the validity of the psychological assessment.

DISADVANTAGES OF ONLINE ASSESSMENT RELATIVE TO TRADITIONAL METHODS

It is clear that online assessment procedures have much to offer. However, there are also drawbacks that must be considered before they are used. One of the questions that bothers many professionals in regard to online assessment has to do with the testing condition. That is, should a test-taker be allowed to take tests while in solitude (usually at home), in contrast to the traditional method, which requires the presence of a test administrator (or a psychologist). One set of possible disadvantages, therefore, relates to diminished control over the testing situation.

Psychometric tests are designed to be administered under controlled, standardized conditions. This may well not be the case in web-based assessments. People might complete assessment instruments under varying conditions: in different locations (late at night in the peace of their own home or in the bustle of a busy Internet cafe), under different physical conditions (alert, tired, or intoxicated; alone or in the presence of others), or under different psychological conditions (relaxed, distressed, bored, mischievous). One has no way of knowing whether any of these conditions apply to a particular instance of assessment. In some applications (e.g., proctored assessments for educational or occupational purposes), one may be able to instruct respondents to complete tests under certain conditions, to use computers situated within a clinic, or to ask them about the conditions under which they completed the questionnaire. In other applications (for instance mass screening, or on self-help sites) this is not realistic. It has been argued (e.g., Reips, 2000) that this variance in assessment context might lead to *greater* ecological validity. However, if assessment results are to be used for any important purpose, one needs to establish that the results have not been affected by this lack of standardization (or that the effect is a systemic one that can be considered when test outcomes are interpreted). While there is sufficient evidence that online and paper-and-pencil versions of tests can measure the same constructs to suggest that results will usually be valid (cf. Barak & English, 2002; Barak & Hen, 2008), there are also sufficient indications of (usually small) differences to imply that this issue is in need of further research (Buchanan, 2002; Buchanan, 2007).

In unproctored assessment situations, there is also an issue concerning the identity of test-takers. Test-takers, when alone, may cheat, misrepresent themselves, or even allow others to take a test for them. This is probably more a concern in high-stakes occupational assessments (cases of assessing candidates for a desired job, study program, and the like), for which the motivation to cheat is obvious (Bartram, 1997; Bartram, 1999). In a psychotherapeutic framework, however, this problem becomes incidental, on the assumption that a patient has a genuine desire to cooperate positively with the clinician. The common solution is to allow test-takers to take tests in a place (and time) of their choosing only if there is no apparent motivation to cheat. Otherwise, online tests may be taken only in a monitored office, or in a different area protected by close surveillance, whether individually or in groups, or under circumstances in which identities can be verified. There are ways in which identity can be established (e.g., national identity numbers, credit card details). However, it is an open question as to whether this will affect some of the phenomena alleged to operate in online assessments (specifically, increased self-disclosure due to anonymity; see Buchanan, 2002; Butler et al., 2010).

The issue of Internet-based test administration under unproctored conditions has brought about professional debates (e.g., Tippins et al., 2006) and has initiated several research studies. The findings of most empirical studies have shown that unproctored test conditions had minimal, if any, effects on test scores (e.g., Arthur et al., 2010; Templer & Lange, 2008), although some other studies have found that, under high-stakes testing conditions, cognitive test scores were inflated (e.g., Carstairs & Myors, 2009).

This leads to another set of issues, related to the psychological effects of different testing situations. There is a growing literature on online psychological assessment, primarily related to its use in research and occupational testing. This includes a number of projects conducted with the aim of establishing whether particular online tests are psychometrically and functionally equivalent to the offline measures on which they are based. Results from such studies, and extrapolation of findings from the large body of research on computer-mediated communication (CMC), have suggested that certain characteristics of the assessment medium (such as reduced social cues, deindividuation, or changes in the focus of attention) may influence the way in which people respond to online tests. In the context of online testing and assessment related to applicant selection conditions, the International Test Commission (2006) has issued clear guidelines to facilitate appropriate testing conditions, so that untrue variance originating from the online situation is minimized (Bartram, 2006; Lievens, 2006).

CMC research (e.g., Kiesler et al., 1984; Walther, 1996) has indicated that, when people interact via computers, their communication may be disinhibited to some extent (as we have already indicated, this effect appears to apply to online communication; see Joinson, 1998; Joinson, 1999; Joinson, 2001; Suler, 2004), hence our earlier suggestion that people's online behavior might reflect their "real personalities" unfettered by normal social constraints.

Disinhibition effects have traditionally been discussed (and researched) in terms of "flaming" – hostile communications – but also seem to impact upon the degree to which people are willing to disclose personal (and often very sensitive) information. Simply put, people seem to disclose high levels of personal information when interacting on the Internet (Barak & Gluck-Ofri, 2007; Joinson, 2002; Joinson & Paine, 2007; Qian & Scott, 2007). There are strong indications that people may reveal more about themselves to an online questionnaire than in an f2f context (e.g., Butler et al., 2010).

There is also evidence that people may respond in less socially desirable ways to online questionnaires; Joinson (1999) randomly assigned college-student participants to complete a social desirability questionnaire (among other instruments) either via the Internet or in a paper-and-pencil format. He found that social desirability scores were lower for the group tested via the Internet. This finding has been interpreted as evidence that people will be less influenced by social desirability concerns when completing online assessments; they may feel free to express socially disapproved aspects of their identities. On the other hand, they may also feel less constrained to provide the information requested by the assessor (Buchanan et al., 2002b).

Possibly as a function of these phenomena (or perhaps the ideas advanced by Bargh et al., 2002, and McKenna, 2007, that people are more able to express their "true selves" on the Internet), a number of studies have reported differences between online and offline respondents, who did not appear to differ in any way other than the medium used to assess them, in mean scores on several instruments (e.g., Barak & Cohen, 2002; Davis, 1999; Fouladi et al., 2002; Joinson, 1999). There are some suggestions that this is the case with respect to measures related to negative affect (in that people report higher levels of negative affect when tested online). If correct, this has clear implications for clinical assessment. In any case, it is an issue on which more research is clearly needed.

One of the implications is that normative data should not be used in interpreting scores obtained with online clinical inventories. This assertion is based on the fact that the vast majority of normative data available will have been gathered offline. Buchanan (2003) has shown that using offline norms may lead to very serious errors of judgment of the meaning of a particular score achieved using an online psychological test (e.g., in the case of one set of data presented, use of offline norms would have led to misclassification of 18 percent of the sample). Clearly, this objection would not apply to normative data gathered online; in that case, one would be comparing the score of an individual with data from the appropriate population. The difficulty here is the heterogeneity of that population; it is possible that one may be called upon to assess people from different cultures or countries (or even *in* other countries). Will appropriate data be available under those circumstances? In the case of screening instruments (e.g., on self-help sites), how does one ensure that the correct norms have been used and correct feedback given to the individual? These issues led Buchanan (2003) to suggest that online tests should not currently be used in a manner requiring the use of normative data, and their main utility would be in applications that did not require such comparisons to be made (e.g., monitoring change during therapy, ipsative measures such as the SDS). This is a situation that is likely to change; as online tests become more widely used, normative data will accrue and the mechanisms that might affect responses will become better understood.

Another potential drawback to online assessment is the current lack of regulation and quality control. In the case of standard offline assessment procedures, a number of mechanisms exist to ensure at least a minimum standard of quality and professionalism, usually regulated by governments and professional organizations. For example, in many countries, publishers of psychometric tests adhere to standards developed by bodies such as the International Test Commission (International Test Commission, 2001) and require evidence (e.g., a recognized qualification in testing or attendance at a course run by the publisher) of competence before they will sell a test to an individual. Most people with access to assessment procedures and the opportunity to use them will have had appropriate training, and in most cases will also be members of a professional body with a code of ethics and disciplinary procedures for anyone found to have acted inappropriately.

This will extend in part to online assessment procedures: those involving commercially published psychometric instruments or employed by trained, qualified therapists. However, a large proportion of the assessments being conducted over the Internet (e.g., via self-help or personality testing sites) do not meet these criteria, and numerous examples of very bad practice can be found (e.g., invalid instruments, data stored without informed consent, misleading information, potentially distressing feedback) (Barak & English, 2002; Oliver & Zack, 1999). It should be mentioned that the International Test Committee (2006; see also Bartram, 2006; Coyne & Bartram, 2006) has proposed clear guidelines intended to deal with and partially prevent such problematic situations. Positive consequences stemming from these guidelines, however, are yet to be documented.

ETHICAL AND LEGAL ISSUES

Codes of ethical conduct for psychologists typically include some statement to the effect that psychologists should only use procedures that are fit for their purposes. For example, the section of the current APA ethics code dealing with assessment states, "Psychologists base the opinions contained in their recommendations, reports, and diagnostic or evaluative statements, including forensic testimony, on information and techniques sufficient to substantiate their findings" (APA, 2002). This principle applies both to therapeutic interventions (which should be evidence-based and empirically supported) and to assessment procedures (which should actually measure the intended constructs).

Although we know much more today than previously regarding the efficacy of online interventions (see Barak et al., 2008, and work presented in this volume), relatively less is known about online assessment. Despite numerous indications that they can work successfully, factors that may impact upon the validity of online tests still require much more investigation. In this sense, there is a great burden of responsibility upon people conducting online assessments to ensure that their tools are fit for their purposes. Unfortunately, many of the "tests" currently available on the web are likely to be manifestly unfit for any purpose whatsoever, and lack any evidence of reliability or validity. These include measures developed by (well-intentioned) amateurs, and even psychologists, who are not aware or sufficiently careful of psychometric issues, and professionals who are aware of psychometric issues but have not fully considered the possible effects of using a new testing medium. Kier and Molinari (2004) mentioned several main ethical issues involved in such testing situations: lack of in-person counseling and guidance, possible misuse and abuse of test results, and lack of informed consent. These authors suggested legal and ethical actions to minimize the unethical use of online amateur tests. Given that many "end users" of online assessments will be unaware of the quality of the test they are using, this may create problems, especially in the (many) situations where feedback is given to users (see also Barak, 2003; Barak, 2006, for discussion of a parallel situation with career-related assessments where people may make wrong career decisions on the basis of flawed feedback).

One possible use of Internet-mediated assessments is for self-exploration and personal development purposes. As already indicated, there is a wide range of instruments available for this purpose, and the popularity of self-testing websites indicates that people are using them. The primary incentive to take a test under such circumstances is to obtain feedback, which the test-taker may then use for various purposes (including making life decisions), perhaps based on invalid grounds.

This makes it very important for people constructing online tests to ensure that the information is accurate and that it will not have a negative effect upon test-takers. Accuracy can only be ensured by using assessment techniques of demonstrable validity and making comparisons with appropriate normative data if required (e.g., when informing someone how their scores on a screening inventory compare to those of other people). The majority of sites presenting online tests do (appropriately) print a disclaimer of some sort, advising people not to place too much reliance on the test results. However, it is an open question whether such disclaimers have much impact, given the strength of the well-known "Barnum effect" (the tendency of people to accept test feedback composed of high-base-rate personality traits as descriptive of themselves, even if the feedback is fictional; Groth-Marnat, 2009). Research is required to establish whether people actually do believe feedback from online tests and to assess whether inappropriate feedback might have any negative effects upon their lives. It is also possible that test feedback might have immediate negative effects, irrespective of any action people take based on it. It has been shown that fairly minor mood manipulations in Internet experiments can influence people's emotional states (Goritz et al., 1999; MacLeod et al., 2007). How might people react to feedback indicating that their level of intelligence is "well below the population average"? Or that their pattern of scores has some negative implications for their physical or mental health? Or that they have a high score on some socially undesirable construct (e.g., psychoticism)? These issues might have an especially large impact upon people with problems or low self-esteem: exactly the kind of people who might be seeking mental health help or information on the Internet.

This observation also applies to the use of online tests by psychologists for diagnostic purposes and is a reason why there might be reservations about the unsupervised use of the tests. The very taking of a psychological test might itself create a detrimental situation. This may result from the client experiencing stress while taking the test, as well as from an unexpected negative evaluation (in cases where immediate results are provided to test-takers, a common procedure in many tests published on the Internet). Therefore, being an unaccompanied test-taker might potentially be painful and even harmful (Kier & Molinari, 2004). A solution to this problem − at least in the context of clinical tests − is to use a computer stationed in a clinic to take Internet-based tests, so that immediate support is available. Another possible solution to provide support when needed, even if a test-taker is in solitude, is through the phone or through synchronous online communication. Clearly, such support is easier to provide within established therapeutic relationships than in cases of mass-screening or self-help sites.

Issues related to the remote provision of mental health services must also be considered. One of the great advantages of behavioral telehealth (or Internet-supported psychotherapy and counseling) is that services can be provided for people in distant locations. This is also an area of potential difficulty, especially given the "emergent" nature of Internet law. In some areas, there are local or national laws relating to telehealth provision. However, there is evidence that a high proportion of behavioral telehealth providers are unaware of (or misunderstand) local legislation that applies to them (Maheu & Gordon, 2000). Maheu and Gordon also found that a high proportion of practitioners provided services to clients in other jurisdictions (in their study, other US states). If one extrapolates this to the (realistic) scenario of people providing assessments to people in other countries, it is clear that there may be legal issues one needs to consider (see Chapter 6). What recourse might a client have in the case of malpractice (e.g., giving misleading or damaging feedback from an online assessment) by a remote practitioner? What legislation applies regarding the secure transmission and storage of data, and access rights to it?

Security of data transmission and storage must also be considered. Much has been made of the "hacker threat": unauthorized interception of, or access to, test data by third parties. The extent to which this is a problem is open to debate. On the one side, it is certainly possible. For example, Reips (2002) observes that configuration errors or certain data transmission techniques result in possibly confidential data being openly available via the World Wide Web in the case of online psychological experiments, and that this happens frequently. Given that psychologists constructing such experiments are likely to be among the more technically proficient and "Internet-savvy" members of the profession, this is a worrying finding. This may cause a problem for online counseling applications if Maheu and Gordon's (2000) prediction that many therapists, who are not computer experts, will find themselves forced to adopt new technologies. On the other side, the extent to which there really is a problem may be exaggerated. Yes, it is possible to intercept data transmitted via computers. It is also entirely possible − and probably easier for most people − to tap a telephone, listen outside a therapist's door, break the lock to a "secure" filing cabinet, and so on. The risk is therefore probably no greater than in traditional assessment contexts (Barak & English, 2002). We are not aware of any incidents where the "hacker threat" has been anything other than a hypothetical problem, so, while it is an issue that people should be aware of, it is possible that its practical importance is low.

A related issue refers to the availability of detailed test information on the Internet. This information − including "good" and "bad" answer examples, tips, and interpretations − could significantly damage assessment validity (Bauer & McCaffrey, 2006; LoBello & Zachar, 2007; Suhr & Gunstad, 2007). This is especially problematic as many test administrators are not aware of such prior knowledge and/or possible practice by test-takers, so they do not take this factor into consideration.

SUMMARY

The current chapter has made an attempt to cover the wide spectrum of issues relating to Internet-supported psychological assessment. No doubt, the Internet has provided psychology with a revolutionary vehicle through which methods of assessment of people − for therapeutic purposes, for appraising a person's suitability for a study program or a job, and for self-exploration − are changing. Thanks to the typical characteristics of the Internet − the "Penta-A Engine" of availability, affordability, accessibility, acceptability, and aloneness − its exploitation as a tool that enables efficient testing and assessment is inviting. Perhaps the central advantage for assessment is its flexibility in terms of time and place, provision of quick and accurate scoring, availability of textual information and web links pertaining to the nature of the assessment results, central control of updating test versions, and Internet-supported non-testing assessment methods. Further, because of the special communication characteristics of people who use the Internet, such as anonymity, invisibility, asynchronicity, and lack of eye-contact, human inhibitions diminish and more candid responses may be anticipated, thus elevating the validity of the assessment.

Although online assessment is useful and valuable, there are several precautions that have to be taken. Perhaps the most problematic issue is that many amateur tests are published on the Internet, and naive surfers cannot differentiate between a professional, validated assessment website and a non-professional one. There is some evidence to suggest, as has been pointed out, that the measurement of specific dimensions online might possibly be erroneous, and perhaps assessments of some people, or people in certain circumstances, might be biased. We have made a special point of addressing the issue of providing assessment feedback online, and of the potential harm that this could cause if done badly.

Online assessment is, relatively, a new territory. Many issues and questions are being raised and only a few answers based on empirical research can be given to date. Until knowledge based on much practice and massive research is accumulated, we should be cautious in routinely applying online assessment. Intensive investigations are needed in order to provide reliable answers to questions regarding basic issues, for example converting traditional tests to online versions, providing feedback to test-takers online, performing chat-based interviews, using synchronous and asynchronous environments as a means of behavioral assessment, and so on. In addition, it would be beneficial to raise public awareness and understanding of online tests so that people will know what to expect and what not to expect, thus obviating potentially harmful situations. We also call for the training of professionals in Internet-related assessment, to provide them with new and advanced tools, on the one hand, and to make them aware of their shortcomings and limitations, on the other.

KEY TERMS

Deindividuation A psychological process characterized by reduced individual self-evaluation and decreased inhibition in crowd situations.

Disinhibition Abolition or reduction of psychological mechanisms that govern spontaneous behavior.

Ecological validity The degree to which findings obtained from research in controlled situations may be generalized and found relevant under other circumstances and more natural environments.

Factor structure The basic main dimensions or psychological constructs underlying responses to a given test.

Myers-Briggs Type Indicator (MBTI) A well-known, widely used personality assessment test based on Jung's typology of personality.

Normative data Statistical parameters of a comparison group by which an individual person's test results are analyzed.

Projective test A psychological test in which people are asked to respond to ambiguous stimuli (e.g., pictures, unfinished sentences) and in which they supposedly express their individual needs and desires.

Psychological assessment A set of various procedures, including written tests, interviews, appraisal of group behavior, and other measures, carried out in order to evaluate a person's personality and various traits.

Psychometric properties Quality of measurement of a psychological test, assessed by several factors, such as reliability and validity.

Qualitative Based on subjective analysis and impression rather than objective, measured assessment.

Reliability The degree to which a test consistently measures a trait or construct.

Rorschach inkblot test A projective test in which people are presented with symmetrical ink stains and asked to tell what they see in them.

Social desirability The general tendency of people to do and say things so others value and like them.

Thematic Apperception Test (TAT) A projective test that is based on creating personal stories stimulated by given standard pictures.

Validity The degree to which a test measures the concept it is supposed to measure.

REFERENCES

Aluja, A., Rossier, J., & Zuckerman, M. (2007). Equivalence of paper and pencil vs Internet forms of the ZKPQ - 50 - CC in Spanish and French samples. *Personality and Individual Differences, 43,* 2022−2032.

American Psychological Association (APA). (2002). Ethical principles of psychologists and code of conduct. *American Psychologist, 57,* 1060−1073.

Amichai-Hamburger, Y. (2007). Personality, individual differences and Internet use. In A. Joinson, K. McKenna, T. Postmes, & U. Reips (Eds.), *The Oxford handbook of Internet psychology* (pp. 187−204). Oxford, UK: Oxford University Press.

Anolli, L., Villani, D., & Riva, G. (2005). Personality of people using chat: An on-line research. *Cyberpsychology and Behavior, 8,* 89−95.

Anthony, K., & Merz-Nagel, D. (2010). *Therapy online: A practical guide.* London: Sage.

Arthur, W., Glaze, R. M., Villado, A. J., & Taylor, J. E. (2010). The magnitude and extent of cheating and response distortion effects on unproctored Internet-based tests of cognitive ability and personality. *International Journal of Selection and Assessment, 18,* 1−16.

Back, M. D., Schmukle, S. C., & Egloff, B. (2008). How extraverted is honey. bunny77@hotmail.de? Inferring personality from e-mail addresses. *Journal of Research in Personality, 42,* 1116−1122.

Baer, L., & Minichiello, W. E. (2006). Internet assessment of obsessive-compulsive disorder. *Journal of Clinical Psychiatry, 67,* 1473.

Baker, J. D. (2007). Queendom online test repository. In R. A. Reynolds, R. Woods, & J. D. Baker (Eds.), *Handbook of research on electronic surveys and measurements* (pp. 352−354). Hershey, PA: Idea Group.

Barak, A. (1999). Psychological applications on the Internet: A discipline on the threshold of a new millennium. *Applied and Preventive Psychology, 8,* 231−246.

Barak, A. (2003). Ethical and professional issues in career assessment on the Internet. *Journal of Career Assessment, 11,* 3−21.

Barak, A. (2006). Internet career assessment. In J. Greenhaus, & G. Callanan (Eds.), *Encyclopedia of career development* (pp. 404−406). Thousand Oaks, CA: Sage.

Barak, A., & Cohen, L. (2002). Empirical examination of an online version of the self-directed search. *Journal of Career Assessment, 10,* 383−396.

Barak, A., & English, N. (2002). Prospects and limitations of psychological testing on the Internet. *Journal of Technology in Human Services, 19*(2/3), 65−89.

Barak, A., & Fisher, W. A. (2002). The future of internet sexuality. In A. Cooper (Ed.), *Sex and the Internet: A guidebook for clinicians* (pp. 267−280). New York: Brunner/Routledge.

Barak, A., & Gluck-Ofri, O. (2007). Degree and reciprocity of self-disclosure in online forums. *Cyberpsychology and Behavior, 10,* 407−417.

Barak, A., & Hen, L. (2008). Exposure in cyberspace as means of enhancing psychological assessment. In A. Barak (Ed.), Psychological aspects of cyberspace: Theory, research, applications (pp. 129−162). Cambridge, UK: Cambridge University Press.

Barak, A., Hen, L., Boniel-Nissim, M., & Shapira, N. (2008). A comprehensive review and a meta-analysis of the effectiveness of Internet-based psychotherapeutic interventions. *Journal of Technology in Human Services, 26,* 109−160.

Barak, A., & Miron, O. (2005). Writing characteristics of suicidal people on the Internet: A psychological investigation of emerging social environments. *Suicide and Life-threatening Behavior, 35*, 507–524.

Bargh, J. A., Mckenna, K. Y., & Fitzsimmons, G. M. (2002). Can you see the real me? Activation and expression of the "true self" on the Internet. *Journal of Social Issues, 58*, 33–48.

Bartram, D. (1997). Distance assessment: Psychological assessment through the Internet. *Selection and Development Review, 13*(3), 15–19.

Bartram, D. (1999). Testing and the Internet: Current realities, issues and future possibilities. *Selection and Development Review, 15*(6), 3–12.

Bartram, D. (2006). The internationalization of testing and new models of test delivery on the Internet. *International Journal of Testing, 6*, 121–131.

Bauer, L., & McCaffrey, R. J. (2006). Coverage of the test of memory malingering, Victoria symptom validity test, and word memory test on the Internet: Is test security threatened? *Archives of Clinical Neuropsychology, 21*, 121–126.

Betz, N. E., & Borgen, F. H. (2009). Comparative effectiveness of CAPA and FOCUS online career assessment systems with undecided college students. *Journal of Career Assessment, 17*, 351–366.

Bhatara, V. S., Vogt, H. B., Patrick, S., Doniparthi, L., & Ellis, R. (2006). Acceptability of a Web-based attention-deficit/hyperactivity disorder scale (T-SKAMP) by teachers: A pilot study. *The Journal of the American Board of Family Medicine, 19*, 195–200.

Blackman, M. C. (2002). The employment interview via the telephone: Are we sacrificing accurate personality judgments for cost efficiency? *Journal of Research in Personality, 36*, 208–223.

Bressani, R. V., & Downs, A. C. (2002). Youth independent living assessment: Testing the equivalence of web and paper/pencil versions of the Ansell-Casey Life Skills Assessment. *Computers in Human Behavior, 18*, 453–464.

Brodey, B. B., Rosen, C. S., Brodey, I. S., Sheetz, B. M., Steinfeld, R. R., & Gastfriend, D. R. (2004). Validation of the Addiction Severity Index (ASI) for Internet and automated telephone self-report administration. *Journal of Substance Abuse Treatment, 26*, 253–259.

Buchanan, T. (2001). Online personality assessment. In U. D. Reips, & M. Bosnjak (Eds.), *Dimensions of Internet science* (pp. 57–74). Lengerich, Germany: Pabst Science Publishers.

Buchanan, T. (2002). Online assessment: Desirable or dangerous? *Professional Psychology: Research and Practice, 33*, 148–154.

Buchanan, T. (2003). Internet based questionnaire assessment: Appropriate use in clinical contexts. *Cognitive Behaviour Therapy, 32*, 100–109.

Buchanan, T. (2007). Personality testing on the Internet: What we know, and what we do not. In A. Joinson, K. McKenna, T. Postmes, & U. Reips (Eds.), *The Oxford handbook of Internet psychology* (pp. 447–460). Oxford, UK: Oxford University Press.

Buchanan, T., Johnson, J. A., & Goldberg, L. R. (2005). Implementing a five-factor personality inventory for use on the Internet. *European Journal of Psychological Assessment, 21*, 115–127.

Buchanan, T., Ali, T, Heffernan, T. M., Ling, J., Parrott, A., Rodgers, J., & Scholey, A. S. (2002a, October). *Psychometric properties of online self-report memory questionnaires: The EMQ and PMQ*. Poster session presented at German Online Research '02, Hohenheim, Germany.

Buchanan, T., Joinson, A. N., & Ali, T. (2002b, October). *Development of a behavioural measure of self-disclosure for use in online research*. Paper presented at German Online Research '02, Hohenheim, Germany.

Buchanan, T., & Smith, J. L. (1999). Research on the Internet: Validation of a World-Wide Web mediated personality scale. *Behavior Research Methods, Instruments, and Computers, 31*, 565–571.

Buffardi, L. E., & Campbell, W. K. (2008). Narcissism and social networking web sites. *Personality and Social Psychology Bulletin, 34,* 1303−1314.

Butler, S. F., Villapiano, A., & Malinow, A. (2010). The effect of computer-mediated administration on self-disclosure of problems on addiction severity index. *Journal of Addiction Medicine, 3,* 194−203.

Cacciola, J. S., Alterman, A. I., Rutherford, M. J., McKay, J. R., & May, D. J. (1999). Comparability of telephone and in-person Structured Clinical Interview for DSM-III-R (SCID) diagnoses. *Assessment, 6,* 235−242.

Carlbring, P., Brunt, S., Bohman, S., Austin, D., Richards, J., Öst, L., & Andersson, G. (2007). Internet vs. paper and pencil administration of questionnaires commonly used in panic/agoraphobia research. *Computers in Human Behavior, 23,* 1421−1434.

Carstairs, J., & Myors, B. (2009). Internet testing: A natural experiment reveals test score inflation on a high-stakes, unproctored cognitive test. *Computers in Human Behavior, 25,* 738−742.

Chinman, M., Young, A. S., Schell, T., Hassell, J., & Mintz, J. (2004). Computer-assisted self-assessment in persons with severe mental illness. *Journal of Clinical Psychiatry, 65,* 1343−1351.

Chuah, S. C., Drasgow, F., & Roberts, B. W. (2006). Personality assessment: Does the medium matter? No. *Journal of Research in Personality, 40,* 359−376.

Chung, C. K., & Pennebaker, J. W. (2008). Revealing dimensions of thinking in open-ended self-descriptions: An automated meaning extraction method for natural language. *Journal of Research in Personality, 42,* 96−132.

Coffee, K., Pearce, J., & Nishimura, R. (1999). State of California: Civil service testing moves into cyberspace. *Public Personnel Management, 28,* 283−300.

Coles, M. E., Cook, L. M., & Blake, T. R. (2007). Assessing obsessive compulsive symptoms and cognitions on the Internet: Evidence for the comparability of paper and Internet administration. *Behaviour Research and Therapy, 45,* 2232−2240.

Correa, T., Hinsley, A. W., & de Zuniga, H. G. (2010). Who interacts on the web? The intersection of users' personality and social media use. *Computers in Human Behavior, 26,* 247−253.

Coyne, I., & Bartram, D. (2006). Introduction to the special issue on the ITC guidelines on computer-based and Internet-delivered testing. *International Journal of Testing, 6,* 115−119.

Cronin, B., Morath, R., Curtin, P., & Heil, M. (2006). Public sector use of technology in managing human resources. *Human Resource Management Review, 16,* 416−430.

Cronk, B. C., & West, J. L. (2002). Personality research on the Internet: A comparison of Web-based and traditional instruments in take-home and in-class settings. Behavior Research Methods, Instruments, and Computers, *34,* 177−180.

Cunningham, J. A., Humphreys, K., & Koski-Jännes, A. (2000). Providing personalized assessment feedback for problem drinking on the Internet: A pilot project. *Journal of Studies on Alcohol, 61,* 794−798.

Davies, J. (2006). "Hello newbie!**big welcome hugs** hope u like it here as much as I do!": An exploration of teenagers' informal online learning. In D. Buckingham, & B. Willett (Eds.), Digital generations: Children, young people, and new media (pp. 211−228). Mahwah, NJ: Erlbaum.

Davis, M., Bolding, G., Hart, G., Sherr, L., & Elford, J. (2004). Reflecting on the experience of interviewing online: Perspectives from the Internet and HIV study in London. *AIDS Care, 16,* 944−952.

Davis, R. N. (1999). Web-based administration of a personality questionnaire: Comparison with traditional methods. Behavior Research Methods, Instruments, and Computers, *31,* 572−577.

Döring, N. (2002). Personal home pages on the web: A review of research. *Journal of Computer-Mediated Communication, 7*(3)Retrieved November 1, 2002 from http://www.ascusc.org/jcmc/vol7/issue3/doering.html

Duggan, A. P., & Parrott, R. L. (2000). Research note: Physicians' nonverbal rapport building and patients' talk about the subjective component of illness. *Human Communication Research, 27,* 299−311.

Elford, R., White, H., Browering, R., Ghandi, A., Maddiggan, B., & St. John, K., et al. (2000). A randomized controlled trial of child psychiatric assessments conducted using videoconferencing. *Journal of Telemedicine and Telecare, 6,* 73−82.

Elgin, P. D., & Clapham, M. M. (2004). Attributes associated with the submission of electronic versus paper resumes. *Computers in Human Behavior, 20,* 535−549.

Elliott, T. R., & Byrd, E. K. (1985). Scoring accuracy of the Self-Directed Search with ninth-grade students. *Vocational Guidance Quarterly, 34,* 85−90.

Erlanger, D., Feldman, D., Kutner, K., Kaushik, T., Kroger, H., & Festa, J., et al. (2003). Development and validation of a web-based neuropsychological test protocol for sports-related return-to-play decision-making. *Archives of Clinical Neuropsychology, 18,* 293−316.

Fortson, B. L., Scotti, J. R., Del Ben, K. S., & Chen, Y. (2006). Reliability and validity of an Internet traumatic stress survey with a college student sample. *Journal of Traumatic Stress, 19,* 709−720.

Fouladi, R. T., McCarthy, C. J., & Moller, N. P. (2002). Paper-and-pencil or online? Evaluating mode effects on measures of emotional functioning and attachment. *Assessment, 9,* 204−215.

Gati, I., & Saka, N. (2001). Internet-based versus paper-and-pencil assessment: Measuring career decision-making difficulties. *Journal of Career Assessment, 9,* 379−416.

Gerjets, P., & Hellenthal-Schorr, T. (2008). Competent information search in the World Wide Web: Development and evaluation of a web training for pupils. *Computers in Human Behavior, 24,* 693−715.

Gill, A. J., Oberlander, J., & Austin, E. (2006). Rating e-mail personality at zero acquaintance. *Personality and Individual Differences, 40,* 497−507.

Gore, P. A., Jr, & Leuwerke, W. C. (2000). Information technology for career assessment on the Internet. *Journal of Career assessment, 8,* 3−19.

Goritz, A, Batinic, B, Goersch, A, & Moser, K. (1999, October). *Induzierbarkeit von Stimmunslangen uber das WWW.* Paper presented at the meeting of German Online Research '99, Nürnberg, Germany.

Groth-Marnat, G. (2009). *Handbook of psychological assessment* (5th ed). New York: Wiley.

Guadagno, R. E., Okdie, B. M., & Eno, C. A. (2008). Who blogs? Personality predictors of blogging. *Computers in Human Behavior, 24,* 1993−2004.

Hamilton, R. J., & Bowers, B. J. (2006). Internet recruitment and e-mail interviews in qualitative studies. *Qualitative Health Research, 16,* 821−835.

Hattrup, K., O'Connell, M. S., & Yager, J. R. (2006). Pre-screening job applicants with interactive voice response and web-based technologies: Are the methods equivalent? *Applied HRM Research, 11,* 15−26.

Hill, B. C., Theis, G. A., & Davison, M. A. (2002). Integration of a web-based behavioral health assessment tool in clinical medicine. *American Clinical Laboratory, 21*(3), 21−25.

Hoffmann, T., Russell, T., Thompson, L., Vincent, A., & Nelson, M. (2008). Using the Internet to assess activities of daily living and hand function in people with Parkinson's disease. *NeuroRehabilitation, 23,* 253−261.

Holland, J. L., Powell, A. B., & Fritzsche, B. A. (1994). *The self-directed search: Professional user's guide* Odessa, FL: Psychological Assessement Resources.

Hunt, N., & McHale, S. (2007). A practical guide to the e-mail interview. *Qualitative Health Research, 17,* 1415−1521.

Hyler, S. E., Gangure, D. P., & Batchelder, S. T. (2005). Can telepsychiatry replace in-person psychiatric assessments? A review and meta-analysis of comparison studies. *CNS Spectrums, 10,* 403−413.

Ihme, J. M., Lemke, F., Lieder, K., Martin, F., Müller, J. C., & Schmidt, S. (2009). Comparison of ability tests administered online and in the laboratory. *Behavior Research Methods, 41*, 1183–1189.

International Test Commission (2001). International guidelines for test use. *International Journal of Testing, 1*, 93–114.

International Test Commission (2006). International guidelines of computer-based and Internet-delivered testing. *International Journal of Testing, 6*, 143–171.

Johnson, J. A. (2005). Ascertaining the validity of individual protocols from web-based personality inventories. *Journal of Research in Personality, 39*, 103–129.

Joinson, A. N. (1998). Causes and implication of disinhibited behavior on the Internet. In J. Gackenbach (Ed.), *Psychology and the Internet: Intrapersonal, interpersonal, and transpersonal implications* (pp. 43–60). San Diego: Academic Press.

Joinson, A. N. (1999). Social desirability, anonymity, and Internet-based questionnaires. Behavior and Research Methods, Instruments, and Computers, *31*, 433–438.

Joinson, A. N. (2001). Self-disclosure in computer-mediated communication: The role of self-awareness and visual anonymity. *European Journal of Social Psychology, 31*, 177–192.

Joinson, A. N. (2002). Understanding the psychology of Internet behaviour: Virtual worlds, real lives. Basingstoke, UK: Palgrave.

Joinson, A. N., & Paine, C. B. (2007). Self-disclosure, privacy and the Internet. In A. Joinson, K. McKenna, T. Postmes, & U. Reips (Eds.), *The Oxford handbook of Internet psychology* (pp. 237–252). Oxford, UK: Oxford University Press.

Jones, J. W., Brasher, E. E., & Huff, J. W. (2002). Innovations in integrity-based personnel selection: Building a technology-friendly assessment. *International Journal of Selection and Assessment, 10*, 87–97.

Jones, W. P. (2004). Testing and counseling: A marriage saved by the Internet? In J. W. Bloom, & G. R. Walz (Eds.), *Cybercounseling and cyberlearning: An encore* (pp. 183–202). Alexandria, VA: American Counseling Association.

Jones, W. P., Harbach, R. L., Coker, J. K., & Staples, P. A. (2002). Web-assisted vocational test interpretation. *Journal of Employment Counseling, 39*, 127–137.

Kelly, K. R., & Jugovic, H. (2001). Concurrent validity of the online version of the Keirsey Temperament Sorter II. *Journal of Career Assessment, 9*, 49–59.

Kier, F. J., & Molinari, V. (2004). Do-it-yourself testing for mental illness: Ethical issues, concerns, and recommendations. *Professional Psychology: Research and Practice, 35*, 261–267.

Kiesler, S., Siegal, J., & McGuire, T. W. (1984). Social psychological aspects of computer mediated communication. *American Psychologist, 39*, 1123–1134.

Kleiman, T., & Gati, I. (2004). Challenges of Internet-based assessment: Measuring career decision-making difficulties. *Measurement and Evaluation in Counseling and Development, 37*, 41–55.

Kluemper, D. H., & Rosen, P. A. (2009). Future employment selection methods: Evaluating social networking web sites. *Journal of Managerial Psychology, 24*, 567–580.

Knapp, H., & Kirk, S. A. (2003). Using pencil and paper, Internet and touch-tone phones for self-administered surveys: Does methodology matter? *Computers in Human Behavior, 19*, 117–134.

Konradt, U., Hertel, G., & Joder, K. (2003). Web-based assessment of call center agents: Development and validation of a computerized instrument. *International Journal of Selection and Assessment, 11*, 184–193.

Kraus, R. (2004). Ethical and legal considerations for providers of mental health services online. In R. Kraus, J. Zack, & G. Stricker (Eds.), *Online counseling: A handbook for mental health professionals* (pp. 123–144). San Diego, CA: Elsevier Academic Press.

Kraut, R., Olson, J., Banaji, M., Bruckman, A., Cohen, J., & Couper, M. (2004). Psychological research online. *American Psychologist, 59*, 105–117.

Landers, R. N., & Lounsbury, J. W. (2006). An investigation of Big Five and narrow personality traits in relation to Internet usage. *Computers in Human Behavior, 22*, 283–293.

Le, H-N, Perry, D-F, & Sheng, X. (2009). Using the Internet to screen for postpartum depression. *Maternal and Child Health Journal, 13*, 213–221.

Lee, H. (2005). Implosion, virtuality, and interaction in an Internet discussion group. Information, Communication & Society, 8, 47–63.

Leung, L. (2002). Loneliness, self-disclosure, and ICQ ("I seek you") use. *Cyberpsychology and Behavior, 5*, 241–251.

Lievens, F. (2006). The ITC guidelines on computer-based and Internet-delivered testing: Where do we go from here? *International Journal of Testing, 6*, 189–194.

Lievens, F., & Harris, M. M. (2003). Research on Internet recruitment and testing: Current status and future directions. In C. L. Cooper, & I. T. Robertson (Eds.), *International review of industrial and organizational psychology* (Vol. 18). Chicester, UK: Wiley.

LoBello, S. G., & Zachar, P. (2007). Psychological test sales and Internet auctions: Ethical considerations for dealing with obsolete or unwanted test materials. *Professional Psychology: Research and Practice, 38*, 68–70.

Lumsden, J. A., Sampson, J. P., Reardon, R. C., Lenz, J. G., & Peterson, G. W. (2004). A comparison study of the paper-and-pencil, personal computer, and Internet versions of Holland's self-directed search. *Measurement and Evaluation in Counseling and Development, 37*, 85–94.

MacLeod, C., Soong, L. Y., Rutherford, E. M., & Campbell, L. W. (2007). Internet-delivered assessment and manipulation of anxiety-linked attentional bias: Validation of a free-access attentional probe software package. *Behavior Research Methods, 39*, 533–538.

Maheu, M. M., & Gordon, B. L. (2000). Counseling and therapy on the Internet. *Professional Psychology: Research and Practice, 31*, 484–489.

Mangunkusumo, R. T., Duisterhout, J. S., de Graaff, N., Maarsingh, E. J., de Koning, H. J., & Raat, H. (2006). Internet versus paper mode of health and health behavior questionnaires in elementary schools: Asthma and fruit as examples. *Journal of School Health, 76*, 80–86.

Marcus, B., Machilek, F., & Schütz, A. (2006). Personality in cyberspace: Personal web sites as media for personality expressions and impressions. *Journal of Personality and Social Psychology, 90*, 1014–1031.

Matthews, J., & Cramer, E. P. (2008). Using technology to enhance qualitative research with hidden populations. *The Qualitative Report, 13*, 301–315.

McCoyd, J. L., & Schwaber Kerson, T. (2006). Conducting intensive interviews using email: A serendipitous comparative opportunity. *Qualitative Social Work, 5*, 389–406.

McCue, P., Buchanan, T., & Martin, C. R. (2006). Screening for psychological distress using Internet administration of the Hospital Anxiety and Depression Scale (HADS) in individuals with chronic fatigue syndrome. *British Journal of Clinical Psychology, 45*, 483–498.

McDaniel, M. A., & Nguyen, N. T. (2001). Situational judgment tests: A review of practice and constructs assessed. *International Journal of Selection and Assessment, 9*, 103–113.

McKee, L. M., & Levinson, E. M. (1990). A review of the computerized version of the Self-Directed Search. *Career Development Quarterly, 38*, 325–333.

McKenna, K. Y. A. (2007). Through the Internet looking glass: Expressing and validating the true self. In A. Joinson, K. McKenna, T. Postmes, & U. Reips (Eds.), *The*

Oxford handbook of Internet psychology (pp. 205–222). Oxford, UK: Oxford University Press.

McKenna, K. Y. A. (2008). Influences on the nature and functioning of online groups. In A. Barak (Ed.), *Psychological aspects of cyberspace: Theory, research, applications* (pp. 228–242). Cambridge, UK: Cambridge University Press.

McKenna, K. Y., & Green, A. S. (2002). Virtual group dynamics. *Group Dynamics, 6,* 116–127.

McKenna, K., & Seidman, G. (2005). You, me, and we: Interpersonal processes in electronic groups. In Y. Amichai-Hamburger (Ed.), *The social net: Human behavior in cyberspace* (pp. 191–217). New York: Oxford University Press.

Medalia, A., Lim, R., & Erlanger, D. (2005). Psychometric properties of the Web-based work-readiness cognitive screen used as a neuropsychological assessment tool for schizophrenia. *Computer Methods and Programs in Biomedicine, 80,* 93–102.

Michinov, N., Michinov, E., & Toczek-Capelle, M. (2004). Social identity, group processes, and performance in synchronous computer-mediated communication. *Group Dynamics, 8,* 27–39.

Miller, E. T., Neal, D. J., Roberts, L. J., Baer, J. S., Cressler, S. O., & Metrik, J., et al. (2002). Test-retest reliability of alcohol measures: Is there a difference between Internet-based assessment and traditional methods? *Psychology of Addictive Behaviors, 16,* 56–63.

Miller, M. J., Cowger, E., Young, T., Tobacyk, J., Sheets, T., & Loftus, C. (2008). Assessing Holland types on the Internet: A comparative study. *College Student Journal, 42,* 270–275.

Mooney, J. (2002). Pre-employment testing on the Internet: Put candidates a click away and hire at modem speed. *Public Personnel Management, 31,* 41–52.

Naglieri, J. A., Drasgow, F., Schmit, M., Handler, L., Prifitera, A., & Margolis, A., et al. (2004). Psychological testing on the Internet: New problems, old issues. *American Psychologist, 59,* 150–162.

Naus, M. J., Philipp, L. M., & Samsi, M. (2009). From paper to pixels: A comparison of paper and computer formats in psychological assessment. *Computers in Human Behavior, 25,* 1–7.

Nordin, S., Andersson, G., Carlbring, P., Klein, B., & Austin, D. (2007, October). *A picture-based online questionnaire for agoraphobia.* Paper presented at the third meeting of the International Society for Research on Internet Interventions (ISRII 2007), Charlottesville, VA.

Nosek, B. A., Smyth, F. L., Hansen, J. J., Devos, T., Lindner, N. M., & Ranganath, K. A., et al. (2007). Pervasiveness and correlates of implicit attitudes and stereotypes. *European Review of Social Psychology, 18,* 36–88.

Ochs, E. P., Mah, K., & Binik, Y. M. (2002). Obtaining data about human sexual functioning from the Internet. In A. Cooper (Ed.), *Sex and the Internet: A guidebook for clinicians* (pp. 245–262). New York, NY: Brunner-Routledge.

Oliver, L. W., & Chartrand, J. M. (2000). Strategies for career assessment research on the Internet. *Journal of Career Assessment, 8,* 95–103.

Oliver, L. W., & Zack, J. S. (1999). Career assessment on the Internet: An exploratory study. *Journal of Career Assessment, 7,* 323–356.

Paulsen, A. S., Crowe, R. R., Noyes, R., & Pfohl, B. (1988). Reliability of the telephone interview in diagnosing anxiety disorders. *Archives of General Psychiatry, 45,* 62–63.

Peris, R., Gimeno, M. A., Pinazo, D., Ortet, G., Carrero, V., & Sanchiz, M., et al. (2002). Online chat rooms: Virtual spaces of interaction for socially oriented people. *Cyberpsychology and Behavior, 5,* 43–51.

Pettit, F. A. (2002). A comparison of World Wide Web and paper-and-pencil personality questionnaires. *Behavior Research Methods, Instruments, and Computers, 34,* 50–54.

Potosky, D., & Bobko, P. (2004). Selection testing via the Internet: Practical consideration and exploratory empirical findings. *Personnel Psychology, 57,* 1003–1034.

Qian, H., & Scott, C. R. (2007). Anonymity and self-disclosure on weblogs. *Journal of Computer-Mediated Communication, 12,* 1428–1451.

Read, J. P., Farrow, S. M., Jaanimägi, U., & Ouimette, P. (2009). Assessing trauma and traumatic stress via the Internet: Measurement equivalence and participant reactions. *Traumatology, 15,* 94–102.

Reips, U-D. (2000). The web experiment method: Advantages, disadvantages, and solutions. In M. H. Birnbaum (Ed.), *Psychological experiments on the Internet* (pp. 89–117). San Diego, CA: Academic Press.

Reips, U-D. (2002). Internet-based psychological experimenting: Five dos and five don'ts. *Social Science Computer Review, 20,* 241–249.

Riva, G., Teruzzi, T., & Anolli, L. (2003). The use of the Internet in psychological research: Comparison of online and offline questionnaires. *Cyberpsychology and Behavior, 6,* 73–80.

Robie, C., & Brown, D. J. (2007). Measurement equivalence of a personality inventory administered on the Internet versus a kiosk. *Applied HRM Research, 11,* 97–106.

Rochlen, A. B., Beretvas, S. N., & Zack, J. S. (2004). The online and face-to-face counseling attitudes scales: A validation study. *Measurement and Evaluation in Counseling and Development, 37,* 95–111.

Rosen, J., Mulsant, B. H., Marino, P., Groening, C., Young, R. C., & Fox, D. (2008). Web-based training and interrater reliability testing for scoring the Hamilton Depression Rating Scale. *Psychiatry Research, 161,* 126–130.

Ross, C., Orr, E. S., Sisic, M., Arseneault, J. M., Simmering, M. G., & Orr, R. R. (2009). Personality and motivations associated with Facebook use. *Computers in Human Behavior, 25,* 578–586.

Russell, D. P. (2007). Recruiting and staffing in the electronic age: A research-based perspective. *Consulting Psychology Journal: Practice and Research, 59,* 91–101.

Sampson, J. P. (2000). Using the Internet to enhance testing in counseling. *Journal of Counseling and Development, 78,* 348–356.

Sassenberg, K. (2002). Common bond and common identity groups on the Internet: Attachment and normative behavior in on-topic and off-topic chats. *Group Dynamics, 6,* 27–37.

Schatz, P., & Browndyke, J. (2002). Applications of computer-based neuropsychological assessment. *Journal of Head Trauma Rehabilitation, 17,* 395–410.

Shermis, M. D., & Burstein, J. C. (2003). *Automated essay scoring: A cross-disciplinary perspective* Mahwah, NJ: Lawrence Erlbaum.

Silvester, J., Anderson, N., Haddleton, E., Cunningham, S. N., & Gibb, A. (2000). A cross-modal comparison of telephone and face-to-face selection interviews in graduate recruitment. *International Journal of Selection and Assessment, 8,* 16–21.

Sinadinovic, K., Berman, A. H., Hasson, D., & Wennberg, P. (2010). Internet-based assessment and self-monitoring of problematic alcohol and drug use. *Addictive Behaviors, 35,* 464–470.

Spek, V., Nyklíček, I., Cuijpers, P., & Pop, V. (2008). Internet administration of the Edinburgh Depression Scale. *Journal of Affective Disorders, 106,* 301–305.

Steenhuis, M-P., Serra, M., Minderaa, R. B., & Hartman, C. A. (2009). An Internet version of the diagnostic interview schedule for children (DISC-IV): Correspondence of the ADHD section with the paper-and-pencil version. *Psychological Assessment, 21,* 231–234.

Subrahmanyam, K., & Smahel, D. (2006). Connecting developmental constructions to the Internet: Identity presentation and sexual exploration in online teen chat rooms. *Developmental Psychology, 42,* 395–406.

Suhr, J. A., & Gunstad, J. (2007). Coaching and malingering: A review. In G. J. Larrabee (Ed.), *Assessment of malingered neuropsychological deficits* (pp. 287−310). New York: Oxford University Press.

Suler, J. R. (2002). Identity management in cyberspace. *Journal of Applied Psychoanalytic Studies, 4,* 455−459.

Suler, J. (2004). The online disinhibition effect. *Cyberpsychology and Behavior, 7,* 321−326.

Suler, J. (2008). Cybertherapeutic theory and techniques. In A. Barak (Ed.), *Psychological aspects of cyberspace: Theory, research, applications* (pp. 102−128). Cambridge, UK: Cambridge University Press.

Tausczik, Y. R., & Pennebaker, J. W. (2010). The psychological meaning of words: LIWC and computerized text analysis methods. *Journal of Language and Social Psychology, 29,* 24−54.

Templer, K. J., & Lange, S. R. (2008). Internet testing: Equivalence between proctored lab and unproctored field conditions. *Computers in Human Behavior, 24,* 1216−1228.

Teng, C-I. (2008). Personality differences between online game players and non-players in a student sample. *Cyberpsychology and Behavior, 11,* 232−234.

Tippins, N. T., Beaty, J., Drasgow, F., Gibson, W. M., Pearlman, K., & Segall, D. O., et al. (2006). Unproctored Internet testing in employment settings. *Personnel Psychology, 59,* 189−225.

Trettin, L. D., May, J. C., & McKeehan, N. C. (2008). Teaching teens to "Get net smart for good health": Comparing interventions for an Internet training program. *Journal of the Medical Library Association, 96,* 370−374.

Tseng, H., Macleod, H. A., & Wright, P. (1997). Computer anxiety and measurement of mood change. *Computers in Human Behavior, 13,* 305−316.

Tucker-Ladd, C. E. (2000). *Psychological self-help.* Retrieved March 27, 2010 from http://www.psychologicalselfhelp.org

Turkle, S. (2004). Whither psychoanalysis in computer culture? *Psychoanalytic Psychology, 21,* 16−30.

van de Looij-Jansen, P. M., & de Wilde, E. J. (2008). Comparison of web-based versus paper-and-pencil self-administered questionnaire: Effects on health indicators in Dutch adolescents. *Health Research and Educational Trust, 43,* 1708−1721.

Volcani, Y. (2000). The tale of SAGASTM: Bringing apperception tests into cyber world. *Cyberpsychology and Behavior, 3,* 303−307.

Wall, J. E. (2000). Technology-delivered assessment: Power, problems, and promise. In J. W. Bloom, & G. R. Walz (Eds.), *Cybercounseling and cyberlearning: Strategies and resources for the millennium* (pp. 237−251). Alexandria, VA: American Counseling Association.

Walther, J. B. (1996). Computer-mediated communication: Impersonal, interpersonal, and hyperpersonal interaction. *Communication Research, 23,* 3−43.

Weekley, J. A., & Jones, C. (1999). Further studies of situational tests. *Personnel Psychology, 52,* 679−700.

Williams, J. E., & McCord, D. M. (2006). Equivalence of standard and computerized versions of the Raven Progressive Matrices Test. *Computers in Human Behavior, 22,* 791−800.

Wolford, G., Rosenberg, S. D., Rosenberg, H. J., Swartz, M. S., Butterfield, M. I., & Swanson, J. W., et al. (2008). A clinical trial comparing interviewer and computer-assisted assessment among clients with severe mental illness. *Psychiatric Services, 59,* 769−775.

Yoshino, A., Shigemura, J., Kobayashi, Y., Nomura, S., Shishikura, K., & Den, R., et al. (2001). Telepsychiatry: Assessment of televideo psychiatric interview reliability with present- and next-generation Internet infrastructures. *Acta Psychiatrica Scandinavica, 104,* 223−226.

Younes, M., Hill, J., Quinless, J., Kilduff, M., Peng, B., & Cook, S. D., et al. (2007). Internet-based cognitive testing in multiple sclerosis. *Multiple Sclerosis, 13,* 1011−1019.

Zlomke, K. R. (2009). Psychometric properties of Internet administered versions of Penn State Worry Questionnaire (PSWQ) and Depression, Anxiety, and Stress Scale (DASS). *Computers in Human Behavior, 25,* 841−843.

Zurlo, R., & Riva, G. (2009). Online group creativity: The link between the active production of ideas and personality traits. *Journal of Cyber Therapy and Rehabilitation, 21,* 67−76.

Chapter | thirteen

International and Multicultural Issues

Adrian EG Skinner and Gary Latchford

After all, when you come right down to it, how many people speak the same language even when they speak the same language?
Russell Hoban, The Lion of Boaz-Jachin and Jachin-Boaz, 1925, Ch. 27

The first author recently flew from the UK to the US. On arrival in the US, purchases were made with credit cards; on return home, the bill was on the doormat. While in the US, emails were sent home.

To accomplish these tasks, flights and reservations were made on the Internet, involving companies in the UK and the US. A "back office" specialist in Canada, to whom one or more of the banks involved had subcontracted this work, processed the credit card transactions. The emails visited servers in a number of countries while making their way to their destinations. On return home, it was necessary to query an item on the account — a "local" call made from the UK was answered by an employee based in Delhi, where the bank had sited its call center.

This tale of everyday life in the twenty-first century illustrates that we now live in the "global village" envisaged by Marshall McLuhan in the 1970s. It now takes no more effort to communicate with someone

257

Online Counseling. DOI: 10.1016/B978-0-12-378596-1.00013-7

across the world than it takes to talk to a neighbor. Many transactions cross international boundaries without the permission or even the knowledge of those involved. Importantly, as McLuhan foresaw, the technology involved has changed the nature of the transaction (McLuhan & Powers, 1992). He would undoubtedly have seen it as inevitable that not only would counseling and psychological treatment be delivered via the Internet but that these services would be delivered across national and cultural boundaries.

The chapter authors are both English, and work providing psychological treatment in the UK National Health Service (NHS).[1] This chapter has been informed by the developments in the therapeutic community in the UK to respond to the needs of a multicultural society, and by the authors' experiences within it.

CULTURAL ISSUES IN COUNSELING

Recent years have seen a clear recognition that ethnicity and culture play a potentially important role in therapeutic relationships, with the publication of guidelines for those providing psychological services to ethnic minorities (e.g., APA, 1993), many insightful works on the mechanisms of action and the potential for racism (Fernando, 1993), and some documents outlining the key areas for training (Patel et al., 1996) and multicultural skills of counselors (Sue et al., 1992).

This short chapter cannot hope to provide a comprehensive summary of this important work; it will focus specifically on the implications for online counseling. Some initial thoughts are necessary, however. First, rather than discussing definitions of different ethnic groups, we would like to encourage you to see culture as something individuals define themselves in relation to. All of us carry the influences of our own culture or cultures. It is important to remember that any discussion of cultural issues is not focused exclusively on the client but takes account of the culture of the therapist and the interaction that results. To begin with, then, take a look at Box 13.1 before you continue.

The second point to note is that cultural diversity means different things to different people in different parts of the world. Mental health services in northern England may focus on providing an adequate service for those whose ethnic background is Pakistani or Indian, for example, while in parts of the US the focus may be on Spanish-speaking Americans. Contemplating online counseling, the reality is that the potential juxtaposition of cultures between client and therapist is

---

[1] The NHS is a government-funded organization that provides most health care to UK citizens, including running the majority of hospitals. Private treatment is available but regarded mostly as a "top-up" and used only by a minority. Psychological treatment and counseling are available through the NHS as well as in the voluntary and private sectors.

Box 13.1 Looking at Your Own Culture

1. How would you define your own culture?
2. What influence does your culture have on you? Think about the following:
   a. Your religion and beliefs
   b. Your choice of food
   c. Your choice of partner/friends
   d. Your choice of places to live/places to travel to
   e. Your sense of security within your society
   f. Your experience of discrimination
   g. Your reaction to someone with a different cultural background
   h. The reaction of those with a different cultural background to you

breathtakingly wide. How, then, might cultural differences between therapist and client influence the process?

Perceptions of the Therapist about the Client

Our own culture influences the way we see ourselves and others. In the context of counseling, the therapist may have a stereotyped view of people from certain cultures, may have limited understanding of the experience of the client (e.g., of racist abuse), or may have limited understanding of the role of culture in the experience of physical or mental illness (e.g., the role of spiritual beliefs in coping with a chronic physical illness).

Perceptions of the Client about the Therapist

The client may have particular expectations of a therapist with a different cultural background, and may be apprehensive or uncomfortable, or fear being misunderstood. In a situation where the client comes from a cultural minority and the therapist from the majority, the "power" status within the therapeutic context may be skewed. The ability to consult "away" from a local situation may actually encourage people from minority communities to seek help via other means such as the Internet.

Language

Most counselors and therapists will have come across situations in which they have seen clients with a different mother tongue. In the majority of f2f transactions, the client will have moved to the therapist's country and neighborhood and will be fluent in the language of his or her hosts. In other situations, there will have been linguistic barriers that will have had to be overcome. In areas where there are large numbers of immigrants using the language of their inheritance, local authorities may have set up special facilities. The success of these enterprises is variable. In northern England, black mental health centers do a good job in providing ethnically appropriate support to the Punjabi- and Urdu-speaking population, but the success of black West Indian mental health centers in London and the Midlands has not protected this population from, for instance, the overdiagnosis of psychotic disorders (Littlewood, 1992; McGovern & Cope, 1991). Even in situations where both participants speak the same language, there are ample opportunities for misunderstandings to arise via the regional or national differences. One can imagine the confusion when an English client with an American counselor announces, "I'm dying for a fag [cigarette]" during an online session! In George Bernard Shaw's words, we are "two nations separated by a common tongue."

The use of the Internet for counseling has, therefore, both potential advantages and potential disadvantages from a multicultural perspective. The absence of visual and auditory cues might imply that both parties are less likely to be swayed in their judgments by cultural factors. What is less clear is whether this is always a good thing.

The Cultural Context of Models of Counseling

Most models of counseling are rooted in Western models of psychology, and this can create problems. Research involving participants from different ethnic backgrounds has not always been methodologically rigorous, leading to common but unsubstantiated stereotypes such as "South Asians are more likely to somatize mental illness." Further, the often-implicit assumption is that non-Western models of psychology are inferior. Other authors have placed counseling in a much wider, international context, arguing that all cultures have developed models of healing based on either medical-physiological, sociopsychological, supernatural, or bodily functional/behavioral intervention, and that in Western societies these have tended to become specialized and distinct (Tseng & Hsu, 1979). It is important to be aware of this context, and open to the experience and beliefs of the client.

The Impact of Online Counseling

Research into the importance of culture in online counseling is in its infancy, and we simply do not have the answers to many questions we would like to ask. It is, however, apparent that the ability bestowed by Internet services may have a profound impact on how people seek counseling and how they experience it.

It is possible that the absence of the visual cues that would otherwise influence people's assumptions of culture (e.g., color of skin) may lead to a degree of cultural blindness. It is also possible, however, that people will rely more on other cues, such as surname. Moreover, the assumptions that individuals have about cultures remain, and it is arguable that the risk of misunderstanding can be even greater. It is likely, for example, that online counselors would, in theory, be exposed to clients from a great many unfamiliar cultural backgrounds, well beyond their expertise. Understanding the beliefs, needs, and social context of the client is important, and to achieve this in such a situation would require counselors to acknowledge their lack of knowledge and skills and to be aware of any assumptions they may make. They need to be prepared to listen with sensitivity and to support their work with appropriate study.

It should also be remembered that future developments will inevitably see the widespread introduction of real-time video, which will again alter the cues available to counselor and client, influencing the assumptions each makes about the other.

Another possibility, of course, is that it may be possible to provide a client with counseling from someone of a similar background more easily than it is at present. For instance, someone of a West Indian background living in London or a Hispanic living in Chicago could conceivably choose to consult a counselor based in the West Indies or Cuba, feeling that they would be more comfortable dealing with their problems in this way.

This would, of course, set new difficulties for the counselor, whose potential ignorance of the culture of his or her clients might be replaced by ignorance about their environment. Would a black Briton of West Indian heritage receive a better service from a white British counselor who lived in the same town than from a West Indian counselor working in Jamaica?

Finally, consideration of these issues raises an important dilemma. Should counselors take cultural background into consideration in the assessment, mindful that not doing so may lead to ignoring a major influence on the client, or should they take advantage of the medium and strive to remain culturally blind, keeping their client's and their own cultural background hidden so that the biases they would introduce are kept from the experience of counseling? Given the many subtle influences of culture and stereotype, the latter option is probably impossible, but we would also like to stress the difficulties inherent in the first option: to really attempt to understand the cultural context of client and counselor is not easy, but we would argue that it is essential.

ETHICS

A number of organizations in the US and the UK have produced ethical guidelines about working on the Internet. The APA's guidelines are quite basic (APA, 1997) and caution the practitioner to exercise care in this new medium; its booklet aimed at the actual or potential consumer (APA, 2000) concentrates on providing guidance on assessing the quality of information on the Internet. The ACA guidelines (ACA, 2005), while making no explicit statement about international practice, make detailed recommendations about issues such as ensuring backup for Internet clients and adhering to "state regulations" that militate against international work. The British Psychological Society's (BPS) report (BPS, 2001) makes specific reference to potential problems in operating outside national boundaries, and although this report does not recommend "banning" such transactions it does suggest that international users be made aware of specific potential problems. Similarly, the British Association for Counselling and Psychotherapy (BACP)'s report (British Association for Counselling and Psychotherapy, 1999) has a number of concerns about Internet counseling that might be made more acute across international boundaries.

The report produced by the ISMHO (ISMHO Case Study Group, 2001) about assessing suitability for Internet therapy faces a number of these issues squarely. Apart from linguistic and cultural concerns, the report stresses the need for online therapy to be potentially part of a treatment package; such a package must inevitably be more difficult to assemble across national boundaries. The group expresses concerns about the effect of concurrent or previous therapy; there are risks that clinicians may have faulty or incomplete understanding of treatments in other countries and cultures. The group is also concerned about cross-cultural practice and recommends that clinicians only practice within cultures with which they are familiar.

Although none of these concerns are necessarily exacerbated by the presence of an international boundary, they might well be. What kinds of issue may be made more acute across international boundaries?

Issues of Security: The Identity of the Therapist

A key area of difficulty for clients obtaining counseling on the Internet is the establishment of the identity and credentials of the person providing the service. How does the client determine that his or her counselor is properly qualified and trained?

These problems also exist in the "real" world, but in the cyberworld they are potentially made more difficult. When we visit the office of a doctor, dentist, or counselor, we are supplied with cues that tell us that we are visiting a properly qualified person. There may be certificates on the wall, the service provider may be sharing premises with other professionals, etc. The cues tell us that the service provider has had their credentials checked by a trusted authority and is who they say they are.

Using the Internet, the client is prevented from making many of these checks. There is no office and no wall of certificates. A number of websites offer "credential checks," such as that offered at Martha Ainsworth's "Metanoia" site (http://www.metanoia.org/imhs/identity. htm). Other websites are less regulated and consist of little more than an advertising service in which therapists describe themselves. Choosing a "credential-checked" therapist will certainly increase the level of protection for a client, but it is perhaps expecting too much for any organization to understand the complexities of a wide variety of therapy professions in numerous countries. It is also difficult to estimate the validity of different "credential-checking" processes offered by a variety of websites. Certainly, some websites offer advertising space to therapists who do not mention any qualifications or whose qualifications are not widely recognized. This is scarcely surprising in view of the enormous task such websites set themselves in making judgments about a variety of professionals from all over the world.

If a client uses a counselor from another country, this problem is potentially much greater. Is the person I am consulting registered with the professional body in his or her own country? What is the professional body in that country?

To illustrate our point, the "qualification" situation in two countries with quite similar traditions and languages (the US and the UK) is radically different. The US has a tradition of state registration of a large number of therapy professions, which both protects the public and allows oversight of the payment of fees by insurers. When US citizens go to a psychologist, social worker, or counselor in the US, they know that an independent authority governs the professional's qualifications and practices. Using the Internet for therapy would not be problematic for these organizations if the therapist and client came from the same state or country, but might be if the two resided in different countries.

The practice of counseling and psychotherapy in the UK is currently mainly unregistered, however, and anyone may call himself or herself a counselor. Since 2009 most psychologists have had to register with the Health Professions Council (HPC). There are a number of counseling and psychotherapy organizations but there is no statutory body, although the HPC has plans to register psychotherapists. People practicing bizarre treatments can and do set up fine-sounding organizations. Some of these are listed on US-based websites.

This may sound hopelessly disorganized, and to some extent it is. Efforts to register psychotherapists and counselors have currently resulted in only partial success, due in part to disagreements among those wishing to be registered. Lord Alderdice, Speaker of the Northern Ireland Assembly and trained psychoanalyst, attempted to introduce a bill regulating psychotherapy to Parliament in 2001 but failed when the government did not support it; instead, action was sought to register psychologists under existing regulations.

The potentially harmful effects of this omission are mitigated by the fact that a substantial amount of counseling and therapy in the UK is organized through the NHS. The NHS only employs or contracts with properly qualified staff and thus undertakes the credential-checking task. Therapy in the private sector is often on the basis of referral from a family doctor, who will have undertaken the same task.

There are, of course, instances where unqualified or maverick counselors and psychologists (and doctors and dentists) have carried on dubious practices, sometimes for many years. It is not our contention that the international use of the Internet for therapy exposes users to a new risk, just that it increases an existing one.

As can be seen from the above account of circumstances in the UK and the contrast between the UK and the US, someone seeking counseling from a practitioner in another country, even when the two countries seem similar in language and tradition, could be quite severely handicapped when judging the qualifications of his or her counselor.

Issues of Security: The Identity of the Client

Just as the client seeking treatment needs to have concerns about his or her therapist, so the Internet therapist must have concerns about the identity of his or her client. Because these transactions are frequently fee-based, the provision of a credit card number provides part of this check. There is, however, no guarantee that the person logging in is the client, although measures can be taken to minimize this problem. There is a risk of a child masquerading as an adult, a male passing themselves off as female, and so on. It is not apparent to us that these kinds of risk are any greater across national boundaries, but it does seem as if the insistence of some US insurance and health maintenance organizations on restricting practice to clients and counselors from the same state may protect against this to an extent.

The drawback of such a stance, however, is that it prevents a resident of, say, Utah from benefiting from the expertise of an online therapist in New York, never mind anywhere else in the world.

Issues of Security: The Transaction

As with other types of Internet transaction, there are concerns about the security of counseling transactions on the Internet. Such transactions need to be protected by measures such as encryption. There is, however, no reason to suppose that international transactions are any more vulnerable than national ones.

Issues of Safety: Protection and Redress of Grievance

In an f2f transaction, or with an Internet transaction with a therapist in the same country, the client has a route to follow if something goes wrong. In both the US and the UK, the therapist will probably have an employer or professional association with whom to lodge a complaint, and the client has the resort of legal action. It is important to note, however, that the therapist is also protected from groundless or frivolous complaints.

This legal protection largely disappears with international Internet transactions. Many sites state that their service is conducted under the laws of the country in which they are based (http://www.psychologyon-line.co.uk). In consequence, a disgruntled client would have to undertake legal action in the resident country of the service, potentially an expensive and confusing task of grappling with an unfamiliar legal system. Interestingly, there are moves toward authorities claiming jurisdiction over Internet transactions involving their residents ("An Act to Amend Chapter 63, Title 40, Code of Laws of South Carolina, 1976, Relating to the Licensure and Regulations of Social Workers," 2002), although it is difficult to envisage a therapist in, say, Australia being prosecuted by the South Carolina authorities. It is also likely that the therapist would claim (perhaps with some justification) that his or her services were governed by the country or state in which he or she were based. In any case, in practice it would be difficult to enforce legislation across international boundaries.

Taking a broader view, it is likely that the question of Internet liability will be addressed first in a more popular area of e-commerce, after which Internet counseling may well be forced to follow whatever precedents are set down.

The other mode of redress for a disappointed client would be to a therapist's professional organization, if he or she is a member of one. Such organizations should be prepared to investigate an international complaint, though this investigation may well be hampered and/or made more expensive and difficult for the client. However, organizations such as the APA and the BPS have extensive investigatory and disciplinary machinery and there is no reason why they should not handle international complaints using the same technology that facilitated the Internet transaction to interview the complainant and therapist.

We are of the opinion that one of the consequences of the Internet revolution may be that these organizations find that they need to be much more cooperative on an international level. We could very well see a future scenario in which the APA asks the BPS to conduct a joint investigation for a case involving both US and UK participants. Such an enterprise would require much closer understanding and appreciation of each other's differing cultures, standards, and expectations.

Limits of Confidentiality

Situations will arise in which therapists have to consider breaching client confidentiality. For instance, a client may confess to a crime or say that he or she intends to commit one. A client may also present with thoughts or behaviors that threaten his or her health or integrity and may, in the extreme, require hospitalization.

For f2f practitioners this problem is familiar (if infrequent) and they have the training, skills, and local knowledge to cope with the situation. The increased distance between therapist and client would potentially create great problems — whom would the therapist call? Moreover, there may well be different expectations with respect to confidentiality in different cultures.

Access to Support

Practitioners of f2f therapy will regularly consult with fellow professionals about clients, almost always with that client's permission. Clients in therapy will often be taking medication prescribed by a psychiatrist or family doctor, and there is usually good liaison with the therapist. If an Internet practitioner becomes concerned about a client's medication or medical care and that client comes from the same country, the problems of distance may well be overcome with the use of the telephone. This would be much less easy across national boundaries where, for example, time zones may impede contact or medications may be differently named. In addition, an Internet practitioner may not have access to information about resources local to the client.

There is significant doubt that an Internet practitioner would be able to exercise a full "duty to protect" his or her client if that client were far distant and in a care system about which the practitioner might know little.

Multicultural Competence

It is reasonable to expect of an online counselor that he or she will consider the implications of working with clients with different cultural backgrounds, as well as the competencies he or she needs to provide an adequate service (see Box 13.2 for a concise outline). As we have emphasized, this process begins with counselors increasing their awareness of

---

Box 13.2 Developing Cross-Cultural Skills

1. Increase self awareness of
   a. The influence of your own culture
   b. Your assumptions about other cultures
   c. Your feelings about working with clients from other cultures
   d. The potential impact of your own culture on clients with different cultural backgrounds
2. Develop knowledge of different cultures; for example,
   a. Acknowledge the importance of the cultural context for the individual
   b. Acknowledge the influence of culture on beliefs about health/mental health
   c. Acknowledge the influence of culture on experience and expectations of counseling
3. Develop culturally sensitive interventions; that is,
   a. Respect individual beliefs and cultural differences
   b. Acknowledge limitations as a counselor
   c. Actively seek knowledge and advice/supervision

Box 13.3 Opportunities and Threats in International Practice

1. What are the advantages and disadvantages for the client?
2. What are the advantages and disadvantages for the counselor?
3. If you were to offer a service to someone from another country, how would you
   a. Ensure your qualifications are accepted by the client?
   b. Follow the requirements of the law where you and/or your client reside?
   c. Take into account the cultural background and context of the client?
   d. Plan to deal with a situation in which you became concerned about your client's wellbeing?
4. How do you think that international practice will affect traditional counseling in the future?

their own cultural influences and their beliefs about other cultures, and then moves on to increasing their understanding of other cultures. They also must focus on the influence of culture on understanding and the expression of mental and physical health problems, as well as on how culture affects the understanding and expectations of counseling. It involves an acceptance of difference and an active attempt to fill the many gaps in knowledge and skill. We strongly recommend that the reader follow up the references given in the present chapter.

"Prepare to be Assimilated!"

Of the messages entered on the e-group run by the ISMHO, a significant proportion concern therapists' worries about practicing abroad or out of state. Often, informal and formal advice is "Don't do it!" The difficulties outlined above, especially legal uncertainties and problems with funding, have led to a widely held view that Internet therapy is fine provided that it is practiced only within national or state boundaries. See Box 13.3 for a summary of key issues.

The decision of whether to offer services across geographical boundaries may not be a decision that counselors have the privilege of making for much longer, however: consumers will exercise their right to choose who to consult, seeking out the most appropriate (or cheapest) counselor regardless of national and international boundaries. Market forces may well determine the way in which online counseling develops in the future.

SUMMARY

Online counseling is already having an impact and has raised important issues regarding areas such as ethics and security. We have argued that the difficulties in addressing these issues are multiplied when an international dimension is added. Although we have recognized the reluctance of many online counselors to take on clients from other geographical areas, we feel that such a change is inevitable in the future.

Responses to the challenges this creates will inevitably be both organizational and personal. Professional and state organizations need to address the legitimate concerns of current and potential users of these services, ensuring that complaints are investigated and services are regulated.

On a personal level, it is up to all online counselors contemplating work with clients from different cultural backgrounds to be familiar with the issues that may arise and to ensure that they are equipped with the skills that will enable them to be competent to practice. We have provided a very short introduction to the field and attempted to raise awareness of the important issues – both practical, such as access to support, and more theoretical, such as the way in which the medium may affect cultural aspects of the therapeutic process.

We feel that an awareness of multicultural issues is fundamental to all practitioners, but would argue that the opportunities afforded by online counseling again add a different dimension. There is a real prospect of clients seeking out specialists with different cultural backgrounds in different countries, or clients seeking out counselors with similar cultural backgrounds but potentially a different understanding of context. In either case, there is potential for confusion in the resulting combination of client and therapist.

One thing is certain, and that is that there is no going back. It is likely that the future of online counseling is one largely without national or cultural boundaries, but one where these will nevertheless impinge significantly on therapy. It is a future of more choice for consumers, more challenges for providers, and a great deal of interest for sympathetic observers of this developing scene.

Editors' Note: While the Internet resembles a global bulletin board where everyone can cross borders with amazing ease to approach an abundance of services and resources, delivery of professional services to the public by licensed clinicians is still governed by state laws and restricted by the clinician's malpractice insurance. Readers are invited to review the ethics chapter in this book (see Chapter 5) as well as visit http://www.EthicsCode.com for more details about existing recommendations.

KEY TERMS

Confidentiality The agreement not to share certain kinds of information or information gathered in a specific setting.

Counseling A term used interchangeably with Therapy meaning the provision of active psychological intervention designed to aid the recipient.

Culture The customary beliefs, social forms, and material traits of a racial, religious, or social group.

Ethics The principles of conduct governing an individual or a group.

Perception The interpretation of the utterances and actions of one person by another.

Therapist A psychologist, counselor, social worker, or any practitioner qualified to provide mental health interventions.

Therapy A term used interchangeably with Counseling.

REFERENCES

Act to Amend Chapter 63, Title 40, Code of Laws of South Carolina, 1976, Relating to the Licensure and Regulation of Social Workers (2002). Code of Laws of South Carolina (Chapter 63, Title 40).

American Counseling Association (ACA). (2005). Code of ethics. Retrieved August 16, 2010 from http://www.counseling.org/Resources/CodeOfEthics/TP/Home/CT2.aspx

American Psychological Association (APA). (1993). APA guidelines for providers of psychological services to ethnic, linguistic, and culturally diverse populations. Retrieved October 27, 2003 from http://www.apa.org/pi/oema/guide.html

American Psychological Association (APA). (1997). APA Statement on Services by Telephone, Teleconferencing, & Internet. Retrieved August 16, 2010 from http://www.apa.org/ethics/education/telephone-statement.aspx

American Psychological Association (APA). (2000). *dotCOMSENSE*. Author. Retrieved August 16, 2010 from http://helping.apa.org/dotcomsense

British Association for Counselling and Psychotherapy (BACP) (1999). *Counselling online: Opportunities and risks in counselling clients via the Internet.* Rugby: Author.

British Psychological Society (BPS) (2001). *The provision of psychological services via the Internet and other non-direct means: A professional report.* London: Author.

Fernando, S. (1993). *Mental health, race and culture.* London: Macmillan Education.

International Society for Mental Health Online (ISMHO) Clinical Case Study Group (2001). Assessing a person's suitability for online therapy. *Cyberpsychology and Behavior, 4*, 675–680.

Littlewood, R. (1992). Psychiatric diagnosis and racial bias: Empirical and interpretative approaches. *Social Science & Medicine, 34*, 141–149.

McGovern, D., & Cope, R. (1991). Second generation of Afro-Caribbeans and young whites with a first admission diagnosis of schizophrenia. *Social Psychiatry and Psychiatric Epidemiology, 26*, 95–99.

McLuhan, M., & Powers, B. R. (1992). *The global village: Transformations in world life and media in the 21st century.* New York, NY: Oxford University Press.

Patel, N., Bennett, E., Dennis, M., Dosanjh, N., Mahtani, A., & Miller, A., et al. (1996) *Clinical psychology, 'race' and culture: A training manual.* Leicester, UK: British Psychological Society.

Sue, D., Arrendondo, P., & McDavis, R. (1992). Multi-cultural counselling competencies and standards: A call to the profession. *Journal of Counselling and Development, 70*, 477–486.

Tseng, W., & Hsu, J. (1979). Culture and psychotherapy. In A. J. Marsella, R. Thorp, & T. Ciborowski (Eds.), *Perspectives on cross-cultural psychology.* London: Croom Helm.

A LOOK IN TO THE FUTURE OF ONLINE COUNSELING

Chapter fourteen

The Future of Health Care and Online Counseling

Ron Kraus
Editor, EthicsCode.com

ON PROPHESY AND PROPHETS

People who in Biblical times prophesied fantastic future events were often feared, either considered to be holy and blessed with God-like powers or to be raving madmen. Distinguishing the qualified prophets from the delusional and psychotics must have been a challenging task for our lay ancestors. It is told that great conflicts often flared up between true prophets

273

Online Counseling. DOI: 10.1016/B978-0-12-378596-1.00014-9

and false ones. Such, for example, was the reported case at Mount Carmel where one prophet challenged others to a debate in the public arena. At first, the crowd was understandably confused, not knowing whom to cheer as the right prophet. But then, Elijah's debate and ensuing fireworks ended up being much more convincing and the case was closed. Regardless of important issues such as monotheistic faith, human conflicts, and the effects of pyrotechnics on the average Biblical spectator, one clear conclusion can be drawn from these historic events — prophesy is a risky business.

Wise people avoid the risk of making prophesies, believing it to be the irresponsible conduct of fools. Indeed, it is easy to see how some prophesies, especially those that turn out to be complete nonsense, are hazardous for one's career, reputation, and self esteem. To avoid potential embarrassment, modern-day prophets prefer to call their beliefs about future events educated guesses, hypotheses, or predictions.

To be safe as well as scientifically correct, educated prophets nowadays make a prediction that they name "hypothesis," as well as a prediction that their initial prediction will turn out to be completely wrong. This way, benefits to science can be established regardless of research results, and researchers can publish to say either that they can predict and prove, or prove that they cannot.

As true prophets are scarce nowadays, one can only speculate about what their message would be if they suddenly dropped by for a visit and gave a few interviews on national television talk shows. Would the old prophets tell us that the Lord is very angry with us about how we treat each other and his world? Would the prophets raise our collective anxiety with apocalyptic predictions of global warming and floods, nuclear holocausts, pollution, and deadly plagues? Would they also assure us that eternal life and prosperity could be ours if only we chose to divert all efforts to fighting ignorance, poverty, and disease instead of each other? One can but wonder, as most reliable biblical prophets are long gone.

And so, with caution and awareness of the above, some educated guesses will be made in this chapter regarding the direction of health care in the coming years, with a specific focus on mental health care online.

HEALTH CARE REFORM IN THE US: WHERE IS IT HEADED?

Many decades have passed since the establishment of federal health programs such as Medicare and Medicaid without significant change being made to the health care system. Under a new administration, elected on a promise of change in 2009, the US recently moved, albeit reluctantly, to enter into a new era. The year 2010 now marks the historic date when most US citizens finally became eligible to receive the benefits of health insurance. What many today take for granted, such as Social Security benefits, public education, and old-age medical care, were once the luxury of the rich. In the same way, it is reasonable to assume that people will look back one day and wonder why it took the US so long to make health care benefits available to all.

It is, however, not only the health care system, people's eligibility, and access to services that will undergo major changes over the coming years, but also the field of medicine itself. A revolution in medical science is foreseen that will alter the field and change the world as we know it. In fact, it seems that, if natural or man-made disasters do not destroy us first, there is a good chance that modern medicine and technology will eventually be able to defeat death. Will our children or their children enjoy health care that is able to stop and reverse the aging process? Will tomorrow's medicine be able to reconstruct tissues and regenerate organs in such a way that people could, at least theoretically, live forever? Quite possibly all this may indeed come true; that is, of course, if we remember the golden rules taught by the ancient prophets and don't self-destruct first.

With some delays, the descendants of Adam and Eve may for the first time in recorded history be on the verge of completing the search for immortality. The ancient quest may not end with the simple digestion of a magical fruit. Rather, it is more likely that a variety of developments in a few fields will produce the cure. Among the areas worth mentioning in that respect are nanotechnology, genetic and stem-cell therapies, and various applications of telemedicine and robotics.

ACCESS TO MENTAL HEALTH CARE ONLINE: DIRECTORY SEARCHING AND SCHEDULING

Where can one find a good psychologist when such is desperately needed? Prior to the days of the Internet, people would usually ask their family or close friends for recommendations. But then, what if one was so unfortunate as to have relatives or friends who had never been in need of mental health counseling? Well, if one had health insurance, for example, a referral might have been generated by the network or the family physician. People who had to search on their own could look up the term "psychologist" in a phone directory and then try calling the clinicians listed there. For some, calling a stranger whom they found in a telephone directory may seem intrusive or difficult. In fact, it may be that many people who felt the need for a professional mental health service before the days of the Internet avoided seeking it due to feelings of shame, fear of exposure, and potential stigma.

The search for a psychologist today, or for any other type of health care provider for that matter, is much easier. In fact, the Internet allows hesitant or disabled customers to stay at home and speak with no one, but still be able to locate and interact with a quality care provider of their choice or have very meaningful clinical sessions online. It is not only phone directories that are now available online; many health insurance companies also list their professionals online for members to connect with. Private and government entities as well as professional organizations make it easy these days for customers to both locate and interact with professionals of their choice online.

Consumers of health and mental health are no longer left in the dark when seeking to consult a professional they have never met or heard of before. Today's clients have the ability to go online and check for themselves what the clinician's record looks like, what they have published — even what their home looks like from all angles. We live in the age of information, and knowledge is accumulating faster and faster every year. Almost everything we wish to know is now available online. Information is accessible from anywhere, at any time, and to anyone like never before. Not only can modern clients find a qualified psychologist online, schedule a meeting, and connect with the professional of their choice; the service itself can be carried out online without ever leaving the home.

Will direct online search, scheduling, and service be made even easier and more common in the coming years? The trend over the past 10 years seems to suggest that the answer may be positive.

The term "digital divide" was used in the first edition of this book to describe the difference between those who have access to resources online and those who do not. When trying to assess the future of online counseling in terms of access to health care resources, it is important to pay attention to this issue, particularly in terms of the following questions:

1. Will all people be able to benefit from services online in the same way?
2. Do all households in the US have an Internet connection?
3. Do all patients have access and/or the skills necessary to operate modern technology?

Not everyone is connected yet, although most of the affluent and healthy people are. Will the future show that we were able to provide equal access for all? Hopefully we will accomplish such a goal, although it may be that, unless we make the elimination of ignorance and poverty a priority, nothing much will change, and the divide may remain an ongoing issue to be resolved. Still, progress is expected as technologies usually follow a pattern of becoming more common. The telephone is a good example of this. For some years after its invention, many people did not have a telephone in the home, while today more and more people walk around carrying smart cell phones.

So, what will the future look like for a person seeking health care service online? If all goes well, patients could look up and select a clinician, schedule an appointment, consult in real time, and then scan their smart medical or credit card to complete the process. Naturally, confirmations for all transactions would immediately arrive online, unless otherwise indicated. Wouldn't such a service be nice, simple, and comfortable?

At this point it may be important to mention professional license and liability insurance limits, and the issue of delivering clinical services across state lines. Before the days of the Internet, finding and scheduling clinicians was done through local resources. As a result, the issue of professionals delivering services to clients residing in states where the clinician is not licensed was not a frequent concern. Today, when resources are online, it is easy to find and communicate with anyone, from anywhere. Providers as well as clients need to remember that professional license and liability insurance only allow clinicians to practice in the state where they are licensed. For more guidance on this matter see Section 4 at http://www.ethicscode.com, as well as the ethics (Chapter 5) and legal (Chapter 6) chapters in this book. Will the license mobility issue be resolved and allow clinicians to serve patients across state lines? Hopefully this will be the case, as some initiatives are already pushing in that direction.

OUR HEALTH RECORDS: PRIVACY, STORAGE, AND TRANSFER

During the past decade, health care providers became interested in bringing services online, but concerns regarding the collection, transfer, and storage of personal information were also raised. Prior to the emergence of any official guidelines, visionary clinicians already worked to define an ethics code for online counseling. One such attempt was EthicsCode. com, which was published in 1999. Later, once the HIPAA regulations had been published, adherence to rules concerning the privacy of patient records online became the required norm for all health care providers in the US. Today, all patients in the US must be informed about possible risks to privacy when data are transferred online, and providers must take certain measures to ensure the privacy of health care records.

Years have passed since EthicsCode.com and the HIPAA regulations were published, but the debate in the US about how health care records should be handled still continues. Some see the potential of keeping and sharing electronic medical records while others are concerned about possible breaches of privacy and misuse. It is easy to understand the arguments made by both sides of this debate. Those in favor believe that, if records were accessible to clinicians online, time and money and even lives could be saved. Supporters of the electronic medical record concept wish to allow all health care professionals immediate access to the full medical file of the patient, including history, all lab work results, tests, medications, and recent procedures. Such access, especially when patients cannot provide the information themselves, is sometimes crucial and potentially life-saving.

Those who oppose the concept of keeping health records online are mostly concerned about issues relating to the privacy of the data and their misuse. If private medical records are exposed to unauthorized use, patients' interests could indeed be harmed. Would we vote for political candidates running for office if we knew that their medical condition includes ongoing or past treatment for paranoid schizophrenia? Would our bank approve our mortgage application if their research into our medical profile suggested that we may become disabled in the coming years? Would future employers screen our job application not only for criminal records but also to evaluate our personal and family medical records? Obviously, there could be situations where public exposure or misuse of people's medical records could be both damaging and upsetting. Can we really trust the safety and security measures to protect the privacy of medical data online at all times? But then, the current system is also not perfect yet we still use it.

The best possible guess regarding the future of health care records online is that we will probably have several options. Even today, some commercial entities offer customers the ability to manage their health records online. If one elects to place one's trust and medical data online, out of one's free will and having been informed of possible risks to privacy, who could be blamed for security failure, if it happened? When it comes to clients of the public system, it may be that their approval will be required for online records storage and transfer, and an alternative system that is not online may still be offered to those who want it.

A simple way to resolve the debate is to give people the option of online or non-online storage, or have them sign an informed agreement, as is done with HIPAA regulations now. Another way to deal with medical records in the future could be to place a microchip in the client's health insurance card, which could be updated at the end of every procedure; all relevant medical data could then be carried conveniently in the wallet, next to cash and credit cards. Such a smart card could also be available to medical and health care staff if the patient were disabled or could not provide information directly.

As to security breaches of medical records in the future, well, these will probably still happen, in the same way that banks will still be targeted simply because they hold money. Today, information is power, and so the need to continuously update the security of private data will probably remain a task in the future.

Access to Resources, Eligibility, and Authorizations Online

In the past, clinicians had to call, fax, or write the patient's insurance carrier whenever a new client came in. Checking to verify the patient's eligibility and level of coverage is an important issue for providers. Sometimes, clinicians and patients had to wait for clearance before treatment could start and frustration would mount. In recent years, more and more of these procedures are done online. Most clinicians can now log into the insurance provider's website online, check the client's eligibility, get authorization, and even fill out periodic reviews of treatment. Though it is not flawless, the whole process of eligibility verification and authorization for service has in recent years been made simple, direct, and in many cases immediate.

In the coming years the trend will likely continue to grow and service-related communications online will probably become the norm. The only problem that may linger is that relating to the digital divide. Some people have access to online resources while others do not. Often, it is the poor, undereducated, old, or disabled that have less access to resources and services online. Paradoxically, these groups are also the most in need. Bridging the gap created by the digital divide is one of the important challenges of tomorrow's health care. It is not only imperative that all citizens are covered by health insurance but also that all citizens have equal access to the available resources.

Submitting Claims and Getting Payments Online

Years before health care and mental health providers considered doing business online, banks were already wiring money across continents. Our credit cards were also active online long before any clinicians started providing consultation services over the Internet. Consequently, the easiest part for the clinical community to accept about Internet-assisted work was the fact that claims and payments could be made online. After all, who would object to sending a claim online with a click of the mouse and seeing the funds appear as if by magic in their bank?

Since early pioneers started consulting and collecting credit card payments online, the field has evolved quite dramatically. Numerous groups now offer online claims submission and direct deposit services to clinicians. In fact, most health insurance companies as well as federal and State health programs in the US actually encourage clinicians to submit claims and even tax reports online. The system online can process claims and payments faster, all steps in the process can be monitored with ease, and errors can be traced more clearly by all sides involved.

Without doubt, claims and payments for health services will continue to be done online. In fact, it may be that handwritten reports will become a thing of the past, and all health care records will be in electronic form.

HOME VISITS ARE BACK — ONLINE

Not many readers will remember their family doctor making a home visit. This observation is not necessarily explained by people's tendency to repress unpleasant childhood memories of long syringe needles and bitter syrups, but rather because such visits became increasingly rare. In the past, when modern health care was still in its infancy, physicians would be called by the family to visit an ailing member instead of the other way around. Ancient physicians, so the legend goes, would pack their medical bag and ride into the stormy night with a mission to care for the sick. Considering the state of health care today, it is no wonder that some people feel sorry that the good old days are gone.

In the era of the industrial revolution, cities built hospitals and a health care system was created. For many years now, patients have been brought to clinics and hospitals, where conditions and equipment are better suited to modern medical care. Even that most natural process, childbirth, has become a medical procedure, requiring hospitalization and rarely done at home. Modern doctors are no longer expected to make home visits, unless circumstances are very special or the wife insists it's time for dinner. But then, all this may change as interaction with health care providers will be possible online. In the future, home visits may return, but these will probably be virtual visits online.

Advances in telemedicine already allow monitoring of patients from a distance. The spread of the Internet to more homes and advancements in medical technology in the coming years will probably make online doctors' appointments common. Patients would be able to see and hear their clinician, who in turn may be able to see the medical file online along with readings from monitors designed to be worn by patients at home or in a facility. Most mental health consultation services could be done online already, even without the more sophisticated technology of the future. Unfortunately, it seems that most clinicians are still not taking full advantage of the available technology. Will this situation change in the future? Probably it will, but gradually.

When online counseling had just been born, hesitant clinicians were at first understandably concerned about the efficacy of text relations. Today, when much evidence exists to prove that online counseling basically works as well as f2f meetings, it is easy to predict that, when video-conferencing becomes the norm, even doubtful professionals will have little left to say against working online. True, it is not quite the same when your client is tearful in their home environment and you cannot offer them a tissue, but then, seeing and speaking online can be as meaningful as a personal meeting in the office.

Does the above suggest that in the future patients will no longer come to the clinician's office? Not necessarily. It is more likely that some will prefer to consult online while others will still wish to come to the clinician's office. After all, even when a few years ago phone consults became feasible, most clients continued to see their therapists in person. Further, the original CPT code 0074T (now replaced by CPT codes 98966 and 98969), which allowed physicians to consult via and bill for online service, limited online service to existing patients only, meaning those who had had an initial f2f assessment in the office. The above indicates that online service is not meant to replace but perhaps supplement or enhance the more traditional forms of service.

CONSULTING MACHINES ABOUT HOW WE FEEL

ELIZA was probably the first attempt to have humans engage in a conversation with a machine (Weizenbaum, 1966). True, some car owners may claim that they had had conversations with their vehicles long before people spoke with ELIZA, but then, unlike automobiles refusing to start, ELIZA answered.

From a review of a brief discussion with ELIZA, one may see how far we are from having truly meaningful conversations with machines. Below is an example of what happened when an attempt to consult ELIZA took place recently (http://chayden.net/eliza/Eliza.html):

>> Hello.
How do you do. Please state your problem.
>> I feel funny speaking about my personal problems with a machine.
Do computers worry you?
>> Not so much. People worry me more.
I'm not sure I understand you fully.
>> I was wondering if a machine could understand me.
Why do you mention computers?
>> Are you human or a computer?
What do you think machines have to do with your problem?
>> Well, I was hoping you could help me feel better
Were you really?
>> Yes. Can you help me?
You seem to be quite positive.
>> Thank you, but I am not sure this is the case.
We were discussing you — not me.
>> Yes, so can you help?
You are sure.
>> No, now I'm confused.
Are you saying no just to be negative?
>> No, I'm saying it to be honest.
You are being a bit negative.
>> Really?
Please go on.
>> Why do you think I'm being negative?
Why do you ask?
>> I wish to know.
You say you wish to know?
>> Yes, please.
I see.

The human mind, it seems, is still too complex for a machine to handle it with care. Our emotions and feelings, our personal associations and subjective perceptions, our motives and dreams, our public and private selves, and the dynamic interaction of all these is something present-day computers cannot yet fathom. To think that a machine can replace a therapist is perhaps a bit ambitious and unrealistic and yet, when one deals with behavior and not emotion, the potential for machines to be useful may in fact be there.

In CBT, for example, the purpose of the process is not necessarily to explore, understand, and compassionately soothe troubling emotions or perceptions. Rather, the focus in CBT is more on a structured plan designed to change behaviors and beliefs. A set of steps gradually guiding patients toward a behavioral goal is effective even if done online, especially if faulty beliefs are replaced with better ones and rewarding incentives are provided for accomplishments. Here is no need to understand complex emotions but rather provide a route toward successful change in behavior. Such strategies can be built with a therapist but can also be done in a self-help-style program online with the client working alone.

It may be that we will not process delicate and complex emotions with machines any time soon, but customer care is already provided by computerized voice-recognition systems today. Could similar technology be used in the future to process calls that come to the clinician's office or hospital? Could sophisticated ELIZA-type programs help guide clients toward recovery or behavior change? Most probably, some aspects of computerized programs would be useful to some.

EDUCATION AND TRAINING VIA VIRTUAL REALITY

Similarly to online counseling, education online was a new concept only a decade ago. Today, most universities offer many online services to students, including classes and even full degrees. It is reasonable to assume that virtual classes and class discussions, case presentations, and clinical supervision sessions will all be part of tomorrow's graduate training programs in mental health.

The concept of "virtual reality" is also predicted to become more common both for the training of clients and clinicians. The technology of virtual reality is much like playing a sophisticated video game, where real-life skills can be practiced but no real damage occurs if the game is over. Pilots can learn to fly planes this way, and clients could learn to confront various fears, respond appropriately to simulated social situations, or practice to become more assertive. Online education and training developed successfully over the past decade and will continue to grow.

REGULATING ONLINE COUNSELING

The issue of license and liability insurance limits when providing clinical services crossing state lines was previously mentioned in relation to license mobility. However, a bigger concern may be the issue of regulation. At this point, there is no official entity that really regulates clinical work online, especially if done as part of private practice. If patients found a clinician online and then wanted to complain or report a problem, it would usually be up to them to find where the clinician is licensed, if at all. Today, anyone can set up a website and claim to be a professional online. The Internet is mostly unregulated, and so caution should always be recommended. More about this subject can be found in Holmes and Ainsworth (2004).

CONCLUSION

Looking at the progress made in the past 10 years, one can assume that online counseling research and practice will continue to expand. Still, even though research is providing sufficient data and CPT codes for the practice are in place, the majority of clinicians today are not yet fully familiar or comfortable with online counseling. As the professional community becomes more comfortable with the concept, and as technology makes online communications easier and more widespread, the field is expected to grow. Of all forms of online counseling, videoconferencing will probably become the most popular as the ability to see and hear each other will give both clinician and client the feeling that they are communicating f2f, as if in the office.

KEY TERMS

Cognitive behavioral therapy (CBT) A mental health treatment method that focuses on changing clients' perceptions and behaviors.

Digital divide A term used to describe how some people have access to resources online while others do not.

ELIZA Probably the first attempt to have a computer use Rogerian/humanistic psychotherapy principles to engage in a therapeutic dialogue with human clients.

Health care reform A plan relating to the expansion of health care coverage to most US citizens. The proposed reform bill was passed and signed into law by the president of the US in March 2010.

Hypothesis and null hypothesis Predictions made by a researcher that describe what the research results may indicate.

Nanotechnology A rapidly expanding technology field that deals with the creation and operation of very minute structures.

Stem cells and stem-cell therapy Stem cells, either adult or embryonic, are cells that are as-yet undifferentiated. Stem cells can grow into any type of tissue or organ. In stem-cell therapy, stem cells grown in the lab are expected to replace or enhance damaged tissues.

Telemedicine The ability to diagnose, monitor, and/or treat patients from afar using machines, computers, or robotic devices.

Virtual reality Similar to sophisticated video games, virtual reality allows users to practice and train skills in a safe online environment.

REFERENCES

Brown, B. D., Venneri, M. A., Zingale, A., Sergi, L., & Naldini, L. (2006). Endogenous microRNA regulation suppresses transgene expression in hematopoietic lineages and enables stable gene transfer. *Nature Medicine, 12*(5), 585–591.

Caspi, O., Lesman, A., Basevitch, Y., Gepstein, A., Arbel, G., Habib, M., et al. (2007). Tissue engineering of vascularized cardiac muscle from human embryonic stem cells. Retrieved August 16, 2010 from http://circres.ahajournals.org/cgi/reprint/01.RES.0000257776.05673.ffv1.pdf

Dekel, B., Zangi, L., Shezen, E., Reich-Zeliger, S., Eventov-Friedman, S., & Katchman, H., et al. (2006). Isolation and characterization of nontubular Sca-1+Lin – Multipotent stem/progenitor cells from adult mouse kidney. *Journal of the American Society of Nephrology, 17,* 3300–3314.

Holmes, L., & Ainsworth, M. (2004). The future of online counseling. In R. Kraus, J. Zack, & G. Stricker (Eds.), *Online counseling: A handbook for mental health professionals* (pp. 257–269). San Diego, CA: Academic Press.

LaVan, D. A., McGuire, T., & Langer, R. (2003). Small-scale systems for in vivo drug delivery. *Nature Biotechnology, 21*(10), 1184–1191.

Morgan, R. A., Dudley, M. E., Wunderlich, J. R., Hughes, M. S., Yang, J. C., & Sherry, R. M., et al. (2006). Cancer regression in patients after transfer of genetically engineered lymphocytes. *Science, 314*(5796), 126–129.

Nie, S., Xing, Y., Kim, G. J., & Simons, J. W. (2007). Nanotechnology applications in cancer. *Annual Review of Biomedical Engineering, 9,* 257.

Weizenbaum, J. (1966). ELIZA – A computer program for the study of natural language communication between man and machine. *Communications of the ACM, 9*(1), 36–45.

Index

Lightning Source UK Ltd.
Milton Keynes UK
UKOW05n0609191016

285630UK00016B/512/P